THE CREDIBILITY FACTOR

Putting Ethics to Work in Public Relations

THE CREDIBILITY FACTOR
Putting Ethics to Work in Public Relations

Lee W. Baker

BUSINESS ONE IRWIN
Homewood, Illinois 60430

© RICHARD D. IRWIN, INC., 1993

Sponsoring editor: Cynthia A. Zigmund
Project editor: Jess Ann Ramirez
Production manager: Ann Cassady
Designer: Larry J. Cope
Compositor: Precision Typographers
Typeface: 11/14 Palatino
Printer: Book Press, Inc.

Library of Congress Cataloging-in-Publication Data

Baker, Lee W.
    The credibility factor : putting ethics to work in public
relations / Lee W. Baker
        p.   cm.
    ISBN 1-55623-885-1
    1. Public relations—Moral and ethical aspects. 2. Public
relations—Corporations—Moral and ethical aspects. 3. Professional
ethics. I. Title.
    HM263.B3157   1993
    659.2—dc20   92-20630

Printed in the United States of America
1 2 3 4 5 6 7 8 9 0 BP 9 8 7 6 5 4 3 2

Preface

Credibility. This book is for executives and managers who want to attach credibility to themselves and their organizations as they plan and conduct public relations programs. Some of you are called public relations people. Others may have one of a diverse number of titles and positions. Whatever your title, you manage communications aimed at publics whose attitudes and actions affect the success of you or the enterprise with which you are associated.

The basic message of this book is that ethics are the foundation for achieving credibility. You find here such words as moral values, standards of conduct, and individual conscience. These can be translated into doing what's right, being fair, honest, open, and careful to avoid conflicts of interest. Putting these ethical factors to work in the programs you develop and present can gain credibility for you. Doing this is not easy. Each problem situation requires careful analysis, time to ask questions and to make deliberate, wise choices.

You'll read about the ethical considerations in the public relations acts of individuals and institutions in the business world, in government, in politics, in education, in health care, in the news media, and in nonprofit organizations. You'll find examples of individuals and organizations whose credibility blossomed because of ethical attention and direction. Contemplate these, and look for what you can put to work to gain a similar benefit. You'll also read of instances in which other individuals and organizations overlooked ethics in their public relations and lost credibility. These are here to help you know what to avoid in your quest for credibility.

In these cases, our branding an individual or organization as acting either ethically or unethically applies only to the situation described. Ours is not a wholesale endorsement or condemnation of all other activities of that individual or organization. Ethical judgments of these others must necessarily be made separately on the basis of surrounding circumstances.

Following these, there are chapters of helpful, practical advice from ethicists and from experts in public relations management who have successfully waged the battles to put ethics to work and win credibility. In the comments and experiences of the PR practitioners, you will glean useful information that you can apply in your own challenging situations.

The book continues with a discussion of ethics programs and codes of ethics, in themselves forms of public relations communications, and describes how they can aid an organization to operate more ethically and be recognized for credibility. These sections will serve PR managers affiliated with organizations that have a program in place as well as with those that are weighing the pros and cons of installing one.

The last chapter addresses a couple of barriers to credibility: the incompetency of some who attempt to operate in the public relations field and the manner in which they can bring harm to the fully qualified; and the failure to achieve true professional status for all practitioners. Views of those who favor and oppose licensing of PR individuals are presented. Would licensure offer a means to weed out incompetents and win designation as a "professional," or would it be unnecessary regulation?

A further word about the audience for this book. It can guide your public relations work and lead you to credibility, regardless of your title or your field of endeavor. You may be a chief executive officer, an administrator or a manager. You may be associated with a business corporation, university, hospital, government or other institution. If you are planning or directing programs that attempt to shape public opinion and influence a segment of society to think or act in a particular way, you are part of a public relations operation, and you can profit from this book.

Lee W. Baker

Acknowledgments

This book might never have been written without the initial encouragement of two leaders and pioneers in public relations, Scott Cutlip and Frank Wylie. Thank you, gentlemen.

The gathering of information, opinions and data took place over more than two years. I am indebted to many individuals and organizations for their assistance and cooperation. For their contributions in conversations, letters and statements that became a part of these chapters I express deep gratitude to Pat Jackson, Chet Burger, Edward Bernays, Dick Truitt, Davis Young, John Budd, Frank Wylie, Scott Cutlip, Joe Epley, Jerald terHorst, Denny Griswold, Joan Taylor, Randy Baker, Beth West, Jack Blake, Fred Alexander, James Lukaszewski and Ron Wall. Many contributed to the research. I particularly want to thank Scott Cutlip, Frank Wylie, Ralph Izard, Hugh Culbertson, Bill Small, Sue O'Brien, Mel Sharpe, Edward Bernays, Joan Bugbee, Marlan Nelson, Don Wright, Raymond Simon, John Luecke, Bill Baxter, Betsy Kovacs and the Public Relations Society of America, the editors of the society's *Public Relations Journal* and the International Association of Business Communicators' *Communication World*, Maria Fort of the IABC Foundation, the Ethics Resource Center, and the Josephson Institute of Ethics. I greatly appreciate the valuable assistance in shaping the direction and content of the book provided by Cynthia Zigmund of Business One Irwin.

And I owe more than words can express to my wife, Jean Otto, whose ideas and encouragement were the stimulus for the start, and the finish, of this work. Nearly, if not equally, as important, she is my favorite editor. The book benefits greatly from her manuscript review.

L.W.B.

Contents in Brief

Contents

Chapter One

The Credibility Factor: Setting the Stage

This book is mainly about developing and keeping credibility as a result of putting ethics to work in public relations. A minor theme, much less expressed, is about the credibility of the terms *public relations* and *PR*. Less important though it be, let's look at the latter first.

While used interchangeably, the labels cover the public relations proposals, actions, and communications of individuals and organizations in many fields. *Public relations* and *PR* appear daily in the news. They are just as ubiquitous in our conversations. Sometimes the terms are used with approval and admiration: "Boy, that was a real public relations coup"; perhaps more often they are intended to criticize or disparage: "That's a bunch of PR garbage." You hear such other remarks as "Let's PR this," "I'll bet this is a PR manipulation," "With the right PR, we'll make this happen," or "That was a PR disaster."

Considering what the public is exposed to in the news, the cartoons, the sitcoms, the talk shows, and soap operas, it shouldn't be surprising that there are those who think of public relations as the term for a quick fix, who see its application to a problem situation as a substitute for forthrightness, candor, credibility, and integrity. As a result, in the minds of many the term calls up visions of fraud and deceit, misinformation and falsehoods, influence peddling and payola. They see self-styled PR experts apply the spin, make things appear just a little different from what was really said or done and more favorable for an individual or organization. For spin doctors, the main prerequisite to practice is a nimble mind.

We are audacious enough to suggest that as the public recognizes and approves credibility in public relations programs, obtained by the dedication of those who put ethics to work, there will be more positive and less negative connotations attached by the public to these two labels. The public will perceive both the perception and the reality of public relations activities, at least largely, as a dignified and forthright vocation, perhaps even a profession. Those engaged in these endeavors will be much more honored, much less scorned. There will be a time when, if you say that you're writing a book on ethics in public relations, there will not be snickers all around and the response, "Isn't that an oxymoron?"

Now to the credibility factor and the individuals and organizations who recognize the value it can attach to their public relations activities and are willing to work to achieve it. Who's involved in this wide world of public relations? What kind of and how many people are we talking about? What do they really do? How much influence do they have? Whom do they influence?

You'll find these people in just about every organized activity you can think of. Chief executive officers, regardless of what they're called—head honcho, chairman, boss, whatever—constitute a sizable portion. They're at the helm; they bear the ultimate responsibility for meeting the goals of their organizations. They are charged with maintaining harmonious relationships with the publics that are important to the success of their operations. This means they're also responsible for influencing change when that change is necessary to maintain constructive relationships. Because of their positions, they are seen as the top public relations persons. If something goes wrong or is perceived to be handled improperly and there is a loss of credibility, they get the blame. On the other hand, they receive credit for the PR successes and the credibility progress of the organization.

Herb Schmertz, formerly of Mobil Oil Corp., in writing about the role of corporate executives, said, "Every top manager should understand the principles of good public relations." He emphasized the value and need for them to develop public affairs–relations skills in dealings with elected and appointed government officials, community organizations, the news media, and special-interest groups.[1] What he says applies equally to the men and women in charge of nonbusiness operations.

Another portion, perhaps the largest, is made up of those in the public relations positions—where so much of the action takes place and so many credibility worries arise. Here again, there's quite a variance in titles. The words *public relations*, or *public affairs*, or *communications* appear on many of their hats—but not all of them. They may be working in or directing departments of public relations, public affairs, public information, investor relations, or corporate communications; with public relations counseling firms; or self-employed as PR consultants. The U.S. government population survey of 1991 reported 173,000 filers of Internal Revenue Service returns who listed their occupation as public relations. Surely, there are tens of thousands more in the field who choose a different term for their work.

And there are additional thousands who serve as contact persons, whose public relations skills rest importantly on knowing how to reach those in desired offices and being able to influence and persuade them. They work for clients to win contracts from private or public organizations, to obtain changes in laws or regulations at one of the several levels of government or to gain special rights, favors, or advantages for individuals or organizations.

The lines of demarcation that separate these groups, all part of the public relations process, are flexible. Many of these people who step across the borders that separate the groups operate even simultaneously in more than one of these categories.

In the lives of all of these, there are pressures as they stand at the crossroads of decision making and prepare to resolve public relations dilemmas rife with ethical overtones. Sometimes the dilemmas are of their own making; other times, they are the result of outside forces over which they had little or no control. Always, credibility is at stake. What currents tear at their consciences? How severe are the torments? How do they arrive at a resolution? How do they respond? What do they say as they describe what has taken place and their part in it? Are they candid, truthful, and fair in their communication? Or do they attempt to cover up relevant facts by misleading or even false statements? Do they weigh the ethical quality of the response, make principles and moral values the victors, and allow ethical influences to shine through to establish credibility? Or is expediency the chief tool that forges the decision?

The drive for credibility in public relations can play on the world scene. And it can backfire if ethics is ignored. When the presidents of the United States of America and the then Union of Soviet Socialist Republics—Presidents Reagan and Gorbachev—planned get-togethers in the 1980s, the airwaves and newspapers talked for days in advance about the public relations angles. You heard about one or both "strengthening position" for the discussions. Much of the grist for the journalists' mills came from White House officials. How would which global leader find a way to come out ahead and win the public relations show? Looking and acting the part of the statesman—or to be perceived as such—apparently counted more than an agreement to mutually trash X number of nuclear warheads. At one meeting of these heads of state, the 1985 summit in Geneva, the press secretary for President Reagan, wanting to be sure his boss received due credit, issued a positive-sounding statement quoting him at the end of a day's talks. The only trouble: The president hadn't read or approved the words.[2] Both suffered loss of credibility, but the press secretary lost the most, after he wrote of the incident three years later. He lost the business position he took after leaving government service.

NOTES

1. Herb Schmertz with William Novak, *Good-Bye to the Low Profile* (Boston: Little, Brown and Company, 1986), p. 5.
2. Larry Speakes with Robert Pack, *Speaking Out: Inside the Reagan White House* (New York: Charles Scribner's Sons, 1988), p. 219.

Chapter Two

Individual Pressures and Ethical Challenges

While there is much in this book about the ethical and unethical acts of organizations, it's important to remember that ethics is an individual, a personal, matter. It concerns one's moral values, standards, and choices. Ethical dilemmas confront individuals, not organizations. The individual is the one who decides whether to put ethics to work in public relations in the interest of credibility, or to move less honorably. This chapter takes up the actions and reactions of individuals as ethical pressures were applied and ethical challenges faced. Put yourself in these roles, analyze what takes place, and consider how you would form a judgment on your proper move.

PRESIDENTIAL PARDON FORCES ETHICAL DECISION—AND RESIGNATION—OF WHITE HOUSE PRESS SECRETARY; CREDIBILITY SURVIVES

Jerry terHorst faced the quintessential ethical dilemma while holding the top public relations post in the White House. He resolved the matter without torment, with a decision formed by his conscience, even though it was "the most difficult decision I ever have had to make."[1] He preserved his credibility.

TerHorst was just 30 days into his job as White House press secretary under President Ford—he was the president's first appointee, named to the post an hour after the president was sworn in. When he learned on Saturday night that the president planned to announce on Sunday morning, September 8, 1974, the granting of a pardon to former President Nixon, terHorst readied his resignation. He handed it to Ford an hour before the president met to inform the press of the pardon proclamation.

In his three-paragraph resignation letter, terHorst said, "It is with great regret, after long soul-searching, that I must inform you that I cannot in good conscience support your decision to pardon former President Nixon even before he has been charged with the commission of any crime. . . ."

"I do not know how I could credibly defend that action in the absence of a like decision to grant absolute pardon to the young men who evaded Vietnam military service as a matter of conscience and the absence of pardons for former aides and associates of Mr. Nixon who have been charged with crimes—and imprisoned—stemming from the same Watergate situation."[2]

TerHorst recalled that momentous day nearly 15 years later in a speech at a Hofstra University forum. He said the fact that the pardon is still the topic for such a program suggested that there is no unanimity of opinion about the merits of the pardon.

"What is there about this single act by President Ford that continues to create arguments?" he asked. His answer: "It is, I think, the issue of morality that keeps alive the issue of the Nixon pardon. It is the ethics of the Ford decision that haunts, that raises questions of right and wrong, that arouses strong feelings about its fairness or unfairness. And thus, I predict, the merits of this particular pardon will forever be with us."

Assuming, said terHorst, the pardon met all constitutional, legal, and political questions, it failed to measure up on ethical grounds. For him, that was the litmus test—and it did not pass— "and still does not."

So, he said, he resigned from "the most important position I had ever held because I could not be a part of an act that I thought was ethically wrong."

In an important matter of principle, as was involved here, terHorst thought a person ought to be guided by inner conscience. Thus, because he felt so strongly that the pardon was ethically wrong, his resigning was the only ethical thing for him to do. "I have no regrets," he told his audience.

TerHorst said he believed the importance of personal conscience was recognized by the Founding Fathers, who saw the individual as superior to the state, rather than the other way around. The precept is in the oath of office taken by all federal appointees, he added. This means a commitment to personal conscience is the highest form of loyalty, in his view, and "it impels us toward ethical conduct for ourselves and society.

"The conscience of the citizenry is the best guardian of democracy's future. Corruption without indignation will be its downfall."[3]

TerHorst took the words of an old proverb, "A good conscience is the best pillow," as the title of an article about the pardon and his resignation that he wrote for a publication of the Josephson Institute of Ethics. In this, he told how many people he respected thought it was wrong for him to resign. They contended that he had a moral duty to stand by Ford and help him defend the pardon against the great controversy it generated. These critics pointed to his 25-year relationship with Ford—they even shared the same hometown background—and his appointment by the president as factors that should rate his loyalty.

To those of this view, said terHorst, his resignation was an act of disloyalty, if not betrayal. Simplistically, they said he had let the president and his personal friend down, and under their value systems this was an unethical act.

The former press secretary countered by saying that their ethical perspective was at loggerheads with his. While he said he believed in loyalty, this matter was not one of mere disagreement over some ordinary political policy. "My beliefs about the justice system are too central to my ethical value system to compromise," he declared.[4]

In his book *Gerald Ford and the Future of the Presidency*, terHorst says that in the weeks following his resignation, there were reports that he left because he was given "misinformation" by Ford and his advisers. He replies to this by saying, "The President never misled me at any time."[5] TerHorst adds, however, that Ford did not include him in any discussions that may have taken place about the possibility of the pardon, which terHorst sees as a separate issue. And he points to his letter of resignation as expressing fully his reasons for resigning.

There are descriptions in the book of the U.S. public's reactions to President Ford in granting the pardon and to terHorst's resigning. Reaction to the pardon was immediate. Phone calls and wire messages poured in to the White House. An hour after radio and television news flashed the word, while the briefing for reporters in the press room was still going on, the tally of opinion received was eight to one against the pardon. TerHorst said that in one short message Ford had wiped out the euphoria that had swept across the nation during his first 30 days in office. To many citizens, the pardon smacked of a "deal," said terHorst. There was no indication that it was, he added, but he pointed out that Ford might have been more sensitive to the public's perception of the event, perhaps more important than the reality.

As for terHorst, he said he "completely underestimated the public impact of my resignation." He said there was a deluge of laudatory letters, phone calls, and telegrams. He said he heard from people in every state of the union: "from housewives, students, servicemen, federal employees, clergymen, factory workers, doctors, attorneys, teachers, judges, and an inmate of Leavenworth penitentiary.

"The theme was constant, suggesting a therapeutic value to my act that I had not anticipated or intended."[6]

The Society of Magazine Writers, an organization of 300 free-lance nonfiction writers, awarded terHorst its first "Conscience-in-Media" medal. The citation was for his "exemplary display of conscience and courage in resigning a highly-coveted position which he felt conflicted with his integrity as a journalist."[7]

Not everyone sided with terHorst. He had some 50 letters from critics who raised the disloyalty issue. He said he was hurt particularly by one who saw his departure as good riddance. He assuaged his pain by remembering that loyalty can breed disloyalty, that if the Nixon men had put loyalty to conscience before loyalty to the administration, the Watergate mess might have been avoided.

The relationship of the two Jerrys, Ford and terHorst, began in 1948. That was the year Ford, a young Republican lawyer, challenged a U.S. representative in the September primary election. TerHorst was a political reporter on *The Grand Rapids Press*. The neophyte in politics won the primary by a wide margin and in November was elected to Congress. TerHorst covered Ford for *The Press* and later when he became Washington correspondent and then bureau chief for *The Detroit News*, and the pair became close friends.

Ford, of course, replaced Spiro T. Agnew as vice president in December of 1973 and, nine months later, succeeded Nixon, as terHorst tells it, "the instant Vice President and then the first instant President."[8] TerHorst was on vacation working on his biography of Ford when he received a call asking him to serve as press secretary, "for a period of transition at least."[9] Could he arrange a leave of absence from the *News?* He could and did.

In his first meeting with Ford in the new post, the two agreed to cleanse the air of what prevailed during the Nixon White House tenure. They would abolish the Executive Office of Communications, which had been a political propaganda arm, and place its responsibilities under terHorst's office. TerHorst accomplished much in the 30 days, and said in his letter of resignation, "The Press Office has been restructured along professional lines. Its staff . . . is competent and dedicated."[10] Noting the changed conditions, an editorial in *The New York Times* said, "He . . . did much in his brief tenure to restore an atmosphere of professionalism and mutual respect to the White House press room."[11]

TerHorst in his book relates some of the reporters' questions at the new president's first news conference and Ford's responses. A query from Godfrey Sperling of *The Christian Science Monitor* asked if Ford planned to write a code of ethics for the executive branch of the government as a way to prevent future Watergates. "The President responded, 'The code of ethics that will be followed will be the example that I set.' "[12]

When terHorst left the White House, he returned to *The Detroit News* as national reporter and writer of a column syndicated to more than 100 newspapers. In 1981 he left the paper to become director, national affairs, for Ford Motor Company in Washington, where he continued to be an observer of government while serving as an advocate for the business interests of his company until retirement at the end of 1990, after which he became a PR consultant.

POINTS

• When you're asked to be part of a decision that means you must act against your conscience, try counseling with those who propose the course. Express your views about the ethical choice as forcibly and clearly as possible. Point out the credibility risks of their recommendation for the organization and for you and other individuals involved. Your reasoning may prevail.

• You may have to put yourself ahead of your organization when it comes to credibility and what your conscience says is right. It's in your self-interest to put yourself first.

• If you want to keep your credibility, be prepared to take whatever action is necessary for its protection. Turning in your resignation may seem to be an extreme one. Be prepared to do this to follow your convictions.

• Don't panic when you come face-to-face with an ethical dilemma. Take the time to weigh your values against the available alternatives.

RELIGIOUS LEADER FALLS FROM PULPIT AND EXPOSES ETHICAL HOLES IN PASTORAL ROBE

James Bakker, leader of the PTL ministry, preached his brand of the Pentecostal gospel to audiences seated before him in a high-tech television studio and those at home before their TV sets. The setting was Heritage USA, which stretched across much of 2,300 acres in suburban Charlotte, North Carolina and over the state border into South Carolina that Bakker bought in 1978 and later.

Bakker had formed his religious-broadcasting network, PTL, a couple of years earlier, when he installed a satellite transmitter at the site and began sending religious programs through the air waves. The significance of the initials seems unclear. Did they stand for "Praise the Lord?" Or "People that Love?" Or "Positive Total Living?"

Regardless, there was rapid growth. PTL became a national enterprise and, by 1984, 1,300 cable systems that served 12 million homes were presenting PTL programs. Its daily television show was broadcast on more than 170 stations. The PTL Inspirational Network offered 24-hour programming. PTL had gross annual income of $66 million and assets of $86 million. Employment had risen to 900. Just two years later PTL had annual gross income of $129 million; employment was at 2,000. Heritage USA had the nation's third most popular theme park, which attracted 6 million visitors.

Bakker headed one of the nation's three richest media ministries—sharing the honor with Jimmy Swaggart and Pat Robertson.[13] Many admired Bakker's charismatic leadership and PR ability, though it had flashes of P. T. Barnum's brand of showmanship.

Expansion in facilities, income, and staff continued until March 1987, when Bakker's brief sexual encounter with a 21-year-old woman in a Clearwater Beach, Florida, hotel room seven years earlier was exposed. The deceit and cover-up were over. Bakker was forced to step down as president; years of spending excesses at PTL and the expensive personal living habits of himself and his wife, Tammy Faye, came to a halt. The Assemblies of God defrocked Bakker, dismissing him as an ordained minister of that denomination. In less than two years, he was to be indicted by a federal grand jury for fraud and conspiracy and was later convicted in a trial and sentenced to 45 years in prison, a ruling reduced to 18 years in 1991.

Perhaps there were clues as to Bakker's eventual fate in a letter Evangelist Pat Robertson wrote to Bakker in September, 1977. Bakker, employed by Robertson from 1965 to 1972, gave leadership and inspiration to the "700 Club" of Robertson's Christian Broadcasting Network. After Bakker launched PTL, Robertson took exception to Bakker's competitive marketing practices, building his TV network at the expense of CBN, and wrote:

"Now this new evidence of duplicity, coupled with recent purchases either in competition with us, or on the same station as we are on, make me question seriously your financial wisdom, your ethics, and your truthfulness.''[14]

In the late 1970s, *The Charlotte Observer*, a daily newspaper in Charlotte, was publishing accounts that all was not as it appeared at PTL. The paper said that the hundreds of thousands of dollars Bakker was raising for overseas missions were never seen by the missions, but went to pay housekeeping bills at home. The Federal Communications Commission took a look at Bakker's affairs in secret hearings and, after a split vote, passed the matter to the U.S. Justice Department, where it died.

Over the next few years, the paper chronicled stories about poor management and fiscal woes. There were said to be financial problems and tax crises as well as wasted funds spent in the construction of Heritage USA. In just the first 10 ½ months of 1987, *The Observer* published more than 600 articles about ''Jim and Tammy Bakker's sullied religious legacy.''[15]

Still other PTL news made headlines in *The Observer* and around the country. There were extravagant purchases by Bakker: a $400,000 Florida condominium, a $600,000 estate in Palm Springs, California. Bakker and his wife were the subjects of stories about their excessive spending for clothes and jewelry, trips, the air-conditioned doghouse for their pet, and the secret suite in the Heritage Grand Hotel. Tammy's ''inch-thick'' makeup also received attention.[16]

In January 1986, to fight back against *Observer* stories which made allegations that PTL had misled its viewers about how some of its funds were spent, the enraged Bakker launched an ''Enough is Enough'' campaign. In a special hour-long program he spoke of ''the most vicious attacks in the history of ministry . . . this ministry has had enough.''[17] He encouraged those in his audience to protest the coverage of *The Observer* and cancel subscriptions to it and other papers in the Knight-Ridder Inc. chain. Protestors responded with more than 2,000 letters, with nine-to-one voicing disapproval of the coverage, but there were few cancellations. Bakker also ordered surveillance of the paper's publisher, Rolfe Neill; editor, Rich Oppel; and reporter, Charles Shepard. Oppel said he later heard from a former PTL security chief that Bakker was angered and frustrated that the tails on the three of us turned up nothing that could be used against us. Three pretty boring guys.''[18]

On December 3, 1984, *The Observer* learned of Bakker's meeting of passion with Jessica Hahn, a church secretary from New York, in a tip phoned in by an anonymous woman, who turned out to be Hahn, herself. But the trail to breaking the story was a long one. Obtaining corroborating details of proof was most difficult. It was not until early March 1987 that *The Observer* had the Bakker-Hahn story together. Bakker and his top aide knew the paper had the goods and began to plan damage control.

Bakker had word that another TV evangelist, Jimmy Swaggart, had known of the Hahn incident for a year. He feared that Swaggart planned a hostile takeover of PTL.

Bakker turned to Evangelist Jerry Falwell, head of the Moral Majority, Lynchburg, Virginia, told him about Hahn, discussed the potential efforts of Swaggart to get control of PTL—and invited Falwell to take over as head of PTL. Falwell, a Fundamentalist Baptist and an unlikely choice to assume charge of a Pentecostal denomination operation, accepted. He too wanted to head off Swaggart, worrying that he could be next. The change of leadership came at an evening meeting of the PTL board of directors on March 18. Bakker, speaking to the board in a conference call from California, resigned. He said he had asked Falwell to replace him. Falwell, on the phone from Virginia, accepted.

The next afternoon, Bakker read his statement of resignation in a conference call with *The Observer*. He said that ''in an isolated incident, I was wickedly manipulated by treacherous former friends and peer colleagues who . . . conspired to betray me into

a sexual encounter." He said he had "succumbed to blackmail
. . . to protect and spare the ministry and my family." His mention of blackmail referred to a $265,000 payoff, including a
$150,000 trust fund, from PTL to Hahn and her advisers. The
following morning the newspaper had headlines about Bakker's
quitting PTL and about his encounter with Hahn. The news-
hungry in Charlotte snatched up 20,000 extra copies.[19]

More revelations flowed through the news media. There was
disclosure of Bakker's sexual activities with male staff members;
of PTL's $68 million in debt; of PTL payments in salary and
bonuses of $1.6 million to Bakker and $300,000 to Tammy in
1986.

Charges in the suit begun by the federal government against
Bakker were much more prosaic—they involved fraud and conspiracy through television, phone, and mail. The suit followed
his indictment by a federal grand jury that convened in September 1987 and met one week a month for 16 months. His downfall
came on October 5, 1989, when a jury in the federal district court
of Charlotte, North Carolina, found him guilty on all 24 counts
against him. Judge Robert Potter sentenced Bakker to serve 45
years in prison and fined him $500,000. Late that month, at age
49, he was moved to a medium-security prison in Rochester,
Minnesota.

The disgraced television evangelist supported his PTL ministry from 1984 to 1987 with a money-raising device that was similar to a pyramid scheme. Addressing his television audiences,
Bakker offered "lifetime partnerships" to donors of $1,000 or
more. The partnerships entitled them to three free nights' lodging a year at Heritage USA, the theme park described as a Christian Disneyland that featured a 163-foot water slide, several
swimming pools, an entertainment center, a shopping mall, and
the Heritage Grand Hotel.

The government charged that Bakker sold tens of thousands
more partnerships than he said he would and that he had failed

to build the promised accommodations. The 500-room Heritage Grand was finished in 1987; a second, the Heritage Towers, was only partly finished, even though Bakker had received more than twice the amount of contributions needed to complete it. Where did the money from the lifetime partnerships go? Most went for operating expenses of Heritage USA; $3.7 million went to Bakker.

The prosecution at the trial presented testimony that Bakker's finance director cautioned him about using the partnership money for operating expenses. The practice violated "financial integrity." Prosecutors also introduced tantalizing highlights of the personal expenditures. There were the $100,000 spent for a private jet to fly the Bakkers' clothes from North Carolina to California; a $500 shower curtain; and, the $100 that bought cinnamon rolls to supply a homey fragrance in the Bakkers' hotel room, though the pastry was not eaten by them.

There were witnesses for the defense who stated their support for and belief in Bakker and who thought the money they gave him was his to use as he wished. Others testified as character witnesses. But the jurors were unimpressed. One said, "The defense didn't really offer a defense." The jury foreman said, "We kept looking for something from the defense and couldn't find anything."

Judge Potter, in delivering the sentence, said, "Those of us who do have a religion are sick of being saps for money-grubbing preachers and priests."[20]

The Observer said editorially the day after the trial ended: "The verdict in the Jim Bakker trial reflects a fundamental distinction in American law. In soliciting donations from his flock, a preacher may promise eternal life in a celestial city whose streets are paved with gold, and that's none of the law's business. But if he promises an annual free stay in a luxury hotel on Earth, he'd better have the rooms available."[21] For *The Observer*, all the time and effort were worthwhile. The paper won the Pulitzer Prize for public service in 1988.

A federal appeals court in Richmond, Virginia, on February 12, 1991, threw out Bakker's sentence and ordered that he be resentenced by a judge other than Potter. The appeals court said Judge Potter allowed his feelings about religion to influence his sentence and quoted the judge's words above, which were described as improper.[22] U.S. District Judge Graham Mullen reduced Bakker's prison time to 18 years and scrapped the $500,000 fine in a Charlotte court on August 23, 1991. In shaving Bakker's term, the judge took note of the evangelist's record in prison, where he had worked with a hospice, raised funds for United Way, and led a stop-smoking class. Bakker was now eligible for parole in 1995 rather than 2001, as under the old sentence.[23]

As well as a televangelist, Bakker was the chief executive officer of the PTL ministry. He made use of a bagful of public relations tactics to attract worshippers and their dollars to the PTL Ministry and to build an institution that provided any desired amenity for his wife and himself. He did this under the cloak of religion. He was greedy, his morality was unacceptable to many, he misappropriated funds, and he misrepresented himself to his live audiences and viewers. Nowhere in his PR productions did he appear to show respect for ethics. He faced a constant barrage of ethical considerations and he dodged them all.

POINTS

• The puzzle: Find where Jim Bakker put ethics to work in his public relations to achieve credibility. A lesson: Don't work for the adulation and support of others unless what you're offering has sound value. Don't build your program on a phony, shaky unethical foundation that may eventually collapse.

- Keep handy a generous dose of skepticism as you watch the rise in the personal successes of others. Many are just as sound as they appear to be. However, if you're part of a constantly expanding operation that seems almost too good to be true, look beneath the surface to be sure all's in order. Ask questions, particularly when you find others are questioning the credibility of the organization; don't accept easy answers.

- What if you're the CEO? You have to decide how much you value your credibility and that of your organization. Recognize there are high risks if you choose to engage in greed, deceit, falsehoods, and breaking the law. How far is the fall, if it comes? There's always the possibility it will.

TANGLES OF PR LEADER OPEN CREDIBILITY GAPS

This is a tale of charges and countercharges, contradictions that may never be resolved. Ripples swirl around executives at the pinnacle of the PR world. Ethical considerations abound. Credibility suffers.

The action centers around Anthony M. Franco, chairman of Anthony M. Franco Incorporated, a public relations firm in Detroit, which he founded in 1964. We focus attention upon him in June 1985, when he was president-elect of the Public Relations Society of America (PRSA). Franco had been a PRSA member for some 25 years and, among activities at the local chapter and national level, contributed three years as a member of the society's Board of Ethics and Professional Standards (BEPS).

On the afternoon of June 11, 1985, Franco was in a meeting at his offices with his senior investor relations executive and representatives of Crowley, Milner & Co., a client. Crowley, Milner, a Michigan corporation, operated department stores in Detroit and its suburbs. The Crowley family held a majority of

the shares, which were traded on the American Stock Exchange.
The purpose of the meeting, according to the Securities and
Exchange Commission (SEC), was to plan a public announcement of an agreement in principle for the sale of Crowley, Milner
to Oakland Holding Company (OHC), a private company.[24]

We leap in time now to an announcement by the SEC on
August 26, 1986, that stunned and shocked many among the
PRSA membership and those in related business services. The
SEC named Franco as defendant in a civil action filed in the U.S.
District Court for the District of Columbia that alleged he violated
antifraud provisions of the Securities Exchange Act. The SEC
said that in a settlement of the action and "without admitting
or denying the allegations in the complaint," Franco consented
to the entry of a permanent injunction.[25] He signed the consent
decree nearly three months earlier, on June 2.[26]

The SEC complaint alleged that Franco purchased common
stock of Crowley, Milner "while in possession of material, non-
public information," commonly known as insider information,
about the acquisition of Crowley, Milner by OHC. The commission further alleged that Franco obtained the information in confidence, in his capacity as a public relations consultant employed
by Crowley, Milner, for the benefit of the client and not for
Franco's personal benefit. After learning about the expected announcement of the OHC acquisition of Crowley, Milner, alleged
the SEC, Franco phoned his broker at home and directed him
to purchase 3,000 shares of Crowley, Milner securities (at $41
per share) for a trust account Franco maintained. The purchase
was said "to have violated a duty of trust and confidence owed
to Crowley" by Franco.[27]

On June 12, 1985, the SEC allegations continued, the American Stock Exchange informed Crowley, Milner that "Franco was
the purchaser" of the 3,000-share block (the size of the sale
triggered an AMEX inquiry). The complaint said Franco denied
to his client that he had been responsible for the trade. Later on

the 12th, said the commission, Franco phoned his broker and asked him to cancel the trade, and the broker did so. The SEC further alleged that on the 12th and later "Franco discussed with his broker various ways in which Franco might avoid having to take responsibility for the trade. The broker declined to follow such a course of action."[28]

Since the stock transaction was nullified within such a short time, it didn't make the transfer sheets. There was no trade. Franco earned no profit.

On the following day, according to the SEC complaint, Crowley, Milner issued a news release, prepared by Franco's staff, announcing the agreement in principle to acquisition by holders of more than 51 percent of Crowley, Milner at $50 a share. Ironically, a month later Crowley, Milner announced that negotiations for its acquisition by OHC had been terminated.

Franco would not comment for this book about the SEC investigation and his signing of the consent decree or the way this affected his position as elected head of PRSA. In a prepared statement on August 27, 1986, he said "a transaction did occur in my family's trust account. It was cancelled the same day it [the transaction] occurred and no financial gain resulted from it. I have decided the best course of action would be to sign the consent decree rather than go through the long and arduous process of litigation."[29]

The following spring, he told *pr reporter*, "When I signed the consent decree, I thought it was more of a benign document than it is. I was naive. Signing it means you neither admit nor deny any of the allegations of the complaint. But that's not understood by most people.

"Often people understand what's perceived over what's real. Once I signed the consent decree, I was perceived guilty. And, by signing the SEC agreement, I am prohibited from comment-

ing on the merits of the settlement. As public relations practitioners know, silence is often perceived as guilt."[30]

Jack O'Dwyer's Newsletter commented, "The SEC has a policy
of nabbing well-known people so that its cases will receive maximum publicity."[31] Could the SEC have pursued the case because
of Franco's position as PRSA president? Was that the lightning
rod?

The problem here centers around the lack of certainty about
what really happened: the SEC allegations that Franco phoned
the broker and asked him to buy the shares of Crowley, Milner,
and Franco's denial of this. Somewhere there's deception about
the purchase of the stock that opens ethical questions. The un-
certainties fog credibility. The SEC consent decree set up another
problem for Franco with officers and board members of PRSA
in 1986.

PRSA, with about 13,000 members at that time, is the world's
largest public relations organization even though it represents a
tiny percentage of the estimated 300,000 employed in the United
States in some aspect of public relations. Still, among PRSA
members are many of the country's highest public relations executives in business and in counseling firms. The society has
worked continuously and assiduously to develop professionalism in its ranks. A Code of Professional Standards was first
adopted in 1954 and has been revised five times since. Specific
procedures in the bylaws provide for enforcement of the standards, investigation of a member charged with a violation, and
disciplinary action as warranted.

The SEC wrote to Franco on October 29, 1985, more than
four months after the alleged stock purchase, while he was still
president-elect, shortly before his election to the top role at the
society's annual meeting in November. The SEC letter was a
request for documents related to Franco's alleged purchase of
Crowley, Milner stock and to preparation of materials by his staff

that announced the proposed acquisition.[32] Franco said later in an interview with *The Wall Street Journal* that he didn't tell PRSA about the probe at that time "because he and his lawyer thought nothing would come of it."[33]

Franco said he accepted the presidency of PRSA at the start of 1986 "because I was advised by counsel that the likelihood of a case being brought was slim. In hindsight, however, publicity brought on by my title and the attention fed by some PRSA members blew it out of proportion."[34] He learned in the spring that the SEC might take action against him.[35]

The first person in PRSA to hear of the SEC investigation of Franco was Betsy Kovacs, the society's executive vice president. She said the first time Franco talked about the SEC investigation with her was on or about May 5. In the conversation, she said, "He did not give me details of the situation but said that the issue was minor and that probably nothing would come of it. He insisted that I must keep everything absolutely confidential because he said he was innocent, and that if the information leaked, he could be in serious jeopardy with even more serious consequences for himself, his business, and his family." Kovacs said she repeatedly urged Franco to discuss the situation with the immediate past president, David Ferguson, the president-elect, Jack Felton, and the chair of the Board of Ethics and Professional Standards. "This is what he ultimately did," she said.[36]

On August 1, 1986, nearly two months after he signed the consent decree, Franco talked with a second PRSA person—David Ferguson—while driving him and his wife to a district meeting of the society in Ohio. Ferguson described the conversation at a PRSA Symposium on Demonstrating Professionalism held September 5, 1986. "He mentioned that he had been specifically barred from discussing the matter, but felt that as immediate past president of PRSA I should know about it. He [said] . . . premature disclosure of what he was about to tell me could be very damaging to him, and asked me to promise him that I would not reveal the subject of our discussion until it had been made public, which I did. He then told me that he had been under investigation by the SEC concerning an incident which gave the appearance of insider trading in the stock of a client's company.''

Ferguson said Franco told him about the SEC investigation and said he was told ''the outcome was that Tony had been given the option of signing a consent decree or having the matter taken to court.'' Asked by Franco for his thoughts about the relative merits of the alternatives, Ferguson said it seemed to him the consent decree ''would be less painful.''

Franco also explained, said Ferguson, that he had requested the SEC to withhold action for a period of time because of a medical problem of one of his children and that the SEC had agreed to the delay of three months.

Ferguson said the conversation turned to the effect of the SEC action on Franco's PRSA activities, and he recalled Franco wondered if he should ask for a hearing before the society's Board of Ethics and Professional Standards. Ferguson said he later learned from the then chair of that board, Don McCammond, that Franco discussed the situation with him and arrangements were made for Franco to meet with the BEPS on September 19.[37]

Franco phoned Jack Felton on August 23, 1986, and, according to Felton, ''Swore me to absolute secrecy and then [said] that he had signed a consent decree with SEC over the purchase of stock for a Franco family trust. . . . He told me his lawyer had advised him not to tell anyone—that his lawyer felt it would be handled as a minor routine matter and that his title as president of PRSA would not appear in any documents filed.''[38]

We've now arrived at August 26, the day the SEC released the information that Franco had signed the consent decree back in June. News that the government had charged the elected leader of organized public relations with wrongdoing sent shock waves through the New York headquarters of PRSA and offices of members around the nation. Ferguson experienced some of this reaction on August 28 at a meeting of the board of directors of the Chicago chapter and "felt the full force of the anger and frustration of these caring members about the developments and their concern for PRSA."[39]

Meanwhile, according to Ferguson, Franco said in a conference call with Kovacs, Ferguson, and Felton late on August 28 that he planned to resign the presidency, an action to be effective at 3 P.M. the following day. Among reasons for resigning, Franco said he didn't want his position as president to interfere with decisions of the Board of Ethics and Professional Standards. There was no mention in his resignation letter of the SEC charges or his signing the consent decree.

Franco met with BEPS on September 19, and a report from that group was before the board of directors at its October 4 meeting. Franco attended a portion of the board meeting, then left to return to his hotel and write his letter of resignation from the society effective that day, and sent it by messenger to the PRSA office. With Franco's resignation, the board terminated its session as it had no authority over nonmembers.

Back to August 26 to 29 and the PRSA headquarters, where there was more to do than answer the barrage of calls from the news media. The membership needed to be informed of what had happened. And, the successor to Franco as president must be announced. Somehow, though, within this organization of communications experts, the first word to the membership failed the test of clarity.

President-Elect Felton signed an August 29 letter to members that told of Franco's resignation but gave no reason for it. PRSA told members for the first time about the consent decree in a

letter signed by Felton as president dated September 11. En-
closed with this was a copy of a letter from the society's attorney
explaining that parties signing a decree neither admit nor deny
the charges made by the SEC. In another letter to members from
Felton on October 5, he announced Franco's resignation from
the society, noting that the action was voluntary and came after
a meeting of Franco with the board of directors. While the letter
said Franco's resigning followed his signing of the SEC consent
decree, it did not speak of the SEC allegations. Felton emphasized that the PRSA bylaws required confidentiality on proceedings of BEPS and the board of directors.

At the time the board received Franco's resignation from the
society, according to a PRSA news release, it was considering
possible violations by him of (1) articles of the society's Code of
Professional Standards that concern dealing fairly, safeguarding
confidences, and not intentionally communicating false or misleading information and (2) Financial Relations Interpretations
of the PRSA Code that address the duty not to buy or sell client
securities when in possession of confidential information, and
the use of inside information.[40]

There was criticism from members that Felton's October 5
letter "should have been more informative about the consent
decree and other public records."[41] Finally, almost three and
one-half months after the story broke, on December 11 the society made a valiant effort to communicate fully with members.
This action came because of a November 8 meeting of the PRSA
assembly, a board made up of members elected by chapters, at
which delegates had questions about restrictions imposed by
PRSA bylaws that hindered communications with members and
the public. (Franco was not invited to appear before the assembly.) The assembly suggested mailing to the membership these
items: Ferguson's remarks at the September symposium; Felton's and Kovacs' remarks to the assembly about the Franco
matter; recommendations of a special task force on procedures,
appointed to review PRSA's handling of the Franco matter, pre-

sented to the assembly; and copies of the consent decree and other papers filed by the SEC on August 26, along with a letter from PRSA's legal counsel defining a consent decree. These materials formed an information packet sent to members, with a cover letter from Felton, on December 11.

A development that turned out to be vital for the future of PRSA was the board's appointment of the special task force, to examine the "crisis in leadership." The introduction of this group's report recognized that "the Society's response and actions have been challenged and criticized by many members in the public media, often with an unfortunate rush to uninformed judgment." The task force identified "six fundamental problems" presented by the Franco case and made recommendations regarding each.[42] The board of directors accepted and acted upon the suggestions.

Regarding communications, the report recommended that the society disclose bad news quickly and fully. To solve the problem that arose when a member resigned while under investigation and PRSA was powerless to act, there was a recommendation that resignations be effective 90 days after they are received by the society, so there would be time to complete an investigation and take action. Another recommendation was for extension of the disclosure policy, adopted by the board for officer and director candidates after the Franco news, to members of the Board of Ethics and Judicial panels, and to officer and director nominees for chapter posts.

In other words, the walls of PRSA shook over the Franco affair. There was confusion, near chaos. But the collective good sense of the leadership, sometimes more absent than present during the crisis days, recognized the dangers and was the source for changes to avoid at least some of the pitfalls in the future.

There was scorching censure of both Franco and PRSA for the bungling and inept handling. A page one headline in *The Wall*

Street Journal charged "PR Society Receives Some Very Bad PR— From Its Ex-Chief." The story led off with, "The public-relations business has an image problem. His name is Anthony Franco."

After noting the SEC charge and Franco's signing of the consent decree, the paper said, "What was worse, in the eyes of many in the industry, was how the PRSA, perhaps the nation's premier organization of communicators, and Mr. Franco, the top-dog flack of them all, somehow failed to communicate." Published a week before the board's October meeting, the paper went on, "The Franco affair is being dragged out, and Mr. Franco and the PRSA are being dragged through the mud, in one of the biggest and most embarrassing PR gaffes in years. In short, it is not a textbook case of effective public relations."[43]

Jack O'Dwyer's Newsletter reported that immediately following the SEC release, the investor relations section of PRSA asked for Franco's resignation as president, and the National Capital chapter asked that Franco step down until the ethics board examined the matter. The newsletter said it had "talked with more than 30 PR professionals in the two days following announcement of the SEC charges, and better than 90 percent said Franco's only course of action was to step aside."[44]

Under the headline "Ethics in U.S. Public Relations: Trouble at the Top," the *International Public Relations Review* in November said, "The Franco episode . . . must have left many readers of . . . publications reporting the case with the impression that public relations associations are more interested in promoting their profession and defending their officers' and members' interests than they are in raising and maintaining levels of ethical conduct."[45]

Further commentary: The *Journal of Mass Media Ethics* in each issue presents a case study of an ethical dilemma, with comments from scholars and practitioners on how they might solve it. The Franco case, "dealing with a variety of ethical dilemmas," was under scrutiny in a 1989 issue.[46] Here are selected comments:

David Ferguson: "Whom do you believe? A trusted friend and colleague who, to the best of your knowledge, had not deceived you in the past? Or an agency of the federal government, which relied on information from third parties whom you did not know and would have no opportunity to question? . . . what is not forgotten is the ethical quandary the situation presented. I learned how difficult it is to make judgments on the ethics of other people."

Scott M. Cutlip, dean emeritus, Henry W. Grady School of Journalism and Mass Communication, University of Georgia, coauthor of *Effective Public Relations:* ". . . for those of us who are members of PRSA, the Anthony Franco case is the most painful and embarrassing of the several instances of unethical behavior that have scarred public relations in recent years. Both PRSA and Franco wound up with plenty of egg on their faces. . . . Franco should have been asked to resign once the SEC charges became public. Surely, PRSA should have sent out a news release . . . when Franco resigned."

Melvin L. Sharpe, professor and coordinator, public relations department, Ball State University: "The Franco case allows us to see how unexpectedly even a professional organization that should have been the most prepared to avoid the kind of problems encountered can find itself unprepared and engulfed in controversy. What might appropriately be called basic standards for the effective performance of public relations were not in place."

Frank W. Wylie, professor, California State University, Long Beach; past president, PRSA; former director of public relations, Chrysler Corporation: "It is the responsibility of the officers and board of directors to (*a*) abide by the bylaws, (*b*) protect the interests of the membership, and (*c*) act promptly in crisis situations. Surprisingly, none of these seemed to happen. The problems of public relations have been caused by the inept, the unscrupulous, and well-intended bunglers. PR has often lacked leadership it needed, and, in various unfortunate ways, PR has earned its criticisms. If we do better, we may merit greater public confidence, but now, post–Franco, it will take a lot of doing."

Deni Elliott, director, Ethics Institute, Dartmouth College: "Franco accepted the PRSA presidency knowing he was under investigation for action directly related to his profession. It certainly was in the best interest of the PRSA membership to have a president untarnished by such an ongoing investigation. . . . When individual PRSA officers failed to inform the membership about the investigation of Mr. Franco or the details of his resignation, they failed to fulfill a professional duty."

For Tony Franco, it has been business almost as usual since 1986. He continues to be active in community service and civic organizations—he served as 1990–91 chairman of the Greater Detroit Chamber of Commerce. *PR Quarterly* selected Franco as 1 of 100 "PR Super Stars," the only one from Michigan, in 1991.

POINTS

• When you're in a bind, when you encounter an ethical dilemma, recognize it for what it is and face up to it.

• Don't postpone an ethical decision you know you must make. Delay can allow matters to get worse and make your attempt to be credible more difficult.

• Don't rely on others to help you out, to give you any aid or comfort. Your problem is an individual matter; the course you decide is based on your own code of standards and behavior.

• Get out all the facts when you communicate with others about a personal or institutional crisis. When information is omitted or delayed, there is the appearance of a coverup. Credibility is hurt.

NOTES

1. J. F. terHorst, "Gerald Ford and the Future of the Presidency" (New York: The Third Press, 1974), p. 236.
2. Ibid.
3. Remarks of J. F. terHorst "Gerald R. Ford—Restoring the Presidency," *Hofstra University Forum*, April 8, 1989.
4. "Ethics—Easier Said than Done," *Josephson Institute* 1, nos. 2 and 3 (Spring–Summer 1990), p. 102.
5. TerHorst, "Gerald Ford and the Future of the Presidency," p. 234.
6. Ibid., p. 235.
7. "Notes on People," *The New York Times*, October 5, 1974, p. 19.
8. TerHorst, "Gerald Ford and the Future of the Presidency," p. vii.
9. Ibid., p. 185.
10. Ibid., p. 236.
11. "Honorable Withdrawal," *The New York Times*, September 10, 1974, p. 40.
12. TerHorst, "Gerald Ford and the Future of the Presidency," p. 191.
13. "Reflections, Jim and Tammy," *The New Yorker*, April 23, 1990, p. 48.
14. Charles E. Shepard, "Forgiven—The Rise and Fall of Jim Bakker and the PTL Ministry," *Atlantic Monthly Press*, 1989, p. 84.
15. *The Bulletin*, American Society of Newspaper Editors, January 1988, pp. 4–5.
16. "Reflections, Jim and Tammy," p. 45.
17. Shepard, "Forgiven," p. 366.
18. *The Bulletin*, p. 7.
19. Shepard, "Forgiven," p. 515.

20. Milo Geyelin and Arthur S. Hayes, ''Jim Bakker's 45-Year Sentence Is Thrown Out by Appeals Court,'' *The Wall Street Journal*, February 13, 1991, p. B4.
21. ''Justice for Jim Bakker: Fraud, not Religion, Was the Issue before the Judge,'' *The Charlotte Observer*, October 6, 1989, editorial page.
22. Geyelin and Hayes, ''Jim Bakker's 45-Year Sentence Is Thrown Out by Appeals Court.''
23. Ann Hagedorn and Wade Lambert, ''Legal Beat,'' *The Wall Street Journal*, August 26, 1991, p. B5.
24. Complaint for permanent injunction, *Securities and Exchange Commission* v. *Anthony M. Franco*, U.S. District Court for the District of Columbia, August 26, 1986.
25. Litigation release #11206, Securities and Exchange Commission, August 26, 1986.
26. Consent of Anthony M. Franco, *Securities and Exchange Commission* v. *Anthony M. Franco*, U.S. District Court for the District of Columbia, June 2, 1986.
27. Complaint for permanent injunction.
28. Ibid.
29. Cynthia S. Grisdela, ''SEC Files Charges of Insider Trading against Publicist,'' *The Wall Street Journal*, August 27, 1986, p. 4.
30. ''Franco Speaks Publicly for First Time about His Case and What Can Be Learned from It by Practitioners and PR Societies,'' *pr reporter* 30, no. 15 (April 13, 1987), p. 1.
31. *Jack O'Dwyer's Newsletter* 19, no. 35 (September 3, 1986), p. 1.
32. Letter from Lise A. Lustgarten, Securities and Exchange Commission, to Mr. Franco, Re: In the Matter of Trading in the Securities of Crowley, Milner & Co. (MHO-960), October 25, 1985.
33. Joanne Lipman, ''PR Society Receives Some Very Bad PR—From Its Ex-Chief,'' *The Wall Street Journal*, September 26, 1986, p. 1.
34. ''Franco Speaks Publicly for First Time,'' p. 1.
35. Lipman, ''PR Society Receives Some Very Bad PR—From Its Ex-Chief.''
36. Remarks by Betsy Kovacs before PRSA Assembly, Washington, D.C., November 8, 1986.
37. Remarks by David Ferguson at PRSA Symposium on Demonstrating Professionalism, Itasca, Illinois, September 5, 1986.
38. Remarks by John W. Felton before PRSA Assembly, Washington, D.C., November 8, 1986.
39. Remarks by Ferguson.

40. "Former PRSA President Anthony M. Franco Resigns from The Society," news release, Public Relations Society of America, October 5, 1986.

41. Report of the Procedures Task Force to the Assembly of PRSA, Washington, D.C., November 8, 1986.

42. Ibid.

43. Lipman, "PR Society Receives Some Very Bad PR—From Its Ex-Chief."

44. *Jack O'Dwyer's Newsletter*, p. 1.

45. "Ethics in U.S. Public Relations: Trouble at the Top," *International Public Relations Review*, November 1986, p. 9.

46. *Journal of Mass Media Ethics* 4, no.1, 1989, p. 106.

Chapter Three

Reacting to a Crisis

How do executives and managers react when a crisis strikes? In many cases, the hit comes from out of the blue. It's a disaster that's unforeseen, that there could be no protection against or planning to prevent. But not always. Sometimes greater diligence in the monitoring of operations could have prevented unwanted exposure and damage.

The response to the crisis, and the way it's viewed by outsiders, enhances or damages the credibility of the crisis-affected organization. By ensuring that it has an ethical basis for the response, the organization can get through the crisis with its credibility flag flying. Consider how ethics in public relations were put to use, or largely ignored, by four corporations as they dealt with crises.

DOW CORNING CAUGHT IN SILICONE IMPLANT CONTROVERSY

A San Francisco federal court jury verdict on December 15, 1991, broke into the open what had been a smoldering story about the safety of silicone gel breast implants. The jury ordered Dow Corning to pay $7.3 million to a woman who claimed implants caused damage to her immune system. Dow Corning, major manufacturer of silicone gel implants, a joint venture of Dow Chemical Co. and Corning Inc., was found to have committed fraud and malice by failing to disclose evidence from its research about potential harmful effects from inserted implants. On January 6, 1992, the U.S. Food and Drug Administration called for a moratorium on surgical insertion of the implants while it gave further study to safety in their use.

Fears heightened among women who had received silicone gel implants. Horror stories surfaced of some women's unpleasant health experiences caused by implants. Still others spoke of their satisfaction with implant results. Since the first breast implant surgery in 1962, more than one million women had undergone implant insertion for reconstruction after breast cancer surgery or for cosmetic reasons.[1] Many women in each category were upset and angry because they were not told of the risks. "There's an underlying sense of rage and betrayal," said Kathleen M. Harris, a Pittsburgh doctor.

Dow Corning released a document that showed "its own researchers were concerned as far back as the early 1970s that the implants could leak—sending silicone through the body with undetermined consequences." This information became public at the 1991 trial.[2] Other materials made public by the firm, responding to an FDA request, revealed complaints from plastic surgeons in the 1980s about problems with the gel product.

"The Dow Corning Corporation revealed itself . . . as a company adrift without a moral compass," commented Steven Fink in an op-ed column in The New York Times. He wrote after learning that for two decades the company had known about the possibility of silicone leaks. "By becoming forthright only after obfuscation, denial, and rationalization failed, the company demonstrated that honesty had been relegated to a backup position."[3]

Fink said the memos and other correspondence written by Dow Corning staff members over 20 years should have served as warning signs. "The company should have created the customer registry that it is only now contemplating and a data base for doctors. It also should have created a crisis management plan guided by a code of corporate ethics."

Columnist Ellen Goodman asked if women had been part of an "experiment"; then she decided that "is too scientific a word for the poorly researched and weakly regulated free market in silicone." She quoted Esther Rome, health activist with the Boston Women's Health Collective, who said, "The manufacturers lied to the plastic surgeons and the plastic surgeons lied to the patients."[4]

There was a management shake-up at Dow Corning in February 1992 that "signals that the company, once inclined to play hardball with opponents, now is shifting toward conciliatory dealings with critics. The move may also indicate a new willingness by the company to acknowledge possible shortcomings in the testing and manufacture" of the implants.[5]

The shift in management brought in as chairman and chief executive officer Keith R. McKennon, who had been executive vice president of Dow Chemical U.S.A. Because implants represented less than 1 percent of Dow Corning's business, the major executive change seemed to recognize the firm's discomfort at finding itself in the crisis spotlight. McKennon's selection, said *The Wall Street Journal*, "appears to support the idea that the company may be taking a softer stance." The paper quoted a security analyst in describing McKennon as "the sort of guy who will lead to compromise solutions, and there's already a change in how Dow Corning is reacting to the public." The story also noted that his "olive-branch approach" might be expensive for Dow Corning. McKennon suggested several steps Dow Corning might take: funding surgery for women who wanted the implants removed but couldn't afford it; continuing research on safety of implants; and setting up a registry with names of women who've had implants as a way to find links to illnesses. The cost of simply removing a high number of implants could be staggering; the cost for one might be as much as $6,500.

The FDA appointed an advisory panel to make recommendations as to future handling of implants and received its report on February 20. In mid-April, the agency announced severe limits on implants. Women with ruptured or leaking implants or other urgent needs and those who required implants for breast reconstruction could be served. However, the FDA restricted the number of implants for cosmetic reasons to 2,000 women. Previously, about 80 percent of the implants were for cosmetic purposes. All women receiving implants would have to enroll in clinical studies to help the FDA gather information about risks.

Dow Corning didn't wait for the word from FDA but took a drastic step to resolve its crisis. On March 19, McKennon told reporters at a news conference that Dow Corning was pulling out of the silicone gel implant business. He said the firm still would be willing to spend up to $15 million for research into health problems caused by implants. Also, Dow Corning would offer $1,200 to a woman who wanted its implants removed but couldn't afford the cost.

McKennon said, "We have made errors. But if we haven't done right up to now, we are sure going to try to do it now." *The New York Times* said the company faced hundreds of lawsuits filed by women with its implants. The CEO also commended the FDA, which "has treated us fairly. They have done the best they could in a difficult situation." This comment was noted by the paper as "a considerable change in tone from when Dow Corning was under different management and company officials said they did not believe the women who were complaining were suffering from anything linked to implants."[6]

Dow Corning covered up unfavorable findings about implants, a serious breach of ethics in public relations. But with the San Francisco trial, it found it could no longer stonewall. With disclosure of the deception, the firm's credibility ebbed. Replacement of the guy at the top, the number one PR person, was not enough to renew the trust. Dow Corning could reduce, though not completely eliminate, the crisis only by quitting the business.

It did this with grace, saying it would continue to be associated with the implant problem on a constructive basis.

POINTS

• Don't sit on unfavorable or unpleasant facts about products or any other aspect of an operation. These are early warning signals not to be ignored.

• If a product can't perform in the way that users are led to expect, take it off the market for further research and testing.

• Keep business and public relations ethics at hand in decision making, and put them to work. Dow Corning could have avoided this crisis, and the shock to its credibility. The company was deceptive in covering up reports of leaks and other implant problems over a 20-year period.

• Be careful in deciding what steps to take to overcome a crisis. Dow Corning said it would pay for removal of implants from women who couldn't afford it. What was the message? Surely some women wondered: If Dow Corning is willing to pay, are they really safe?

COMPANY GIVEN LOW RATINGS FOR ETHICS AND SOCIAL RESPONSIBILITY IN REACTING TO OIL SPILL

There were immediate and strong opinions, mostly critical, of the company involved in the oil spill caused by the grounding of the tanker Exxon Valdez in Prince William Sound, Alaska, on March 24, 1989. The worst such disaster in North American history, the accident emptied 11 million gallons of crude oil into the waters, eventually fouling 2,600 square miles of the sound.

The environment suffered the loss of thousands of birds and hundreds of animals.[7]

How swift and dedicated was the initial reaction of the executive management of Exxon Corporation, owner of the torn tanker? Did those at the top commit all possible resources on a timely basis? Were there thorough, continuing efforts to communicate as fully as possible with all government bodies, environmental groups, employees, shareholders, the news media, and other publics of interest? How well did Exxon put to use the basic elements of ethical public relations—those that establish integrity and credibility?

Critics of Exxon pointed to the tardiness of Chairman and Chief Executive Officer (CEO) Lawrence Rawl in becoming publicly visible after the spill. His "delay in responding drew criticism from analysts and consultants," said *The Wall Street Journal.* It was a week after the accident before he commented publicly, and when he did, he told a news service "that the U.S. Coast Guard and Alaska officials were to blame for the holdup in efforts to clean up the water. 'I don't want to point fingers, but the facts are, we're getting a bad rap on that delay.' " Hardly an acceptance of responsibility.

An analyst, Bruce Lazier of Prescott Ball & Turben, was quoted: "We've heard from the president of the U.S. faster than we've heard from the chairman of Exxon." The paper said "early public relations efforts were sketchy" and the president of Exxon U.S.A., William Stevens, "didn't fly to the site of the spill until President Bush decided to send three representatives to survey the situation." On this point, Exxon President Lee Raymond said that although Stevens did meet with the Bush emissaries, he had other reasons to go to Alaska. "We came to the conclusion that we needed a senior executive on the scene."[8]

"Public relations practitioners view the Valdez as a classic case study of what can go wrong when proven public relations wisdom is underutilized," said the lead-in for an article published in the October 1989 issue of *Public Relations Journal*, the voice of the Public Relations Society of America.

From a public relations practitioner's perspective, it continued, the number one rule in disaster communications was ignored: "Quickly take charge of the news flow and give the public, by way of the news media, a credible, concerned, and wholly committed spokesperson."

The coauthors, E. Bruce Harrison and Tom Prugh, listed points that come into play in a disaster-emergency plan, starting with, "The CEO makes or breaks the public relations outcome." Particularly with environmental incidents of such magnitude, they said, public opinion focuses on the executive "who personifies the company and will communicate for it. He or she must be credible, concerned, and wholly committed—and must be immediately presented to the public via the media."

Exxon CEO Rawl, they went on, "drew heavy fire for failing to inject himself more forcefully, or with the appearance of greater force, into the news coverage immediately after the accident. Since conditioned consumers now more than ever expect to hear from the corporate persona, the longer they wait, the faster the opportunity to present the company's side melts.

"In the Valdez situation, there was a disconnect—a vacuum that created confusion, mistrust, and a field day for other spokespersons."[9]

Corroborating views were expressed by other public relations experts to *The New York Times:* "Exxon seriously worsened the damage to its public standing by failing to seize control of developments after the spill and establish itself as a company concerned about the problems it had caused." These experts said Exxon's biggest mistake was that Rawl "sent a succession of lower-ranking executives to Alaska to deal with the spill instead of going there himself and taking control of the situation in a forceful, highly visible way." Rawl's failure to do this left the impression that the problem just wasn't big enough for top management to get involved.[10]

Let's hear from Rawl. Why didn't he "inject himself more forcefully"? He was at home on Good Friday when the phone rang at 8:30 A.M. and he learned that the Exxon tanker was aground and spilling oil. He told *The Wall Street Journal* that his instinct was to head for Alaska, but he let his colleagues talk him out of it. "What are you going to do?" fellow executives asked Rawl. "We've already said we've done it, we're going to pay for it, and that we're responsible for it." He said he was swayed by the argument that he would "just get in the way . . . now he sometimes wishes he had gotten in the way. . . . I wake up in the middle of the night questioning the decision to stay home."

Another decision made by Rawl and his associates on that first day caused problems in communicating with the news media, and hence the public. The Exxon executives decided information from the company would be issued in Alaska through Exxon people at Valdez, rather than from the corporate offices in New York. Technical difficulties and time differences slowed the flow of news. Phone lines to Valdez quickly became overcrowded and jammed and even Rawl, said the paper, "concedes he couldn't always find a knowledgeable Exxon official there to brief him." Exxon representatives at Valdez held news conferences on a local time basis, failing to take into account the four-hour difference between Alaska and television news and press association headquarters in New York. When the news lagged, and the amount was limited, the public wondered if there was coverup or other manipulation in the handling of information by Exxon.[11]

Rawl's signature was at the bottom of a full-page ad, an "Open Letter to the Public," sponsored by Exxon in some 100 magazines and newspapers in early April. The message said,

"Exxon has moved swiftly and competently to minimize the effect this oil will have on the environment, fish, and other wildlife. . . . I want to tell you how sorry I am that this accident took place." Public relations practitioners pointed out that in the ad the company did not take responsibility for what had happened. They said the ad seemed platitudinous to some and "failed to address the many pointed questions raised about Exxon's conduct."[12] Among letters to the editor printed by *The Wall Street Journal* in response after it published the ad, one reader asked, "Where is he [Rawl] getting his information? During the first three days, little was done to contain the spill." Another said, "Hogwash! Every news account I have read states that Exxon has done less than nothing—even to the point of getting in the way."[13]

Exxon's response to the spill was "prompt and consistent with the contingency plan previously approved by federal and state authorities," according to President Stevens of Exxon, U.S.A. He said in testimony before the Senate Environmental Protection Subcommittee on April 19, 1989, that "within three hours of the spill, Exxon Shipping Company set up a Casualty Response Center in Houston." He said that in the first few hours arrangements were made for the first 5 of over 80 flights needed to airlift more than 2,000 tons of equipment to Alaska. Key response team managers were at the spill site 18 hours after the grounding and dozens more trained people arrived daily. He termed the Exxon effort "probably the largest buildup of equipment and personnel ever assembled to combat an oil spill." He also spoke of the firm's mitigation of the economic impact on communities in the area by opening claims offices and placing funds in local banks to give advance payments to fishermen and others requiring support while claims were being processed.[14]

Countering this was a comment that the company "compounded the damage to its image by initially misleading the press and local residents with assurances that its beach cleanup and booming operations were well under way" at a time when they hadn't started.[15] There also was criticism from Richard Go-lob, publisher of *Golob's Oil Pollution Bulletin*, that Exxon's statements were "erratic and contradictory" and that there was an understatement of the problem. "A spokesman said there would be minimum environmental damage. Anyone who follows these things knows that cannot be true."[16]

Shareholders at the firm's annual meeting on May 18, 1989, in Parsippany, New Jersey, or at least a portion of the 1,700 who attended, had not accepted all the company's explanations. Some fired hostile questions at Rawl and others asked for his resignation. In advance of the meeting, representatives of pension funds holding large blocks of Exxon stock had met with company officials and exacted two promises: "that management would recommend a person with an environmental background be named to the board and that the board form an environmental committee." Prior agreement on these eliminated some potential controversy. Despite the voices of anger at the meeting, shareholders were friendly enough to Rawl and the company to reelect him and other directors and approve management proposals by large majorities. Outside the hotel where the meeting was convened, environmental demonstrators shouted protests and carried placards with messages critical of Exxon.[17]

The voices of the environmentalists were less outraged and more muted overall than might have been expected, according to *Business Week* magazine. It wasn't that they held Exxon blameless, "but by focusing on the company, they contend, critics ignore the real problem: U.S. dependence on oil." Andrew Davis of Greenpeace U.S.A., said, "Sure you can vent a lot of anger, but it's a little misguided."[18]

Others in the United States expressed their frustration with the way Exxon was handling the oil spill by responding as consumers. Radio talk show hosts in some cities asked listeners to boycott Exxon products. The hosts also asked listeners to cut up their Exxon credit cards and send them to the stations or directly

to Rawl. One station in Seattle received more than 1,000 muti-
lated cards.[19] In the House of Representatives, New York Democrat James H. Scheuer stood on the floor and cut his card in half.

In attempts to assess blame for the cause of the accident that
took the Valdez aground, attention narrowed to the ship's captain,
Joseph J. Hazelwood. A felony charge of criminal negligence and
three misdemeanor charges, including operating a vessel while
intoxicated, were lodged against him. A jury in the Anchorage
Superior Court, on March 22, 1990, after six weeks of testimony,
found the captain guilty on only one misdemeanor count, negli-
gent discharge of oil. Superior Court Judge Karl Johnstone on the
following day sentenced Hazelwood to 1,000 hours of community
service, specifically to clean oil from the beaches of Prince William
Sound, and ordered him to pay a fine of $50,000. The sentence
was suspended pending an appeal to the Alaska Court of Appeals,
which announced the overturn of the conviction on July 10, 1992.

The National Safety Board released findings on July 31, 1990,
that spread the blame for the spill; the ship's captain, the third
mate, and Exxon Shipping Co., as well as the Coast Guard and
state and local authorities were found culpable. The board
charged that the third mate failed to navigate the vessel properly
"because of fatigue and excessive workload." His boss, Captain
Hazelwood, wasn't supervising, said the board, because of his
"impairment from alcohol." Exxon failed to "provide a fit master and a rested and sufficient crew," said the board. The Coast
Guard received blame for the ineffectiveness of its traffic-
tracking service and lack of effective piloting services. Alaska
was found at fault for not having piloting rules that called for a
federally licensed pilot familiar with the waterway to be aboard.

Exxon bargained a $1.03 billion settlement with the U.S. Justice
Department and the state of Alaska for civil claims and criminal
charges. Federal Judge H. Russel Holland, who approved the
agreement on October 8, 1991, said his decision took into account
the $3 billion already spent by Exxon for clean-up of the spill.

Claims against Exxon from those who had suffered losses, including fishermen and landowners, still were in court. Through all of this, Exxon needlessly suffered a tremendous loss of credibility. *Business Week* magazine gave a succinct explanation for the Exxon behavior with the comment that Rawl was "never much of a hand at public relations."[20] Too bad that Rawl hadn't worked harder at it—that he did not have a deeper understanding of the public relations role of the CEO. By displaying greater expertise of this kind in the Valdez disaster, Rawl could have saved Exxon from heavy criticism for lacking in business and public relations ethics.

POINTS

• Remember the importance of perception, especially in a crisis, and its effect on credibility. If involvement by the CEO is missing or not obvious, the perception may be that he or she is not interested, doesn't care enough.

• Work with the news media from the beginning. Be open. Give them and the public the facts as they become available.

• Keep ethics in mind in day-to-day operations. For Exxon, this would have meant providing a refreshed crew and a fit master.

• Accept responsibility for what has happened if it rightly sits on your doorstep or that of your organization.

MIGHTY INDUSTRIAL EXPLOSION REVERBERATES 12,000 MILES—ETHICAL RESPONSE IS BLOCKED

Just after midnight on December 3, 1984, in Bhopal, India, leaking poisonous gas, methyl isocyanate (MIC), at a pesticide plant touched off an explosion. It was the worst industrial accident in the history of the world. The plant was one of several facilities in India owned and operated by Union Carbide India Ltd. (UCIL).

At 4 A.M. eastern standard time on the same day, Union Carbide Corporation's media relations staffers in Connecticut began receiving phone calls at their homes from wire services and radio newspeople with questions about the disaster. By 7 A.M. executives of Union Carbide (UCC) were assembling at headquarters in Danbury, Connecticut, greatly frustrated in their attempts to get information about what had happened.[21]

Early estimates of the number of deaths ranged beyond 2,500, and later it was determined the toll was approximately 3,800. In the first days after the tragedy, there were fears that as many as 100,000 survivors would suffer permanent disabilities, but authorities later found the seriously injured numbered about 20,000. The greatest casualties were suffered by those who lived in shantytowns near the plant. These slum homes, incidentally, were erected illegally. The plant was built on the outskirts of the city on land leased by UCIL from the government and surrounded by cleared land. But plant workers began building shelters for their families, and other Indians moved into the area. UCIL asked the government to move the people off the property, but officials at first ignored the request and then changed the law to make the shantytowns legal.[22]

In February 1989, the Supreme Court of India directed a final settlement of all litigation arising out of this disaster in the amount of $470 million—many times larger than any previous damage award in the history of India. The court granted criminal immunity to Union Carbide, an action taken because the Indian government had asked that the UCC chairman and chief executive officer, Warren M. Anderson, stand trial in India on murder charges. The court did not, however, assess blame for the accident. The decision asked for $425 million from Union Carbide Corporation and $45 million from UCIL. Full payments of the settlement were promptly made. Court hearings on appeals of the decision delayed the Indian government's distribution of funds to victims and their families until after the Supreme Court upheld the settlement in October 1991. While that court pronouncement also lifted the immunity from criminal prosecution, legal observers anticipated no further legal steps.

There were damage actions aplenty during the years 1985 to 89—suits totaling more than $250 billion were filed against UCC. Involved were lawyers representing the victims, the government of India and Union Carbide, and judges in federal courts of United States and India. At one point, a federal district court judge in New York obtained a tentative agreement between UCC and victims' lawyers to settle for $350 million. India rejected this and the judge transferred the case from a U.S. court to an Indian court. Three quarters of the half-million claims were from parts of Bhopal not designated by the government as gas-affected. About 250,000 claims had been rejected at the time of the settlement.

Union Carbide India Ltd. and Union Carbide Corporation— What was the relationship between them? What were the responsibilities of one to the other? What were their relationships with the government of India? What kind of ethical dilemmas arose from the explosion? What were the aims and content of the public relations communications of the interested parties?

Union Carbide formed UCIL in the 1920s to provide a legal structure under which it could manufacture products in India. The first production plant was a small operation in Calcutta that made flashlight batteries. After India gained its independence from the British in 1947, the Indian government began increasing the pressure on the country's business affiliates for greater Indian ownership. Union Carbide had reduced its share of ownership in UCIL to 50.9 percent by the time of the Bhopal accident. Indian government segments owned about 25 percent, and more than 23,000 private citizens of the country owned the balance.

Over these years there were changes in the management of UCIL. Indian managers and engineers gradually replaced Americans. By 1982, all the jobs at every level were held by Indians. A U.S. engineer who was the last non-Indian employed there returned home that year.

When the Bhopal explosion occurred, UCIL employed 9,000 in 14 manufacturing plants, 50 warehouses, and sales offices. The product lines included flashlights as well as batteries plus chemicals, plastics, pesticides, and fertilizers. There's an ironic side to the Bhopal production of pesticides. The Indian government required these products and other agricultural chemicals to nourish its "Green Revolution," whose goal was to enable India to feed itself. There were large strides toward food self-sufficiency.

Construction of the Bhopal plant, which opened in 1977, was controlled by regulations of the Indian government. "Union Carbide Corporation transferred preliminary process design packages to the Indian company," said J. J. Kenney, director, federal government affairs. "From there on, by government decree, it was an Indian operation."[23]

The UCC representative said blueprints and detailed design plans were prepared by UCIL and a consulting firm with headquarters in Bombay, which also served as general contractor. Government agencies approved the designs, drawings, and blueprints. After the plant opened, it faced the scrutiny of regulators from more than two dozen government agencies.

A seven-week inquiry, conducted by reporters of *The New York Times* immediately after the MIC leak, found it resulted from numerous flaws, faults, and failures that endangered safety. For example, because the Indian government had wanted the plant to be as labor-intensive as possible, it did not employ the computer system in use at UCC plants in the United States to monitor functions. Instead, management relied on workers to sense escaping MIC by watering of the eyes. This practice violated specific orders in the parent corporation's technical manual, said the paper. The managing director of UCIL said enforcement of safety regulations was the responsibility of the Bhopal plant managers, rather than placing the blame on UCC executives in the United States.[24]

On that morning of December 3 at the UCC corporate headquarters in Danbury, Connecticut, the little news there was of the Bhopal disaster came either from the press or through the affiliate's headquarters in Bombay. "The city of Bhopal had just two trunk telephone lines going in and out of it," said Ronald S. Wishart, UCC vice president, public affairs. "With thousands of Indian citizens plus hundreds of journalists trying to use those lines, getting through to our plant was impossible."[25]

With the meager knowledge available, Union Carbide management made some decisions. CEO Anderson declared that the company would be open with the public. He held his first press conference the afternoon of December 3, and more in succeeding days. Meeting with the press, Anderson said his company accepted moral responsibility for the tragedy.

"Why did we accept moral responsibility while denying legal responsibility?" asked Wishart. "Why not simply let the government sue us?

"To world opinion, Union Carbide is the company involved. It is our logo on the plant gate. And turning our backs on the victims under those circumstances would have compounded the damage to our reputation. We are better than that. Carbide is a concerned corporation and we wanted the world to know it. We didn't want to be the victims' adversary. And we would still rather put the legal issues aside and concentrate on getting help to the victims."

Another decision made on day one was to send a team of technical and medical experts to Bhopal. Wishart said the team's assignment was threefold: to see what was needed to help the victims; to render harmless any of the poisonous gas that might be remaining; and to begin investigating the cause of the accident.[26] Anderson decided to go with the team. He wanted to get an on-the-spot feel for the investigation as well as offer relief for the victims through the financial and medical resources of UCC: "We stand ready to do our part," he declared, in advance of his departure from the United States.[27]

Officials of the state of Madhya Pradesh, of which Bhopal is the capital, had other ideas. Law enforcement agents of the state were at the Bhopal airport to meet Anderson, who arrived there with the chairman and the managing director of UCIL. The authorities arrested the three on charges of criminal and corporate negligence, including "culpable homicide." They were taken to UCC's guesthouse and held under "heavy security" for interrogation. Anderson was released after some six hours following the intercession of the central Indian government. The other two were held for 10 days.[28]

Newsweek magazine termed the arrests "a clumsy political stunt." The arresting order came from the state's chief minister, whose ruling party was facing a major election.[29] Another source suggested the party wanted to demonstrate toughness.[30] Whatever the reason for the detainment, Anderson's good intentions in making the trip were not allowed to be put into play. At a news conference December 10 on his return to Danbury, Anderson said he was treated with "the utmost courtesy and consideration."[31]

Also on that day, UCC offered $1 million to the Prime Minister's Relief Fund, which was accepted. Four months later, UCC offered $5 million in humanitarian aid, which the Indian government turned down. The funds were turned over to the American Red Cross for Bhopal relief efforts and disbursed through the Indian Red Cross.

The Wall Street Journal, in an article published nearly a year after Anderson's frustrated trip, said, "By all accounts, Mr. Anderson's immediate reaction to the disaster was humanitarian. Speeding to Bhopal, he envisioned cutting through corporate and government bureaucracies to provide aid to those injured. Hospitals, orphanages, and vocational schools would be built, help given to all who needed it."[32]

Commenting on Anderson's journey, UCC Group President Robert D. Kennedy told a conference at Wesleyan College in March 1986 that though Anderson's trip "ended without the resolution we all hoped for . . . that doesn't diminish the effort or, in my opinion, the courage involved. It was a moral thing to do. Warren did not have to refer to a code of conduct; he simply did what he felt was necessary."

Kennedy also talked about some of the downside effects of Bhopal. He said that in a year and one half, Union Carbide had moved from a company that less than 20 percent of the public could identify to one "that most people have heard of, but in an awful context." Several communities had turned down UCC applications to build facilities, he noted. He spoke of the need for UCC to earn back "some of the moral credit" lost after the tragedy.[33]

In the weeks after the accident, the company was unable to explain the reason for the gas leaks. The cause was a matter of concern, particularly for employees and residents who lived in areas surrounding the UCC plant at Institute, West Virginia, where the same gas, methyl isocyanate, was used in the manufacturing process. Production and distribution of MCI was stopped there immediately after the Bhopal explosion and did not resume until early May 1985. UCC, as part of its policy of openness, conducted the news media on tours of the Institute plant and another of UCC in the United States where employees handled MIC. Bruce Morton of CBS News, who covered one of the plant tours, said companies could choose either an open or closed information policy, and Union Carbide had chosen to be open.[34] (In August 1985 six persons were hospitalized and 135 treated in emergency rooms after toxic chemical fumes escaped from the Institute factory. UCC accepted full blame for the incident, which resulted from violations of plant procedures.)

There was wide circulation given by reporters to an early theory, later proved false, that failure of an employee to follow correct procedures prior to water-washing filters led to water entering the MIC tank and starting a reaction. It was only after two and one-half years that investigations disclosed a credible real cause. On August 8, 1986, UCC was able to announce that "our investigations to date demonstrate that Bhopal tragedy was a deliberate act." Probers found that the accident could have happened only as the result of employee sabotage—"the deliberate introduction of large quantities of water into the MIC storage tank."[35] UCC also reported that there was a cover-up after the explosion "by certain operators on duty that night."[36]

Independent investigation by the consulting engineering firm of Arthur D. Little, Inc., announced May 10, 1988, "shows 'with virtual certainty' that the Bhopal incident was caused by a disgruntled employee who introduced a large volume of water by connecting a water hose directly to the tank."[37] Identity of the employee responsible for the accident is known to UCC and to the Indian government, but the individual has not been prosecuted.

Court records in the litigation shed light on the responsibilities of the Indian government, of UCIL and UCC, as perceived by each. UCC claimed that Indian companies involved in the building of the Bhopal plant changed its design and "Carbide itself had little control over the plant's construction or operation even though it was the majority owner." Countering this was an official of the Indian government who said UCC had financial and managerial control over the subsidiary. The Indian government argued that its courts were less experienced in personal injury law than those in the United States and also overloaded, and its citizens could not get a fair trial there. UCC termed this "absurd" and quoted the chief justice of the Indian supreme court as saying that compensation for Bhopal victims "could be 'speedily adjudicated' in India."[38]

The public relations surrounding this disaster, the communications and viewpoints of the numerous participating parties, moved across two continents, encompassed different cultures, posed quandaries for two governments. How well did UCC face up to the ethical pressures forced on it? How well did it maintain credibility? One answer is found in the early decision of CEO Anderson for UCC to accept "moral responsibility." This was unequivocal. The company offered substantial aid to the victims, though India refused to accept it. For another response to the question, look to the decision to be open in giving information to the news media and the public. Taken together, these judgments rule out deception and deceit and show concern for fair and honest treatment of others, though the consequences of such an approach were unknown.

POINTS

• Plan for the CEO to be in the limelight, in the leadership role, from the beginning of the crisis.

• Establish communication lines immediately after a crisis with the news media, and keep them open.

• Push for systems that monitor all operations and keep them running as planned. To do less is unethical and can reduce credibility in a crisis that results from an operational failure.

• It's many times harder to regain credibility after a disaster than to maintain it in normal times.

ETHICAL PUBLIC BEHAVIOR SPRINGS
FROM CORPORATE CONSCIENCE

The Johnson & Johnson reaction to the discovery of bottles of Extra-Strength Tylenol capsules laced with cyanide poison, which killed seven people in the Chicago area in 1982, is a classic case in corporate handling of a crisis. This pain reliever represented $450 million in annual sales for McNeil Consumer Products, one of the Johnson & Johnson companies, and approximately 40 percent of those products were in capsule form. Before the scare ended, 31 million bottles representing $100 million in sales had been removed from shelves of supermarkets, drugstores, and other outlets across the country.

Much has been written applauding the firm for its public relations and marketing expertise that successfully weathered this unprecedented tragedy. A lesser measure has been taken of the ethical dimensions involved, enormous as they were. Guiding the management of Johnson & Johnson in the first critical decisions and through those dark days was the business philosophy of the Johnson & Johnson Credo, and the "ethical principles" embodied therein.[39] The credo, a masterful public relations document, is composed of four paragraphs written in the late 1940s by Robert Wood Johnson, who was the company's leader for nearly 50 years. Said by some to be a maverick for his day, Johnson had a deep-grained philosophy about how a business should be run. He thought the corporation should be socially responsible, with responsibilities to society that went far beyond the usual sales and profit motives.

Johnson's credo defines the responsibility of his company to four primary constituencies: consumers, including medical professionals and all others who use the company's products and services; employees, for whom, among other expressions of concern, "we must provide competent management, and their actions must be just and ethical"; the communities in which Johnson & Johnson people work and live and "the world community as well"; and stockholders.

Here was something for James Burke, the chairman of the board and CEO of Johnson & Johnson at the time, and his staff to turn to when the bad news hit. As one account said, "Later we realized that no meeting had been called to make the first critical decision: to be open with the press and put the consumer interest first." To which Burke added, "There was no need to meet. We had the Credo philosophy to guide us." David R. Clare, president and chairman of the executive committee, contributed further: "Crisis planning did not see us through this tragedy nearly as much as the sound business management philosophy in our Credo."[40]

"Mr. Johnson felt deeply that unless business recognized these responsibilities, it could not be successful in the long run," said Lawrence G. Foster, then corporate vice president of public relations. "He thought that paying attention to these priorities would be not only moral, but profitable as well."[41]

It's one thing for the originator of a philosophy to keep the viewpoint alive in his lifetime. Johnson did personally see to it that the intent of his credo was carried out while he was living. But it's another thing to maintain the sense and motivation of the credo at the forefront of management decisions after the passing of that person. Ways were found to do this, after Johnson's death in 1968, that assured continued adherence to the credo and the corporate culture it spawned at Johnson & Johnson.

In the spring of 1972, the company decided to refuel the inspiration of its words with two major actions. The credo provided the theme for the 1972 annual report to stockholders, and the distribution of this document touched members of other basic audiences: consumers, employees, and communities. Johnson & Johnson conducted a refresher on the credo for more than 4,000 management employees in a series of dinner meetings led by former Chairman Philip B. Hofmann.

Hofmann's message to stockholders in the annual report applauded the "rare perception" of Robert Wood Johnson in writing the credo and noted that 'your Company is as dedicated to fulfilling the Credo's objectives as we were when it was first adopted as our guide to greater responsibility." He also reported on the credo meetings with management: "It was an exciting experience . . . everyone present was encouraged to ask questions about the Company's operations . . . more than a thousand (did) and I endeavored to answer every one."[42]

Three years later, Burke "proposed and led Credo challenge meetings" attended by all of top management in the worldwide Johnson & Johnson family of companies. And "challenge" appears to be highly appropriate for the kind of meetings these were. The credo, its philosophy and wording, was debated. Opinions were asked for and expressed. Some of Johnson's original words and phrases were changed to update the language. But at the end, the thrust was unchanged. Since, indoctrination on the credo has been part of the orientation for new management employees.[43]

A phone call from the *Chicago Sun-Times* to James Murray of the McNeil public relations staff the morning of September 30, 1982, was the first word of the tragedy for the Tylenol manufacturer, in Fort Washington, Pennsylvania. Jim Ritter, a consumer reporter, had learned from the Cook County Medical Examiner's office that three people had been killed after ingesting cyanide in Tylenol capsules. Burke and Clare were meeting together at the Johnson & Johnson headquarters in New Brunswick, New Jersey, when they heard the news just minutes later.

As the Tylenol crisis grew, the credo philosophy provided guidance, and the decisions came rapidly, according to Foster. Things happened almost simultaneously on many fronts: "The public and the medical community were alerted immediately. The Food and Drug Administration authorities were notified. Production was halted. Complete cooperation was given to the news media [the press, radio, and television were key to warning the public of the danger]. Tylenol capsules were withdrawn from the national marketplace."[44]

Coverage by the press, radio, and television was almost without parallel. It was said to be the greatest dissemination of news since the assassination of President John F. Kennedy. The Associated Press and United Press International rated the Tylenol story as second in impact in 1982. First place went to developments in the nation's economy, then beset by double-digit inflation and high interest and unemployment rates.

Besides the news coverage, there was media comment and opinion praising Johnson & Johnson for its response to the crisis. From *The Washington Post*: "Though the hysteria and frustration generated by random murder have often obscured the company's actions, Johnson & Johnson has effectively demonstrated how a major business ought to handle a disaster. This is no Three Mile Island accident in which the company's response did more damage than the original incident. No one at the McNeil Consumer Products subsidiary has tried to pretend that nothing is wrong, as Firestone Tire and Rubber Co. officials did when the Firestone 500 tires were disintegrating. From the day the deaths were linked to the poisoned Tylenol . . . Johnson & Johnson has succeeded in portraying itself to the public as a company willing to do what's right regardless of cost."[45]

Tylenol came back—with a flourish and speed that astounded many marketing experts. In six weeks from the finding of the first cyanide-poisoned capsule, Johnson & Johnson conducted a 30-city press conference via satellite to announce the introduction of new triple-safety-sealed packaging that was tamper-resistant. Again, there was widespread coverage. Customer acceptance came quickly. Five months after the start of the crisis, Tylenol had recaptured nearly 70 percent of its previously held market, and within a year it was back to its former preeminent position.

Looking back, Burke found positive results to which he could point: "Two things are clear to us. The first is that the value system, as articulated in the credo, now permeates the company in a way that could not have been possible without the crisis. The credo was tested—and it worked. Further, we learned that the reputation of the corporation, which has been carefully built for over 90 years, provided a reservoir of goodwill among the public, the people in the regulatory agencies, and the media, which was of incalculable value in helping to restore the brand."[46]

There was more horror to come. The next to impossible happened on February 8, 1986. Tylenol was the target for disaster again, this time in Westchester County, New York. Again it was cyanide, added to a capsule, and a 23-year-old woman died. A second contaminated bottle was discovered two days later.

This tragedy was painfully familiar to Johnson & Johnson, which immediately called for the removal of all capsule forms of Tylenol from the market. And again, CEO Burke played a highly visible role as he faced the press: "It is our collective opinion, ourselves, the FBI, the FDA, and the local New York police, that this is a local event."[47] The bottle that took the life of the woman was part of a batch of 200,000 packages shipped to retailers the previous August. Cyanide placed inside the gelatin capsules would have destroyed them within 10 days. Authorities investigating the case said they were convinced this was an isolated case of tampering.

At a second news conference on February 14, Burke called the tampering "an act of terrorism, pure and simple."[48] He said Johnson & Johnson was offering a $100,000 reward for information leading to the arrest and conviction of the poisoner. On February 17, Burke told a news conference that the company was discontinuing the sale of all over-the-counter medications in capsule form. He also announced that the firm would replace, at no cost, all capsules in the hands of consumers and retailers with Extra-Strength Tylenol caplets, a new product in solid dosage form. "We feel the company can no longer guarantee the safety of capsules to a degree consistent with Johnson & Johnson's standards of responsibility to its consumers."

Amid speculation that the cost of the withdrawal of the capsules might exceed $100 million, Burke said: "While this decision is a financial burden to us, it does not begin to compare to the loss suffered by the family and friends of Diane Elsroth (the victim)." The press reported his voice quivered as he referred to the woman who died. He said he expressed, on behalf of the company, "our heartfelt sympathy to Diane's family and loved ones."[49]

There was balanced media coverage and editorial opinion favorable to the company. Said *The Miami News*: "J&J is in business to make money. It has done that very well. But when the going gets tough, the corporation gets human, and that makes it something special in the bloodless business world. Whatever the stock market thinks of it now, moralists are rooting for it."[50] The Council on Economic Priorities selected Johnson & Johnson for its "American Corporate Conscience Award" in 1986.

The marketing efforts of the company, which again established a consumer hotline, nurtured strong consumer support. Within five months, the brand had recovered its position as the leading pain reliever. Another comeback. Once more, the credo had been there when needed!

POINTS

• You and your organization will benefit from an ethical philosophy, a conscience to guide you.

• Take advantage of calmer days to talk about and develop a code and a plan to implement it.

- Apply this ethical point of view in a crisis to maintain credibility.

- Make sure managers understand the code, know its ramifications, and will abide by it.

NOTES

1. Clare Ansberry, Joan E. Rigdon, and Bruce Ingersoll, "Breast Implant Debate Is Pitting Women against Other Women," *The Wall Street Journal*, February 14, 1992, p. A1.
2. Ibid.
3. Steven Fink, "Dow Corning's Moral Evasions," *The New York Times*, February 16, 1992, p. F13.
4. Ellen Goodman, "Quest for Beauty Has Led to Some Ugly Choices," *Rocky Mountain News*, January 27, 1992, p. 26.
5. Thomas M. Burton and Joan E. Rigdon, "Management Shake-up at Dow Corning Signals a More Conciliatory Attitude," February 12, 1992, p. A3.
6. Philip J. Hilts, "As it Quits Implant Business, Maker Says Product Is Safe," *The New York Times*, March 20, 1992, p. A8.
7. Paul M. Barrett and Allanna Sullivan. "U.S. Indicts Exxon in Alaska Oil Spill; Fines Could Be in Excess of $600 Million," *The Wall Street Journal*, February 28, 1990, p. A3.
8. Allanna Sullivan and Amanda Bennett, "Critics Fault Chief Executive of Exxon on Handling of Recent Alaskan Oil Spill," *The Wall Street Journal*, March 31, 1989, p. B1.
9. E. Bruce Harrison, APR, with Tom Prugh, "Assessing the Damage: Practitioner Perspectives on the Valdez," *Public Relations Journal*, October 1989, p. 40.
10. John Holusha, "Exxon's Public-Relations Problem," *The New York Times*, April 21, 1989, p. D1.
11. Allanna Sullivan, "Rawl Wishes He'd Visited Valdez Sooner," *The Wall Street Journal*, June 30, 1989, p. B7.
12. Holusha, "Exxon's Public-Relations Problem."
13. Letters to the editor, *The Wall Street Journal*, April 21, 1989, p. A15.
14. News Release, Exxon Company, U.S.A., April 19, 1989.

15. George L. Church, reported by Jay Peterzell, David Seideman, and Paul A. Witteman, "The Big Spill," *Time*, April 10, 1989, p. 38.

16. Holusha, "Exxon's Public-Relations Problem."

17. Matthew L. Wald, "Angry Shareholders Confront Exxon Chief over Alaska Spill," *The New York Times*, May 19, 1989, p. B5.

18. Andrea Rothman, with other staff members, "Who's that Screaming at Exxon? Not the Environmentalists," *Business Week*, May 1, 1989, p. 31.

19. "Radio Hosts Urging Exxon Boycott," *The New York Times*, April 17, 1989, p. D11.

20. Chris Welles, "Lawrence Rawl," *Business Week*, Special Issue, April 13, 1990, p. 101.

21. Remarks of Ronald S. Wishart, vice president, public affairs, Union Carbide Corporation, "Managing Trouble," Blumenthal Conference on Business Ethics, Little Switzerland, N.C., May 2, 1987.

22. Remarks of J. J. Kenney, director, Federal Government Relations, Union Carbide Corporation, Center for Asian Studies, University of Texas, Austin, April 13, 1989.

23. Ibid.

24. Stuart Diamond, "The Bhopal Disaster, How It Happened," *The New York Times*, January 28, 1985, p. 1A.

25. Wishart, "Managing Trouble."

26. Ibid.

27. William Marbach, with other staff members, "A Company in Shock," *Newsweek*, December 17, 1984, p. 37.

28. Ibid.

29. Mark Whitaker, with other staff members, "It Was like Breathing Fire," *Newsweek*, December 17, 1984, p. 29.

30. Remarks of Kenney.

31. "Bhopal Chronology," Union Carbide Corporation as of November 30, 1989.

32. Barry Meier and James B. Stewart, "A Year after Bhopal, Union Carbide Faces a Slew of Problems," *The Wall Street Journal*, November 26, 1985, p. 1A.

33. Remarks of Robert D. Kennedy, Wesleyan College, March 31, 1985.

34. Wishart, "Managing Trouble."

35. "Bhopal Chronology."

36. "Union Carbide and Bhopal: Setting the Record Straight on Employee Sabotage and Efforts to Provide Relief," Union Carbide Corporation, undated.

37. "Bhopal Chronology."

38. Stuart Diamond, "Carbide Says Indians Altered Bhopal Design," *New York Times*, December 21, 1985, p. 33D.

39. Lawrence G. Foster, "A Company that Cares," Johnson & Johnson, New Brunswick, New Jersey, 1986, p. 143.

40. Lawrence G. Foster, "The Johnson & Johnson Credo and the Tylenol Crisis," *New Jersey Bell Journal* 6, no. 1 Spring (1983), pp. 2–4.

41. Ibid., p. 2.

42. "1972 Annual Report," Johnson & Johnson, p. 2.

43. Foster, "The Johnson & Johnson Credo and the Tylenol Crisis," p. 5.

44. Ibid., p. 3.

45. Jerry Knight, "Tylenol's Maker Shows How to Respond to Crisis." *The Washington Post*, October 11, 1982, p. 1.

46. Foster, "The Johnson & Johnson Credo and the Tylenol Crisis," pp. 5–6.

47. Michael Waldholz, "Johnson & Johnson Calls Tylenol Case Isolated Incident," *The Wall Street Journal*, February 12, 1986, p. 2.

48. "J & J Halts Tyl Capsules," *New York Daily News*, February 15, 1985.

49. Robert D. McFadden, "Maker of Tylenol Discontinuing All Over-Counter Drug Capsules," *The New York Times*, February 18, 1986, p. A1.

50. "A Capsule History of Corporate Morality," *The Miami News*, February 21, 1986.

Chapter Four

Using Ethics to Restore Credibility

When credibility is damaged, it need not remain so forever. An ethical approach to public relations can help restore credibility and repair the loss. The damage may occur through a variety of circumstances, as illustrated in the next three examples. And the road to recovery differs in each case. There is no easy formula; each must be tailored to suit the problem. In all instances of cracked credibility, there is a need to renew the trust and faith in an individual or organization that has been weakened or even destroyed. The public needs to be convinced both in the perception and reality that positive steps for change have been taken.

PRODUCTS THAT INJURE HEALTH OF THOUSANDS, PLUS BANKRUPTCY, DAMAGE CREDIBILITY; ETHICAL DECISION LEADS WAY TO RECOVERY

Manville Corporation had been the world's biggest supplier of asbestos-based products. So there was no place to hide, even if it had tried, when the dangers to health from exposure to asbestos became apparent. The huge PR problems that resulted affected the company's ties with every one of its publics—employees, especially those directly involved in the manufacture of asbestos products; customers, and their employees who worked with the products; shareholders; suppliers; communities in which plants were located; and its creditors and banks.

With headquarters in Denver, Colorado, but operations worldwide, Manville in 1991 employed 16,000 people. Assets were $3 billion. Its businesses, operated through two subsidiaries, included insulation, reinforcements, filtration and building products; and a forest products company providing machinery-based packaging systems.

Manville's financial liability resulting from the thousands of lawsuits filed by those who claimed asbestos-induced disease risks, and the firm's program for coping with this, were the basic pieces of a major business story of the 1980s that continued into the 1990s. How did Manville and other concerned groups learn about the risks posed by exposure to this mineral? Who were those at risk? How badly was credibility hurt? What was the ethical decision of Manville that was significant in the plan it adopted to handle the financial liability?

The possibility of hazard associated with asbestos dust had been known since the early 1900s. There were discussions on the dangers in medical reports, insurance studies, and government publications. Industry sought to reduce dust levels in plants that made asbestos products and sponsored health studies on the hazards.

Unfortunately, the focus was on victims inhaling visible asbestos fibers, much as miners contracted silicosis by inhaling coal dust. But this attention was misdirected; the invisible fibers that people breathed were the culprits. Further, the lag between exposure to and symptoms of an asbestos-caused disease, which can be as much as 40 years, was not known.

Industry did less than it could have, according to W. T. Stephens, president and chief executive officer of Manville, to explain the dangers of exposure to asbestos to employees involved in the manufacture of asbestos products and customers who installed them.[1] His comment seems an admission that Manville, and perhaps other asbestos manufacturers, had practiced questionable business ethics on this issue. Among those endangered were workers in shipyards during World War II. Asbestos is highly fire-resistant, and great quantities were installed in ships to contain fires. Asbestos was a common insulation material in construction projects, too, and workers who insulated pipes were another group at risk.

Research that led to public recognition of a direct link between asbestos and cancer started in 1962 under the direction of Dr. Irving Selikoff and his colleagues at Mount Sinai Medical School, New York City. Dr. Selikoff, who was director of Mount Sinai's Environmental and Occupational Health Division, published findings in 1964 that documented asbestos-related lung disease and cancer. He found that certain groups of workers exposed to asbestos suffered unusually high rates of cancer, most often cancer of the lung.

That same year, Manville began to put warning labels on its asbestos products. But the message of caution came too late for the thousands of people already exposed.

Manville and other asbestos manufacturers were, beginning in 1974, the targets of suits filed by asbestos workers. By August 1982, the backlog of cases at Manville had grown to more than 17,000; there were new ones filed at the rate of 500 per month and, as Stephens put it seven years later, "the race to the courthouse was on."[2]

Executives at Manville sought the answers to many questions in the summer of 1982 as they deliberated the proper course. They asked a consultant to estimate Manville's probable liability for asbestos claims in connection with possible legal action to bring against its insurance carriers. The estimate of liability was $2 billion, based on 50,000 claims at a cost of $40,000 each. There also was word that "asbestos cases may continue unabated for a number of years."[3]

The estimated $2 billion sum exceeded Manville's assets at the time by a wide margin. Yet, applicable rules of accounting obligated Manville to record the amount as a liability. Assuming this $2 billion as a debt would wipe out the company's net worth and ignite a default on all outstanding debt. Insolvency and collapse of the company could be just around the corner.

Facing up to such dire possibilities, the Manville board of directors appointed a special committee of outside directors to study the complex situation and make recommendations. A principal recommendation, adopted by the board, was to file for reorganization under Chapter 11 of the bankruptcy laws. The company took this action in the U.S. Bankruptcy Court for the Southern District of New York on August 26, 1982.

Filing for bankruptcy was a bold action, and an ethical one. The determination to take this course was an ethical decision because it recognized the plight of those who were sick, or might become so, from asbestos exposure, as among those who should be protected. Manville placed persons who had filed claims, and potential health claimants, on an equal footing with all creditors, such as banks and suppliers of goods and services. This course also protected the jobs of Manville employees and assured an uninterrupted flow of products to customers. Operating under Chapter 11 gave Manville a respite from creditors while hammering out a plan of reorganization. The first of two reorganization plans was filed in November 1983, but many court dates were to follow. The next January, Bankruptcy Judge Burton Lifland ruled the Chapter 11 filing "clearly justifiable" and denied motions for dismissal sought by various creditors.[4]

It was not until November 28, 1988, that Manville emerged from Chapter 11 with a court-approved plan of reorganization. The plan provided for creation of the Manville Personal Injury Settlement Trust to be funded by Manville with $2.5 billion over 26 years. Manville was told to contribute nearly $1 billion in cash immediately. Insurance proceeds were a large part of this settlement. The firm also promised to pay the trust $75 million from net earnings annually, beginning in 1991; to turn over 20 percent of profits as long as needed to pay claims, beginning in 1992; to allocate up to 80 percent of its common shares and make preferred stock allocations to the trust.

The trust, established to pay all asbestos health claims against the company, is governed by five independent trustees who evaluate and settle claims. Manville is not involved in disposition of the claims. The bankruptcy court issued a permanent injunction that protects Manville from future asbestos litigation.

The provision that Manville be free of all claims is of benefit to both the trust and the company. This protection, if believed in the financial markets to be truly firm and enduring, is an attractive point for prospective buyers of Manville stock and serves to sustain a fair market price that maintains the value of the trust's assets. On the other hand, uncertainty about further liability for the company could depress the price of the shares and reduce the value of these assets. For Manville, the protection assists it in operating competitively and in gaining access to capital markets.

The trust met two of Manville's major goals in Chapter 11: to find a way to efficiently provide compensation to those who were injured and to pay those who were injured according to the nature of their illnesses. The plan that created the trust also recognized the need for a healthy and growing Manville with a steady stream of profits that would benefit asbestos health claimants.

Bankruptcy Judge Lifland gave high praise to New York Attorney Leon Silverman as the principal person who brought interested parties to agreement on the mechanism for settling claims. Clearly, the trust set a precedent for handling such claims. Silverman's bill to Manville for his work was $2.3 million. Judge Lifland awarded him a 100 percent bonus, despite complaints from Manville's lawyers that a 10 percent premium was adequate.[5]

Following Manville's emergence from bankruptcy, its commercial creditors were paid in full, plus interest. Holders of common shares took a beating. They found their ownership interest in Manville diluted to 2.2 percent. They might have faced a total wipeout, however, if Manville had become insolvent in 1982. During the six years of court litigation, shareholders who disagreed with the terms of the plan of reorganization filed several actions seeking to protect their investments. The court turned down each of these attempts. It was, of course, the shareholders' company that had given cause for the claims.

By 1990, there were 150,000 health claims, three times the 1982 estimate. The trust had settled about 22,000 with an average payment of $43,500—but it had run out of cash. Some attorneys for claimants said the trust had paid out too much to those with early claims. The trust's executive director Marianna Smith said, "Everybody knew that we would have no income in 1990 . . . knew this was going to be troublesome."[6] There was the possibility that the trust would borrow on its assets until funds started flowing in from Manville in 1991.

Manville, now a profitable corporation with three consecutive years of record earnings, proposed in 1990 a plan to pay the trust an additional amount of as much as $520 million over seven years, a step that would hasten payments to victims. Other holders of common stock would receive dividends of approximately $130 million over this period. Stephens said, "Our strong performance since the consummation of the plan of reorganization in 1988 has put us in the position to be able to accomplish this distribution program."[7] The proposal responded to an order of U.S. District Court Judge Jack B. Weinstein in Brooklyn for Manville to come up with new financing after the trust ran out of money. The court approved this restructuring of the trust in May 1991.

Insight into Manville management's philosophy of ethics as related to the asbestos issue, and product and environmental safety in general, is found in remarks of Stephens, who joined the company as an engineer in 1963 and became chief executive in 1986. "Our board had the courage to do what they should . . . [directors] made the right decision and the ethical decision," Stephens said at a meeting of the National Association of Corporate Directors in Washington in October 1989. He noted that the board acted despite "strong objections" of those who then served as president and chairman.

Stephens continued: "If [directors] don't have the courage to promote actions that reflect what is ethically right and in the interest of all constituent groups . . . then they are unprepared to accept the responsibility that comes with service . . . Manville's board won't tolerate anything less than the highest ethical standards."[8]

Earlier that year, Stephens told a meeting of attorneys that "you can't inspect quality into a product and you can't lawyer ethical conduct into an organization. Quality and ethics are a function of the collective attitudes of people." Turning to hazardous exposure levels, he said, "If we wait for workers to get sick or die before setting exposure standards, we have waited too long. That is the ethic of today. But many companies, and even some government regulators, haven't heard it yet."[9]

Speaking in Switzerland in early 1990, Stephens said that from the liability-bankruptcy experience Manville learned "we must have the courage to promote actions that reflect what is ethical, not just what is expedient. Words don't find environmental solutions and they don't initiate proper product testing. Actions do! Health, safety, and environmental issues are not like wine. They do not improve with age. Left to the course of least resistance, they get worse not better. . . . We must have the courage to promote actions that are ethically right even when the short-term pressure is to turn and look the other way."

Stephens added: "To give new meaning to the cherished business acronym of CEO, I agree with the chairman of duPont, who refers to the job of chief executive officer as also being that of chief environmental officer and as chief ethics officer."[10]

There was not universal support for the creation of the trust and other features of the reorganization plan. Perhaps those most opposed were the unhappy shareholders. Stephens acknowledged that there were critics who said Manville used bankruptcy to avoid its responsibilities. To those, he said, "The results speak for themselves."[11]

POINTS

• You sometimes need strong courage to make an ethical business and public relations decision. But don't back away from what seems the right thing to do.

• You'll not always get total agreement on what is an ethical decision. At Manville, the board overruled the company's two top officers.

• You can't foresee all possible crisis situations (e.g., bankruptcy). However, you can apply ethical standards to deal with whatever arises.

• Regaining credibility may take time, but it can be done.

GOVERNMENT CONTRACTOR BOUNCES BACK INTO FAVOR AFTER SWALLOWING STRONG DOSE OF ETHICS

General Dynamics had some deep soul-searching and self-examination to do. This manufacturer of airplanes, submarines, and tanks had worked its way to become the second largest

U.S. defense contractor. But along the way, illegal and unethical practices had developed. The company had become "to many . . . the symbol of waste and corruption in military spending . . . after being the target of embarrassing revelations and allegations."[12] Gaping holes in the General Dynamics' blanket of ethical business practices had come to the attention of government agencies that were customers of General Dynamics products.

Secretary of the Navy John F. Lehman, Jr., in May 1985, ordered a temporary ban on the department's contracting with General Dynamics and he cancelled contracts with two divisions. He saw at General Dynamics "a pervasive corporate attitude that we find inappropriate to the public trust."[13] Lehman's order affected the company's electric boat division at Groton, Connecticut, a major supplier of nuclear submarines to the navy, and its Pomona, California, division, a producer for the navy's missile programs.

The navy also charged General Dynamics, through its electric boat division, with faulty billings and bestowing gifts over a period of 17 years on Adm. Hyman Rickover, who directed the navy's nuclear submarine program until he retired in 1981. Among items misbilled to the Pentagon were charges for boarding the dog of a General Dynamics executive and air transportation by an officer of General Dynamics from St. Louis to his farm in Georgia. The Pentagon withheld $437.8 million from General Dynamics as a way to take back money in improper charges billed by the firm. The gifts to Admiral Rickover, now 85 years old, included diamond earrings for his wife. In June, General Dynamics paid a fine of $672,238, or 10 times the value of the gifts. The navy censured Rickover but permitted him to keep the gifts.

Just one day after Lehman's announcement of the actions against General Dynamics, the firm's chairman and chief executive officer, David S. Lewis, said he would retire at the end of 1985. There was a relationship between the public statements of the two. In April, the Pentagon's inspector general, Joseph H. Sherick, recommended that Lewis and two other high-ranking officials of the firm be disbarred from contracting with the military. Lehman's announcement included his rejection of this recommendation. Lewis had told stockholders at the annual meeting of General Dynamics held in Pomona on May 2 that the company would fight the government's efforts to ban him from doing business with the Pentagon. Now, the matter became moot, but the fact that the issue arose reflects on the scope and intensity of the problems General Dynamics faced at the time in its relationships with Uncle Sam. General Dynamics said Lewis' successor would be Stanley C. Pace, vice chairman of TRW, Inc., who would join General Dynamics June 1 and become chairman in January. Pace "has built a reputation for honest dealings with the government," said *U.S. News & World Report*, a quality that might be among the most needed for the leadership role he was to assume.[14]

At General Dynamics, the signs of strayed ethics in public relations—conflict of interest, lying, coverup—and other faulty business practices endangered future business with its largest customer, the Pentagon. How, if you're General Dynamics, do you fight your way back? How do you gain, or regain, credibility? Secretary Lehman gave the company a clue at the same time he suspended it from bidding on contracts. Get yourself an ethics program that will work, was the message in his letter of May 21, 1985, to the company. There should be "a rigorous code of ethics for all General Dynamics officers and employees with mandatory sanctions for violations."[15]

General Dynamics lost no time in reacting. Gary Edwards, director of the Ethics Resource Center, a nonprofit organization in Washington, D.C., said, "General Dynamics called us the day after the navy banned its contracts."[16] In August, General Dynamics introduced to employees a formal ethics program, a full-blown public relations plan, and acknowledged the assistance of the Ethics Resource Center in its organization and preparation.[17] Edwards termed the General Dynamics ethics campaign the most comprehensive of its kind in the United States.

Announcing in mid-August that he was lifting the navy ban on contracting with General Dynamics, Secretary Lehman said the company had "developed a comprehensive ethics program that will apply to all employees."[18]

Push for assembling the ethics program came from the very top officers of General Dynamics—from Lewis and from Pace, who joined the firm in time to have a hand in its development, and from the president, Oliver C. Boileau. It was ironical that Lewis, so recently threatened with disbarment by the Pentagon, led the drive to clean up unwholesome business and public relations practices in his firm. He appeared to treat lightly, even to cover up, the forceful order of the navy in his comments on the 1985 second-quarter operations, published in the August issue of the employee newspaper, *General Dynamics World*: "Because the Navy has also been dissatisfied with the rate of progress being made in the negotiation of several long-standing issues between the Navy and the company, on May 21st it imposed several conditions that had to be met before any new contracts could be awarded to the Pomona and Electric Boat divisions. Most of these issues have been resolved and we are hopeful that the remaining negotiations will be completed in the near future." Is that all that bothered the navy: "several conditions that had to be met?" This same issue of the newspaper announced the new ethics program in an adjoining column.[19]

To head up the ethics effort, General Dynamics in October 1985 appointed a corporate ethics program director, Kent Druyvesteyn. Previously, he was dean of students and director of the master of business administration program at the University of Chicago's School of Business. Druyvesteyn became vice president of ethics at General Dynamics. "Ethics is conduct," he emphasizes. "The question in ethics is not do you know what the truth is, but do you tell it. . . . The way to teach this is by example."[20]

General Dynamics got more than its feet wet in programming for ethics—it took the deep plunge. A code for responsible practices in business relationships with the government—its principal customer—was part, but only part, of its new standards. The program recognized corporate commitments not only to customers but also to suppliers, employees, shareholders, and the communities of which it was a part. And it recognized the vital requirement of infusing all employees with the spirit of ethical behavior. The firm took a total approach to honoring ethics in relationships with all of its publics.

In announcing the program, the company said extensive employee training and communications will be "an integral and continuing part. . . . Discussions of general business ethics and the Standards will be conducted regularly at all levels." Employees were told that the board of directors had established a committee on corporate responsibility that would review and approve ethics policy.[21]

Centerpiece of the program was the General Dynamics Standards of Business Ethics and Conduct. The standards covered 19 points: conflicts of interest; gifts, gratuities, and entertainment to customers; inside information; outside interests; former government employees; selling and marketing; antitrust; pricing, billing, and contracting; time card reporting; suppliers and consultants; quality and testing; expense reports; company and customer resources; technology and information; cash and bank accounts; security; political contributions; environmental actions; and international business. The conflicts-of-interest section warned employees to consider themselves as persons in positions of trust and "be particularly sensitive to the many situations, on and off the job, where a conflict of interest or even a perception of such a conflict could originate." In the section on gifts, gratuities, and entertainment, employee use of these or other favors to seek a competitive advantage is called a "serious violation" of the standards.[22]

General Dynamics packaged the standards in a 20-page booklet that led off with a letter signed by the three top officers urging employees to "have a personal commitment to meeting the highest ethical standards, as well as meeting the more obvious requirements for quality, schedule, and budget." Outlining the responsibilities of the company, supervisors, and all employees, this ethics information pamphlet told employees about designated personnel—supervisors, ethics program directors, and company attorneys—who would assist them in resolving questions involving ethics and conduct. Employees could reach the program directors, who were at each location, by an ethics hotline or by regular phone, letter, or personal visit. An important part of the director's job was to establish and maintain open channels of communication for all employees at the location. "Inquiries," said the booklet, "will be treated with courtesy and discretion."[23]

Each of the nearly 100,000 employees, as a condition of employment, was asked to sign an acknowledgement card that states: "I have received and read the General Dynamics Standards of Business Ethics and Conduct. I understand that these Standards represent the policies of General Dynamics." New employees also sign up. Supervisors have the responsibility to train employees in the meaning and application of the standards and to ensure that refresher programs are provided as necessary.

The second edition of the booklet issued in 1987 was "updated and improved," said the introductory message from now-Chairman Pace, "based on what we heard from you through ethics awareness workshops, the employee surveys and communications with the ethics program Directors." Pace said the standards were unchanged except for some points of clarification in meaning, the modification of one of the standards and the addition of two—safety and health, and proper use of the ethics program.

"The Standards contained in this booklet are like road signs," said Pace. "They give directions in areas of daily business activity where possible problems of conduct could occur.

"Every employee has a role to play in upholding the Standards. The Standards depend on the sense of honesty, fairness, and integrity brought to the job by all employees. Our values as individuals, applied to everything we do on the job, help determine what the values of General Dynamics are perceived to be. Our values are the values of the company."[24]

There are those who question the effectiveness of corporate ethics programs and ask: Is it just public relations (using the term in a derogatory sense)? Just window dressing? Pace gave a response in the second edition by declaring the program made significant progress in the first two years and by adding, "The program has already had an important impact on strengthening our administrative performance and on improving our image as a company with our customers and the general public. . . . We are determined to maintain the high standards of conduct set by these Standards."[25] From the standpoint of ethical public relations and business practices, the firm had moved to a higher plane.

Support for the effectiveness of the program came from Lehman, when he resigned as secretary of the navy in 1987. "There is not a better relationship today between the Navy and a contractor, and I would submit between any service and a contractor, than we have with Electric Boat," he said.[26]

Pace told the Armed Services Committee of the U.S. House of Representatives in August 1988 that General Dynamics had stressed the need for a personal commitment by all employees to understanding and applying the standards. He said that through the ethics program the company had made it clear that "General Dynamics management believes that any unethical business decision or action is not only unacceptable, but also not good for business, the company, or the shareholders." Pace also told the committee, as an example, that there was training for more than 30,000 people in the details of properly reporting business expenses, "and I do mean details—our guidelines deal with such small items as the nonallowability of laundry costs and shoeshines."[27]

Figures give another view of the ethics program's effectiveness. In 1986, the first full year after its initiation, employees contacted the ethics directors 3,646 times. The company imposed 123 sanctions. Sanctions in order of increasing severity consist of warnings, reprimands, probations, demotions, temporary suspensions, and discharges.

The following year there were 5,482 contacts and 205 sanctions, and the figures were roughly comparable in the next three years. From the beginning, through 1991, there were 1,355 sanctions, including 157 firing of employees, 55 that required refunds for losses or damages, and 8 referrals for further legal action.[28]

The biggest job after five years of the program appeared to be wiping out employee misconceptions about confidentiality and reprisals. Ethics directors do not identify a hot-line caller to a third party without the caller's permission, and no action is taken against callers for using a hot line. Still, in a survey of employees, "38 percent of the respondents believed they would be hurt in some way for using an ethics hot line." This led Druyvesteyn, corporate director of the program, to say, "Our first priority, therefore, is to make sure reprisals don't occur and to prove our commitment by our actual performance."[29]

Ethics and public relations joined at General Dynamics to head the company down a constructive road and restore credibility with the government, and create benefits in its relationships with other vital publics. There was a prod. General Dynamics moved only under forces exerted against it. But what counts is the responsive action taken by the firm's executives. There is no indication they tried to make half-way measures do in meeting the ethics specifications laid down by Navy Secretary Lehman. The company gets credit for initiating a full-scale program to

instill ethical attitudes and to improve business and public relations ethics. On balance, it succeeded.

POINTS

• When you plan to repair or fix shattered credibility, don't
take half measures. Find a comprehensive solution, one that
recognizes all aspects of the problem, and go to work.

• Launch a public relations program that will enlist the support of all who can help pave the road to restored credibility.
Convince them of ways they will benefit.

• Make sure that you have more than a paper program. Monitor to verify it's accomplishing its purpose.

• Find ways to maintain support for the program from the
participants after it's no longer new.

CORPORATION ACCEPTS SOCIAL RESPONSIBILITY, SUCCEEDS IN PR FIGHT TO REGAIN CREDIBILITY AGAINST ACTIVISTS WHOSE TACTICS BYPASS ETHICS

An "ethical, social, and socio-economic debate" is the way one
author characterized the infant formula controversy that swirled
about the head of Nestle S.A., a Swiss multinational firm, in the
1970s and early 1980s.[30]

A medical doctor in the thick of the fray "described promotion
of formulae by commercial concerns as unethical in communities
where there is *no possibility* of such formulae being purchasable
in adequate quantities or used in a cleanly fashion, and/or where
breast-feeding is still the norm."[31]

The dispute raged over the relative values and dangers in the use of infant formula by mothers in Third World nations. The main providers of steam to propel and enlarge the wrangle were activist groups, forming at first in Europe and then in the United States. In no-holds-barred attack communications, their principal target was Nestle, the largest of the suppliers of the product. The activists called upon harsh and emotional words for attention-grabbing headlines and provocative slogans: "The Baby Killer," "Death in the Bottle," "Milk and Murder," "Breast against Bottle," "Profit at any Cost," and "Nestle Kills Babies."[32] How ethical was the public relations campaign waged by the activists, principally against Nestle? What about the ethical position of Nestle in its public relations and marketing stance, at the beginning of the controversy and as the heat waxed more torrid and it struggled to restore credibility? Did the parties involved base their actions on responsible positions? Was this a case of a pox on both their houses, or were there ethical differences in the conduct of the antagonists as they sought public acceptance of their views?

An early event that provoked this intercontinental struggle lasting part of two decades began rather quietly in England with publication of an article, "The Baby Food Tragedy," in the August 1973 issue of *The New Internationalist*, a rather little-known journal concerned with Third World issues. Based on interviews with two child-health specialists, the article on many points questioned practices of the infant food industry that supplied formula. It did, moreover, zero in on Nestle's marketing of the product. Certainly, the firm was the target of the magazine's cover, a deliberately cruel illustration that presented a photograph of "an infant's grave on which had been placed an empty feeding bottle and a crumpled container of Lactogen, a Nestle product."

Among the charges in the *New Internationalist* article, Nestle and other manufacturers of infant formula were accused of reducing breast-feeding by mothers in developing nations through the promotion of their products. And there were said to be problems for babies created by the mothers' use of the infant formulae: malnutrition, gastroenteritis, and higher infant mortality were by-products because many mothers couldn't read the instructions, even in their own language; they often used contaminated water; and they tended to dilute the relatively expensive product to extend its life, thereby reducing its value to infants.[33] For its part, Nestle had long said that breast milk was the best food for a baby, and a message to this effect was on product labels.

"The Baby Food Tragedy" referred to Nestle, as well as the industry in general, and "many damaging assertions were made." It was "very negative" for the industry. Nestle sent a letter of clarification to the editor, but the publication omitted the letter's most important sections. The company then invited the editor to visit the Swiss headquarters and discuss the issues. The *New Internationalist* in an editorial turned down the invitation to a headquarters briefing, "objecting as much to the symbolism as the substance."[34]

Well, that was just the beginning. The dispute was to lead to a major public relations campaign by the activists, the formation of a coalition of activists around the world, and a boycott of Nestle products, and to involve the scientific community and health agencies of more than 150 countries. Also, it led to an unprecedented International Code of Marketing of Breast Milk Substitutes adopted in 1981 by the World Health Assembly after a series of meetings sponsored by the World Health Organization (WHO) and United Nations International Children's Emergency Fund (UNICEF).

Nestle found a way for what it hoped would be a resolution to the conflict and at the same time a demonstration of its ethical intentions. In the spring of 1982, it proposed to fund an independent Infant Formula Audit Commission, to be chaired by Edmund S. Muskie, former U.S. senator and secretary of state. The commission was to be a check on Nestle by investigating complaints about Nestle's marketing of infant formula. Of greater significance, the commission was to be advisory to Nestle in putting into practice the provisions of the code. Muskie accepted the appointment in April of that year and other members of the commission were confirmed in a few weeks.

Retreating now to those early days in 1973, there was a development with a more devastating cumulative effect on Nestle than the British journal article. A free-lance British journalist, Mike Muller, visited Nestle in Switzerland late in the year to gather information for another infant formula story. He was on assignment for War on Want, a British charity organization whose disaster relief and medical aid activities were joined with "research at home and observation in the field." Muller met with and quizzed Nestle managers responsible for infant formula. There was a later exchange of letters in which Nestle provided more information and clarified points. Muller promised to send a proof in advance of publication, but it didn't arrive.

Nestle saw Muller's piece after its publication in June 1974 under the title, "The Baby Killer." There was much for Nestle to object to, including the stated objective: "To make known to a wider public the dangers that follow from the promotion of powdered baby-milks in communities that cannot use them properly." The article also spoke of " 'unethical and immoral' promotion practices, such as the use of 'unqualified sales girls dressed in nurses' uniforms.' " While Nestle in talking to Muller had ascribed this sales practice to competitors, readers could easily have the impression Nestle was guilty of the offense.[35]

Worse for Nestle was to come. War on Want granted to other groups the rights for translation of the article. When a German-language version shortly appeared in Switzerland under the auspices of Third World Working Group–ADW, it bore a new title, "Nestle Kills Babies." In the translation, there were the omission of a disclaimer and misrepresentations from the original article and other revisions.

Nestle reacted in less than a month after the publishing of "Nestle Kills Babies" by filing a libel suit in Bern, Switzerland, District Court. After a series of court hearings from 1974 to 1976, the judge decided the title was libelous and the ADW defendants were guilty. He fined each 300 Swiss francs and ordered them to pay part of Nestle's legal costs. Unfortunately for Nestle, the judge provided fuel to continue the controversy by observing that, yes, there were practices that the company should change to avoid the immoral and unethical charge in the future.[36] Commenting in a speech in 1982, Rafael D. Pagan, Jr., president of the Nestle Coordination Center for Nutrition, Inc., said the "long-drawn-out trial was a public relations disaster that led directly to the boycott."[37]

It was perhaps inevitable that there would be a banding together of people in the United States who believed what they had heard and read about Nestle, true or not. These found a home for their anti-Nestle feelings in the Infant Formula Action Coalition, or INFACT, formed by the Interfaith Center on Corporate Responsibility, for which the National Council of Churches was a major sponsor, and the University of Minnesota Third World Institute. INFACT announced a consumer boycott of Nestle products on July 4, 1977. It didn't matter that no infant formula was manufactured or sold by Nestle in the United States.

As a well-organized boycott group, INFACT had its demands. Nestle should quit promotion and advertising of infant formula, including promotion to the medical profession, end distribution of free samples to hospitals, clinics, and homes, stop service by milk nurses, and "assure that infant formula does not reach 'people who do not have the means or facilities to use it safely.' " Two meetings between Nestle and INFACT in October 1977 and February 1978 were fruitless.[38]

INFACT then moved its attention to Washington and the political arena. The group urged members to send letters to Democratic Senators Edward M. Kennedy of Massachusetts and Frank

Church of Idaho, chairmen respectively of the Subcommittee on Health and Scientific Research and Subcommittee on Foreign Economic Policy, asking them to hold hearings on the use and promotion of infant formula in Third World countries. A hearing would be a chance for INFACT to get nationwide exposure on television. Senator Kennedy was obliging, scheduling a hearing in May 1978 with representatives from the industry, health professionals, and activists to be heard. Nestle didn't make too many points at the hearings; the activists did much better, mixing emotion with data.

There was a constructive follow-up. The International Council of Infant Food Industries, of which Nestle was a member, wrote to Kennedy proposing that the idea of worldwide practices be taken up by a more proper agency, the World Health Organization. Kennedy accepted the idea and contacted the WHO director-general, Dr. Halfdan Mahler. A conference on infant feeding, sponsored by WHO and UNICEF and held at Geneva in October 1979, led to the WHO Code, adopted by the World Assembly in 1981. By the time of the Geneva meeting, Nestle was doing away with advertising and most sales promotion and restricting marketing personnel to educate on better feeding practices—not pushing the products—in talks with health professionals and mothers.

A development during 1980 is viewed by some as being crucial in the tangle between Nestle and INFACT. The United Methodist Church (UMC), which had never joined the National Council of Churches in supporting the boycott, decided to take a look at it at the 1980 UMC general conference. Upshot was the delegates' approval of a minority report that recommended forming a task force to carry on a ''constructive dialogue'' with the infant formula industry. Nestle, invited to comment on a comprehensive background paper completed for the task force in September, returned a detailed response, which led to a meeting of Nestle and task force representatives.[39]

Following the adoption of the WHO Code in 1981, Nestle gave the United Methodist task force a paper outlining the company plans for working with the code. To keep a check on Nestle, the task force asked for documented information to substantiate Nestle's voluntary marketing changes before the code and to changes made to meet the code, plus a "country-by-country analysis of Nestle policy toward the Code." The request troubled Nestle, because its fulfillment would require handing over confidential information. What if some of this should fall into INFACT hands?[40] Nestle decided to accede to the request, hoping its cooperation would begin to build a trust between the parties, which, in fact, it did. The relationship grew more constructive at a meeting in February 1982, to which Nestle took a draft of a policy statement with details of its implementation of the code.

The company organized to better handle the hammering criticism of the activists with creation of the Nestle Coordination Center for Nutrition, Inc. (NCCN), a strategy center, in Washington in 1981. This office brought together a small staff of corporate affairs professionals and nutrition scientists whose job was to tell the public of Nestle's efforts on behalf of Third World mothers and babies and to coordinate nutrition research. NCCN moved Nestle into a more assertive and also more active role. It recognized that the infant formula dilemma was a political as well as nutritional issue, and took its case to opinion makers, to public officials, education and church leaders, and others.

Nestle began to find support from the news media. *Pediatrics*, published by the American Academy of Pediatrics, in its September 1981 issue, said: "The crucial point for pediatricians to realize is that during more than five years of debate and hearings, no substantial, sound scientific data were ever set forth by the critics of industry or officials of the WHO to support the claim that marketing practices for infant formula have actually been a significant factor in decline in prevalence of breastfeeding in the Third World or anywhere else."[41] A related view was set forth in an editorial of *The Washington Post*, published in November 1982: "Upon closer inspection, the data linking formula marketing and infant mortality turn out to be sketchy at best."[42]

Nestle became more innovative. In a "brilliant stroke,"[43] the company in early 1982 proposed establishment of an "infant formula marketing ethics audit committee." This would be a monitoring group whose members would be persons of respect in the clergy, science, and law. Nestle would regain credibility through the association. Up to now, INFACT and its followers had been the monitors. Nestle suggested Muskie, former senator and U.S. secretary of state who was generally well respected, as committee chair. Both WHO and UNICEF gave a green light to the idea. The United Methodist task force commended Nestle for "an especially welcome development."[44] A Washington news conference in early May 1982 announced the Nestle Infant Formula Audit Commission. The commission's members, besides Muskie, included leaders of the American Baptist and Presbyterian churches, whose denominations had endorsed the boycott, and medical experts and scientists. While funding for the commission came from Nestle, its independence was guaranteed by charter.

Nestle's persistent efforts in working with the United Methodist task force attained the desired ends. By a two-to-one majority, the United Methodist General Council on Ministries voted in October 1982 to accept the recommendation of the task force that the UMC refrain from boycotting Nestle. The following January, a major member of the boycott movement, the American Federation of Teachers, withdrew support and the boycott ranks were thinning. Further credibility was restored.

The INFACT boycotters railed against the audit commission concept and formation, but they were unable to discredit it. The United Methodist task force dealt them a major blow in its April 1983 report. There were "serious flaws" in the boycott campaign, said the panel, continuing: "Boycott leaders sought strenuously to prevent the formation of the Nestle Infant Formula Audit Commission, subjecting it to public ridicule and seeking to prevent religious and medical leaders of independent mind from serving. . . . Nestle policies and actions have been subjected to substantial and sometimes gross misrepresentation. . . . INFACT and other boycotting organizations have recently intensified their campaign with inflammatory rhetoric.

"Such facts," the report concluded, "make us regret that some United Methodists supporting the boycott have apparently acquiesced in tactics of vilification without publicly holding critics of Nestle to standards of fairness and truthfulness."[45] This was a strong swat by the United Methodist Church at the communication ethics of the boycotters.

INFACT and its campaign against Nestle were now on the ropes. The international boycott committee made overtures toward calling it off in December 1983. It admitted there was progress by Nestle in many areas, but there were still four areas of concern: educational materials, hazard warnings on labels, gifts to health professionals, and free supplies to hospitals. Nestle suggested that discussions on these points take place with WHO, UNICEF, and the Muskie Commission joining the international committee and Nestle; the parties met in January 1984. There were thorny matters of language and interpretation to be worked out with each of the points, but finally there was an understanding, and a joint statement signed on January 25 announced the suspension of the international boycott. INFACT, the U.S. arm, also called it quits.

The 10 members of the Nestle Infant Formula Audit Commission (NIFAC), incidentally, are active in carrying out their responsibilities. At least one is in a Third World country at any given time on an investigatory trip relating to Nestle's implementation of and compliance with the code. Members monitor Nestle's marketing practices by conducting fact-finding missions at hospitals and other medical facilities in Asia, Africa, and Latin America and check out third-party complaints about Nestle's marketing. The commission issues reports every three months.

The peace that Nestle reached with the boycotters is occasionally cracked. In the fall of 1988, a group in the United States called Action for Corporate Accountability (ACA), supported by the International Nestle Boycott Committee of Europe, asked for resumption of a boycott against Nestle on the basis of three allegations: promoting infant formula "by dumping supplies of formula on hospitals and maternity wards," breaking the agreement signed in 1984 and "violating the trust of concerned organizations," and failing to "provide a business plan . . . detailing how the company would implement the Code, including an end to the free supplies."

The commission responded to the charges with a report that said in effect it did not agree with ACA on any of its accusations, and offered its reasons for the reply to each. NIFAC added that in correspondence and through meetings with ACA, it had responded to ACA about the allegations before the preparation of its report, which was publicly distributed.[46]

With the rekindling of old charges by ACA, Nestle called in a public relations firm, Ogilvy and Mather, for advice. The PR counselors proposed an aggressive, combative program called Pro-active Neutralization. The recommendations to Nestle included setting up an early warning system through which Nestle would gain awareness of actions planned by boycotting groups. Implementation of this suggestion would amount to "infiltration of groups organizing and supporting" a boycott, said *The Wall Street Journal*, and it appeared "too overzealous" for Nestle. The firm rejected the proposal, contained in a confidential report to Nestle that somehow found its way to the press. Putting the recommendations into action would have opened Nestle to charges of unethical public relations practices and hurt its hard-won credibility.[47]

During this lengthy clash, Nestle remained relatively calm in the face of taunts. It showed a sincere interest in acting socially responsible, in being open and responsive, and in maintaining its public relations words and actions at ethical levels. Give Nestle credit too for absorbing the bruises of the battle and fighting on for a product line that was only 2.5 percent of its total business.[48]

A sum-up comment appeared in a June 1990 column in *The Wall Street Journal*: "The company worked hard to separate the genuine concerns of church people and nutritionists from mere political sharpshooting and then set up a code of marketing conduct. The issue has largely been laid to rest."[49]

POINTS

• Your credibility can suffer in a confrontation, particularly when those who attack you wage a public relations campaign outside the bounds of ethics.

• Maintain an ethical public relations stance regardless of the unethical ploys of an aggressive adversary. Don't try to match deceit, misrepresentation, and dishonesty.

• Look for opportunities to form alliances with groups that have respect and credibility.

• Search for different and novel ways to move positively as you challenge your opponents, for example, the formation of the Nestle Infant Formula Audit Commission.

NOTES

1. W. T. Stephens, "From Handmaiden to Visionary: The Evolution of Today's Corporate Director," speech, National Association of Corporate Directors, Washington, D.C., October 30, 1989.

2. Ibid.

3. Manville news release, background information, October 1987.

4. Ibid.

5. Stephen Labaton, "The Bitter Fight over the Manville Trust," *The New York Times*, July 8, 1990, p. F1.

6. Marj Charlier, "Manville Tries to Build New Identity as a Firm Keen on Environment," *The Wall Street Journal*, May 31, 1990, p. A1.

7. Manville news release, September 7, 1990.

8. Stephens, "From Handmaiden to Visionary: The Evolution of Today's Corporate Director."

9. Tom Stephens, "Preventive Management: The Best Medicine for Maintaining Your Legal Health," speech, 1989 Corporate Legal Health Program, Denver, July 13, 1989.

10. Tom Stephens, "Health, Safety & Environment: The Worldwide Bottomline Challenge," speech, World Economic Forum, Davos, Switzerland, February 5, 1990.

11. Stephens, "From Handmaiden to Visionary: The Evolution of Today's Corporate Director."

12. Fred S. Worthy, "Mr. Clean Charts a New Course at General Dynamics," *Fortune*, April 28, 1986, p. 70.

13. Wayne Biddle, "Ethics according to General Dynamics," *The New York Times*, August 16, 1985, p. A12.

14. "General Dynamics Raises a White Flag," *U.S. News and World Report*, June 3, 1985, p. 14.

15. "Lehman Letter Sparked Ethics Planning," *General Dynamics World*, August 1990, p. 4.

16. Biddle, "Ethics according to General Dynamics," p. 14.

17. "Priority Given to Implementation of Updated Standards of Business Ethics and Conduct," *General Dynamics World*, August 1985, p. 1.

18. Biddle, "Ethics according to General Dynamics," p. 14.

19. "Priority Given to Implementation of Updated Standards of Business and Conduct," p. 1.

20. Adam Goodman, "Ethics Codes Help Raise Awareness," *St. Louis Post-Dispatch*, January 23, 1989, p. 1.

21. "Priority Given to Implementation of Updated Standards of Business and Conduct," p. 1.

22. "General Dynamics Standards of Business Ethics and Conduct," 1985.

23. Ibid.
24. "General Dynamics Standards of Business Ethics and Conduct,"
    2nd ed., 1987.
25. Ibid.
26. John H. Cushman, Jr., "Lehman Packs His Bag, Abrasiveness
    Intact but No Resentments," *The New York Times*, March 11, 1987,
    p. B6.
27. Stanley C. Pace, statement, House Armed Services Committee,
    August 10, 1988.
28. Phone conversation of the author with Joseph P. Sutherland, April
    20, 1992.
29. "Lehman Letter Sparked Ethics Planning," p. 4.
30. J. Dobbing, ed., *Infant Feeding: Anatomy of a Controversy 1973–1984*,
    (Berlin Heidelberg: Springer-Verlage, 1988), p. 149.
31. D. B. Jellife, "Advertising and Infant Feeding," *Journal of Tropical
    Pediatrics*, November 21, 1975, p. 161.
32. Dobbing, *Infant Feeding: Anatomy of a Controversy 1973–1984*, p. 96.
33. Ibid., p. v, p. 1, pp. 36–7.
34. Ibid., pp. 37–8.
35. Ibid., pp. 39–40.
36. Ibid., p. 55.
37. Rafael D. Pagan, Jr., speech, Public Relations Society of America
    National Conference, San Francisco, November 8, 1982.
38. Dobbing, *Infant Feeding: Anatomy of a Controversy 1973–1984*, p. 62.
39. Ibid., pp. 111–12.
40. Ibid., p. 117.
41. C. D. May, "The 'Infant Formula Controversy': A Notorious
    Threat to Reason in Matters of Health," *Pediatrics*, September 1981,
    p. 428.
42. "Revisiting the Formula Fight," *The Washington Post*, November
    5, 1982, p. A14.
43. Richard L. Barovick, "Activism on a Global Scale," *Public Relations
    Journal*, June 1982, p. 29.
44. L. M. Perryman, *United Methodist Communication News*, April 5,
    1982, p. 1.
45. J. P. Wogman, ed., " Fourth Report of the Infant Formula Task
    Force to the United Methodist General Council on Ministries,"
    April 28, 1983.
46. "Report on the Infant Formula Controversy by the Nestle Infant
    Formula Audit Commission," undated.

47. "Nestle Rejects Militant PR Plan to Combat Renewal of Boycott," *The Wall Street Journal*, April 25,1989, p. B6.
48. "The Dilemma of Third World Nutrition," *Nestle S.A.*, 1982, p. 20.
49. George Melloan, "Nestle Courts the LDC Middle Class," *The Wall Street Journal*, June 4, 1990, p. A11.

Chapter Five

How the Credibility Factor Affects the Not-For-Profit Sector

What's a not-for-profit? Who are the members of the not-for-profit sector? Some might respond that they are the do-gooders who run the community agencies that provide services to the needy. At best, such an answer is only partially correct. A diverse group of organizations with a wide range of budgets form this sector: the national health and social agencies that operate at local levels; churches and other religious bodies; independent schools, from kindergarten to university; associations formed to express particular points of view, and others. Each carries on public relations activities tailored to its program.

The charters of the not-for-profits may speak of lofty ideals, and these are commendable, but in the nitty-gritty of daily operations, gliches can occur that may spell trouble for credibility goals. Managers associated with not-for-profits and those who someday may be associated with them will learn in this chapter about credibility problems they may encounter in these organizations and receive suggestions on avoiding such pitfalls.

COMMUNITY DONORS RAISE QUESTIONS OF ETHICS AFTER LEARNING THEIR BLOOD SOLD TO NATIONAL BANKS

There's a lot of PR involved in the work of community blood banks. You've heard the messages many times—the call to those with compassion for their fellow man and woman to give their blood that others in the area, perhaps their relatives, friends or neighbors, might be saved. A local blood alert may base its plea on seasonal factors. For example, blood supplies are low because so many people are away for summer vacations, or too busy with Christmas holiday schedules to keep appointments at the blood bank. Those who can donate are asked to do so at once to ease the emergency. It's all part of a practical, sensible nonprofit community cooperative that serves the needs of patients, doctors, and hospitals. Where are the ethical and credibility problems?

The problems in these public relations activities arise when (1) the local blood bank sells donor blood to a national blood bank hundreds of miles away—and the blood is resold one or two times; and (2) those who gave the blood free to the blood bank are led to believe they are performing a community service that will aid fellow citizens, and are unaware of the sales and shipments of their blood to other locations. Deceit and deception taint the public relations calls. The practice at some blood centers of selling blood outside the community without the knowledge of the donors was exposed by Gilbert M. Gaul, staff writer for *The Philadelphia Inquirer*, in a series, "The Blood Brokers," published September 24–28, 1989. His stories earned him the 1990 Pulitzer Prize for public service reporting.[1]

Gaul found in interviewing 70 blood bank officials that "none told donors explicitly that their blood might be sold elsewhere at a profit." Here are figures from a couple of those banks:

- Nearly one half of the blood collected from donors at the Community Blood Center in Appleton, Wisconsin, in 1988 and 1989 was sold outside the area.

- The American Red Cross in Waterloo, Iowa, sold 6 of every 10 pints it collected in 1988 to other blood banks.

A donor at the center in Appleton, Lynne Nelson, upon finding out that some blood from her and other donors was sold, said, "I didn't give blood so someone else can make money from my blood. I gave it to be used at the least expense by anyone who would need it."

Gaul quoted the view of one representing a buyer of blood, who also was critical of the practice. Dr. Aaron Kellner, a former president of the New York Blood Center, which bought 300,000 pints of blood a year, said, "People are being fooled. Nobody is telling them that their blood is going to us. They would be furious if they knew about it. If you're going to do it, you have to tell people up front, publicize the fact. People . . . don't know. It's unethical."[2]

At the Community Blood Center in Appleton, donors found out that their blood might be sold only after the visit by an *Inquirer* reporter. Gaul said the center then starting handing out a written statement to donors saying that "only leftover blood and blood components that would otherwise be lost" are sold. "The needs of our local hospitals and their patients have, and always will, come first; they are why the Community Blood Center exists."

But don't these explanations dodge the issue to some extent? Apparently so. The *Inquirer* found in interviews with a dozen Appleton donors that they took the words to mean that only a small amount of blood was sold.

As one donor said, "As I understand it, the only way it would be sold is if they have an overabundance at the blood bank here and instead of throwing it out . . . they would sell it." And, of course, the facts disagree with this impression. In 1988, the blood center sold 6,800 pints to other centers, or 46 percent of the 14,700 pints it distributed that year. In 1987, it sold 6,900 out of 14,600 pints—47 percent. The center earned $10 on each pint sold above the regular charge to hospitals.

There were hypocrisy, misrepresentation, and deception in the failure of the Appleton center to be fully open with its donors about the fate of their donations. "I confess," said Alan Cable, executive director, "there's a lot about any blood program the donors are not aware of. It's not as a result of not wanting to tell somebody. It's a matter of (their) not asking the right questions." The kind of appeal used by the center is also open to question. In December of 1988, the Appleton center told the local newspaper, "We've never had it quite this tough." Gaul questioned Cable about his statement. Well, said Cable, the recruiters were having to work harder to get donors. "When my staff has to make twice as many phone calls to get in that number of donors, that becomes a real concern," said Cable.[3]

Cable's center supplies blood to four area hospitals. Cable said it is difficult to project the needs of the hospitals. To make certain there is always enough, the blood bank collects more than it needs. The older blood is sold, he said. The *Inquirer* gave as an example the sale by the Appleton center of 50 pints of whole blood a week in 1988 at $48 a pint to the Central Kentucky Blood Center in Lexington. That center extracted the platelets, a component that helps blood clot. The remaining red cells were sold to the Broward Community Blood Center near Fort Lauderdale for $47 a pint. Broward sold these and other red cells from blood centers around the country to hospitals in New York. The price on average was $63 a pint.

Overall, said Gaul, the buying and selling of blood is a multi-billion dollar industry. "Nobody disputes the value of sharing blood," wrote Gaul. "But in the last 15 years, this trading in blood has become a huge, virtually unregulated market—with no ceiling on prices, with nonprofit blood banks vying with one another for control of the blood supply, with decisions often driven by profits and corporate politics, not medical concerns."

He added that the vital resource that is blood gets less government protection "than grapes, or poultry, or pretzels."[4]

Realizing they may be sitting on a powder keg of backlash, the executives who head the nonprofit blood banks have started to take a look at the ethics of their public relations. At a meeting of what you might call their trade association, the Council of Community Blood Centers, in March of 1990 at Clearwater, Florida, there was discussion around the question: What are the ethical responsibilities to donors whose blood is collected in one region and sold to centers elsewhere? Gaul, who attended the meeting, said that Ronald Bayer, a medical ethicist at Columbia University, addressing the gathering on these responsibilities, advised it was time "to clean house and confront these issues.

"It does a profound injury to individuals if you ask them to donate blood to help their neighbors, implying the blood is to be used (by) those with whom they share a geographical identity, when what is meant is that the blood will be used by neighbors in a more figurative sense," Bayer told them. He said it is deceptive to conceal the practice. He also pointed out that the blood centers run the risk "that the deception will be uncovered. From that point on, potential donors will have no reason to trust you."

A more open operation should include disclosure of financial data to donors, urged Bayer. "Bureaucracy is necessary and that necessity must be explained," he said, in reference to administrative and other costs. "But a bloated bureaucracy is not necessary."[5] Bayer said "deception is always wrong" and gave this advice to those who direct community blood centers: "It would be a welcome experience if those responsible for blood banking systems did not respond defensively to the kinds of exposes that have appeared in *The Philadelphia Inquirer* but rather took the opportunity to discuss in open forums the need for, as well as the limits of, reforms, the needs for and the limits of sharing."[6]

Dr. Jeffrey McCullough, an official of the American Red Cross in St. Paul, Minnesota, said that as a representative of a blood center that was a major exporter, "we still are quite aware that there are substantial segments of our donor population that do not take [to] the concept that the community they should support is a very broad one." He suggested that blood banks promote collection as a national program rather than a local one, speak frankly about the use of their blood at some distant place. Bayer thought donors would accept this explanation. "I cannot for a moment imagine that the blood services would be hindered in any marked way were the broader definition of community stressed and openly explained."[7]

These comments to blood bank directors may be the first breeze in a wind of change. If so, there might be an end to the unethical conduct of deceit, misrepresentation, and deception in the public relations of many of the banks. The Gaul series indicated that, to a large degree at least, there was a deliberate cover-up of such basic information as how and where the donated blood was used. Those who were guilty of the deceit and coverup can be criticized for their past unethical conduct, but they also can be applauded if they change their policies to ones of greater candor and openness.

You might like to know that Gaul was a blood donor, giving four times a year, when he began research for his series in 1988. After he finished and the series was published, he still donated blood. He further expressed the hope "that people will keep donating but put pressure on their legislators to monitor this system better. When you donate blood, you deserve to know what happens to it."[8]

POINTS

• Level with the community about what goes on in your operation.

• Avoid the use of deceitful ploys to gain the community's attention if exposure of them will cause backfires.

• State your cause or need fully, without holding back on portions so the statement is skewed in your favor.

• When you ask for the cooperation and support of the community, remember that you need to return the same qualities.

SCANDALS IN UNITED WAY

United Way of America is the collective granddaddy of all fundraising organizations in the country. Located in Alexandria, Virginia, it's at the head of a network of 2,100 local United Way independent associates whose annual fall drives attracted $3.1 billion from donors in 1991. Supported by about 1 percent of the dollars donated by 1,400 affiliates, the national organization in return provides lobbying, training and education, coordination of advertising and publicity for national campaigns, and management services.

Planning and conducting one campaign for contributions that are divided among and benefit dozens of member groups, the local United Way saves the much greater expense and manpower that separate campaigns for each would demand. Givers in the communities answer only one appeal instead of many. Each community's United Way relies heavily on broad-scale public relations efforts for its success. Communications about the need for funds—words and visuals about those who benefit—are packaged and distributed to the news media and publicized in other ways. The public spotlight is directed toward workers who ask others for their dollars and to those who donate, and their reasons for giving. In these and other ways, the United Way has a great deal of visibility. Citizens have high expectations for its manner and method of operations. After all, they feel, it exists because of them.

Volunteers on the board of directors, who set the policies, and the paid executives, who manage and administer the programs of the local agencies, often find themselves in public view. Board members frequently are individuals of clout selected from cross-sections of the community. The mix of men and women may include representatives from business, whose base may be manufacturing, research, finance, retail, or services; from law, accounting, medicine, health care, and labor unions; from college and university faculties; from other social service agencies; and from minority groups.

All of this is background for the shock felt in the local United Way offices—and throughout their communities—in early February 1992, when accusations of lavish spending and free-wheeling management practices were leveled against William Aramony, president of United Way of America (UWA). The news revealed that Aramony, 64, was the highest-paid executive in the charity field, receiving $463,000 in salary and benefits, and entitled to $4.4 million in pension benefits. Stories told of his trips on the supersonic Concorde jet, use of chauffeured limousines, and creation of several for-profit spinoff organizations, one headed by his son. Aramony had been president of UWA for 22 years and with the organization for 37 years, and earned credit for the growth and success of the United Way concept across the nation. Now, scandal was emerging from his office.

Amid "a wave of anger over revelations of high expense-account living and questionable management practices," Aramony resigned on February 27, saying he would take an early retirement but remain in charge until a successor was found.[9] Just two days later, however, the board named an Aramony deputy as acting president and on March 5 appointed an interim president and chief executive officer, Kenneth W. Dam, a former IBM executive. The board of directors asked a Washington law firm to conduct a broad review of UWA operations, to be completed by April 2.

Officials of local United Way affiliates were dismayed and upset. Many voted to withhold monthly payments to the national office until they heard answers to their questions about allegedly extravagant spending by Aramony and plans for stricter financial controls. They also expressed concern about the effect on donor support.

The investigative report substantiated early spending reports. Among disclosures regarding Aramony's use of UWA funds: He had taken 29 trips to Las Vegas between 1988 and 1991; spent $92,265 on chauffeured limousines from 1988 to 1991 and $40,762 for fares on the Concorde between 1987 and 1990. "The report showed a pattern of financial manipulation of hundreds of thousands of dollars for consulting fees, the creation of spinoff organizations and lavish expense accounts," said the *Times*, "all with vague or nonexistent documentation."

Dam acted immediately. He announced internal changes to regulate setting of salaries and benefits, and arrangements with consultants and spinoff organizations. Regarding expense account travel, he said staffers should travel on airline coach fares; he banned use of limos and placed a maximum per diem on travel expenses. He pledged to "take every legal step to obtain reimbursement of all monies owed to United Way of America."[10]

United Way credibility suffered at national and local levels. Aramony appeared to have violated standards of public relations and business ethics, though final assessment of blame awaited further disclosures.

Warts and blemishes are also found in local United Way operations. Perhaps the most notorious case was that of the country's largest United Way, in Los Angeles County, California. Here the ethical and credibility questions also centered around the charity's president and chief executive, Francis X. McNamara, Jr., who had held the post 19 years. Troubles with McNamara's leadership became public in April 1986 through news reports about a study of the agency's public affairs and marketing that he commissioned. The consultant who prepared the study found problems of dissatisfaction and low morale in interviews with more than 100 professional employees and volunteers. Those interviewed described McNamara as an anachronism, as out of touch, aloof and "they wished he would depart gracefully and with full honors—before it was too late."[11] Employees who participated got rid of pent-up grievances and made candid comments about the president and the way the place was run. His critics did, however, give him credit for diligence that led to achievement of annual increases in fund collections.

A controversy ensued about release of the study. When the media asked for copies, his PR staff urged him to distribute the report, to show United Way had nothing to hide. He refused to do so. For a while he even tried to deceive and manipulate by denying the existence of the findings.[12] McNamara did discuss the report with a subcommittee of the board and later the *Los Angeles Times* obtained a copy from the consultant.[13]

McNamara was in a favorable position, however. In suppressing the report, he had the support of his board, whose chairman was Roy A. Anderson, retired chairman of the board and former chief executive officer of Lockheed Corp. If the board put McNamara on the spot, were the members admitting their lack of oversight, and putting themselves on the spot? Such a thought may have been in their minds. Also, they anticipated McNamara's retirement at the end of 1987, and may have decided just to wait it out.[14]

The Los Angeles United Way was the object of another volley, released on June 11, 1986. In the news were stories that more than $300,000 of the charity's funds had been loaned to five former and current members of the professional staff during the years 1980 through 1982. The money was loaned almost interest-free, and unsecured. The largest amounts—$62,900 and $165,328—went to two executives who moved to Los Angeles from Ohio United Way agencies in 1980 and obtained loans from First Interstate Bank, then United California Bank, for relocation costs. Neither borrower made any repayment to the bank. In 1981 United Way paid off the bank and took over the loans. McNamara said United Way did not cosign for the loans but did ask the bank to approve them, and he felt the agency had an obligation to make good on them. He added that the loans were necessary to attract top-level talent. He also said he had cleared the loans with the board chairman at the time, but not with the full board.[15]

Editorials in the press asked for fuller explanations. They saw the erosion of credibility and public confidence and the need to restore them.

Anderson didn't help quiet his questioners when he told a television interviewer that there were no plans to discipline McNamara or to encourage the 61-year-old president to retire. The day after the loan story made headlines, the state attorney general asked the Los Angeles County Board of Supervisors to conduct a probe, which was assigned to the county counsel. In hopes of quieting the outcries, Anderson announced at a news conference on June 13 that United Way would call on a citizens' committee to examine charges in the loan scandal. He said the review would cover "management policies, procedures, and internal controls."[16] There was also an announcement from McNamara, who said he was taking a paid leave of absence. Anderson took over as unpaid acting president. Replacing him as chairman was William F. Kieschnick, retired president of Atlantic Richfield.

Robert Dockson, chairman of the board of California Federal Savings & Loan Association, accepted the chairmanship of the citizens' committee and reported on the inquiry at a news conference in early September. The committee found "flawed judgment" on the part of McNamara and key volunteers who approved of lending donated money to staff executives but, said Dockson, there was "nothing indicative of dishonesty or flagrant misrepresentation." There was a call for reforms in management of the United Way, with Dockson commenting that "I would immediately have a very careful evaluation of all the top people of this organization."[17] One recommendation was to divide the top job of McNamara between at least two persons, with one assigned responsibility for day-to-day operations and the other for long-range planning. The committee also asked the agency to adopt a policy on extending credit or making loans to employees.

The report brought to the attention of the public United Way's use of $260,000 of donated funds to bail out a defunct credit union, money that had not been recovered, and lending $150,000 to an East Los Angeles human services agency, which had made no repayment.

The United Way board voted to study some recommendations, accept others, such as those asking for creation of a new and stronger audit committee and a personnel and development committee. The board, however, faulted no one; there may have been some bad judgment, but made in good faith. McNamara would be called back—he was needed, as the annual campaign was behind schedule because of the loan squabbles. He would, however, advance his retirement six months, and leave in June of 1987. Kieschnick disclosed that individuals and corporations would contribute to a fund that would repay United Way the amount of the outstanding employee loans, and the group would assume the debt.

There were more editorials, this time indignant that the board failed to call for more sweeping reforms and that it reinstated McNamara. His hometown daily, the Pasadena *Star-News*, delivered a direct blast at him: "This breach of public trust should not be condoned simply because the (Dockson) panel found that McNamara 'acted in good faith.' McNamara should give United Way the best gift he possibly can. He should resign—immediately."[18] The *Los Angeles Times* observed that McNamara "has wisely indicated that he will retire next June" and looked forward to "new leadership, new policies, new procedures."[19]

Within a month came the report of the investigation by the Los Angeles County counsel's office, which criticized management practices of the agency in connection with the loans but found no illegal acts. Investigators said there was insufficient authorization to lend much of the money and too few steps to be sure borrowers met pay-back schedules. The report was also critical of the bailout of the credit union and the expense reporting methods of McNamara. His expenses included membership in the California Club, which had no women or black members.

Kieschnick, the board chairman, commented on the county counsel's investigation: "Nobody said there weren't some problems in administration. The good news is they weren't ethical and moral problems."[20] His was hardly a justifiable conclusion since the investigation looked for violations of the law, not at ethical and moral problems. The words ring of spin control.

Kieschnick, Anderson, and McNamara—in their actions and their words—were major PR communicators in the scandal and contributed to the ethical dilemmas created. Of the three, McNamara showed the greatest disregard for ethical behavior and concern about credibility. The results of the first report, the one that had interviews with staff and volunteers about the United Way operation, were never released, even though donors' money paid for the study. McNamara first denied existence of the report, a lie. Then he withheld it, concealed it—a cover-up that surely is an act of deceit and of bad faith. McNamara was deceitful in failing to inform the full board of directors of the loans, and acted against the interests of this social service agency in holding membership in a club whose members were all white males.

Throughout these incidents there was too little sensitivity for the public's right to know—the right to be informed how the charity, to which thousands made contributions, was managed and allocated their dollars. Indifference of this kind in itself is less than ethical.

As a postscript, the 1986–87 campaign did finally get off the ground. But it failed to reach its goal, a failure blamed on the months of unfavorable publicity. Fortunately, those who used the services of the agencies were not hurt as much as they might have been, as the United Way made up the deficit from its strong reserve fund.

POINTS

• Maintain your operation in a manner that meets the expectations and perceptions of your supporters.

• Keep always in mind the sources of income for your budget and present programs that are keyed to the sensibilities of these contributors.

• Plan to spend time away from your office to meet with those who pay for the services you offer and those who use them. Be frank in such talks and ask for an evaluation or grade on how well they think you're doing.

• Open informal discussions with staff members. Draw out their views with questions about what's good and bad in the organization and where improvements can be made.

DONORS WHO GIVE MONEY DON'T ALWAYS KNOW WHERE IT GOES— FUNDRAISING PR MINUS ETHICS

When you're solicited over the phone to give money to a charity and decide to write out a check for $50, how much of that do you think the charity receives? Ninety percent? Fifty percent? Ten percent? Somewhere between one of those numbers? There is no correct answer. It depends upon the charity and its method of fundraising. But the answer could be less than 10 percent. That's right. There are instances in which the soliciting organizations keep more than 90 cents of every dollar donated! Reports of this kind of fundraising dim the credibility for the vast majority of charities whose costs for attracting funds are in a reasonable range.

The *Rocky Mountain News*, Denver, reported in a copyrighted story on July 23, 1990, that professional fundraisers in Colorado "kept 83 percent of the $4.6 million they raised for charity and non-profit groups." The number was based on 60 completed financial statements filed with the secretary of state over the previous two years.

Examples of the percentages of dollars that remained for the charities from the total dollars raised by their paid solicitors (the fundraisers, of course, received the remainder):

Colorado Professional Firefighters Association, 9.96 percent.
Civil Air Patrol, 10.12 percent.
Fraternal Order of Police (Denver metro area) 12.94 percent.
Longmont Lions Club, 15.15 percent.
March of Dimes Birth Defects Foundation, 15.69 percent.
Paralyzed Veterans of America, Mountain States Chapter, 15.71 percent.
Alternatives to Family Violence, 19.58 percent.[21]

In November 1991, the *News* took another look at reports of the state's telemarketing and direct-mail fundraisers and uncovered two charities that received even lesser splits. These were Colorado Jaycees, Estes Park, with 6.7 percent, and New Bridges, Inc., Fort Collins, with 9.6 percent.[22]

Is it ethical in these public relations campaigns for authorized representatives of the charities to call you and ask you to give to the causes described? Of course. But is it ethical, or is it deceitful and deceptive, to let you, perhaps even encourage you to, assume that the chief beneficiaries are the charities, when really they are the fundraisers? It's unethical, because of the deceit and deception, which in many of these instances lead to manipulation and perhaps even cover-up (of the net revenue that goes to the charity). The charitable agency that agrees to accept a small percentage of contributions will suffer loss of credibility, however, only when the practice is exposed.

Some phone solicitors can be so appealing: A typical approach might go like this: "You wouldn't want to deprive underprivileged children the opportunity to see a real circus, with trained animals doing tricks, clowns and skilled acrobats, now would you?" From the number of calls you receive from the phone solicitors, you'd swear these poor kids get taken to the circus or similar shows at least three times a year. The solicitor's playing for the sympathy of the potential giver compounds the unethical charge.

Colorado law requires charitable organizations to make figures on fundraisers public, by filing with the state, information on gross proceeds, expenses and disbursements, and the amount turned over to the charities. While this gives contributors the opportunity to find out what the percentage breaks are, it doesn't mean that they'll go looking for them. And they may never know. Most likely. And they may continue to give year after year to one of those pleas that results in a skim-off of 80 or 90 percent. The law fails to restrict the amount the professional fundraiser can keep of the total gifts.

The state's reporting demands on fundraisers were in a law passed by the Colorado legislature in 1988. The measure's chief sponsor, Republican Sen. Dottie Wham, said, "The bad ones would be put out of business if people would just be critical. I know it's not easy to ask someone . . . say a blind person, 'Are you legitimate?' You feel bad. But that's what we all have to do."[23]

Further appropriate comment came from Neal Richardson, Denver Deputy District Attorney: "I'll be frank. It's very dangerous to give money to charities that solicit by phone.[24] The problem (with current law) is it throws the ball into the court of the contributor to check people out and find out how much (they are getting). If you question them enough, they will either hang up or they will start to do a tap dance that they don't know until all the money comes in." He warned against accepting such an excuse.[25] Richardson suggested givers contribute directly to the charity of their choice.

Those in the organizations that benefit from the efforts of the professional solicitors apparently don't feel ethical pangs. Their rationalization seems to be that, whatever the amount raised, this is money they wouldn't receive otherwise. The executive director for Alternatives to Family Violence, Barbara Hutton, said, "In the ideal world I would rather have the $66,000 [instead of $12,900]. But the money we get allows us to provide service we wouldn't ordinarily be able to provide. And (the telemarketing company) is reaching people who normally wouldn't know about us."[26]

Those hired to do the phoning on behalf of the charities believe they provide worthwhile services. Said Mike Brady, a supervisor for the Gehl Group, which raised $764,207 for the Fraternal Order of Police, which received 12.94 percent: "This is a corporation in business to make money. But it is a mutually beneficial relationship."[27] Being a business, of course, the Gehl Group and other soliciting firms have such expenses as manpower, phone lines, and office rental. Being a business, however, doesn't mean it's an ethical enterprise.

The major nonprofit service organizations, which have staff members who direct annual giving campaigns, are not affected by the state law, as they file financial statements with the Internal Revenue Service. Their cost of conducting campaigns for funds is in a much more modest range, and the percentages of income available for their service programs are much higher. In Denver these include, for example, the local chapter of the Red Cross, which holds campaign costs to about 10 cents of every dollar raised, and United Way, which may take out up to 16 cents. They publicly report their fundraising costs. No cover-up for them.

The fat percentages to phone solicitors and thin returns to charities is by no means limited to Denver. *Money* magazine told of a 1988 Connecticut study that showed "of nearly $9 million raised for charity by 191 telephone campaigns, only 26 cents of each dollar, on average, reached the intended groups. The remaining 74 cents was kept by the fundraisers." The article offered givers a few precautions to observe before writing contribution checks, or giving over the phone by providing a charge card number. In fact, giving your credit-card information to a phone solicitor is a no-no; so is sending money before you ask for and receive information about the organization with its hand out. One suggestion in the article was to check with such watch dog agencies as the National Charities Information Bureau or the Philanthropic Advisory Service of the Council of Better Business Bureaus or the local Better Business Bureau.[28]

Prospective givers should work harder to find out who the big skimmers are and refuse to have a part in their unethical activities. They should withhold their giving and protest to the charities, steps that would take away credibility from the agencies and perhaps force them to change. The continued existence of such unethical public relations gives observers the excuse that they can do the same. It's another case of "doesn't everybody?"

POINTS

• Be a volunteer for credibility in your community. Help to direct attention to agencies that settle for pennies on the dollars raised in their behalf and work for better informed prospective contributors.

• If you're asked to provide public relations counsel to one of these agencies, warn of the potential pitfalls and seek to change the practice.

• Endorse those in agencies that invest reasonable amounts for fundraising.

STANFORD COPES WITH ETHICS BLAME AND CREDIBILITY LOSS

Universities, which have well-stoked public relations factories as well as educational muscle, sometimes find credibility hazards on the campus. At Stanford University, investigations of its use of government research money uncovered alleged overcharges up to $200 million over 10 years. After two years of fighting against accusations and putting into action an ethical clean-up, Donald Kennedy, university president, announced in July 1991 that he would resign at the end of the coming academic year.

In a letter to the school's trustees, Kennedy said, "It is very difficult, I have concluded, for a person identified with a problem to be the spokesman for its solution." He "had the courage and vision to subordinate his ego for the good of the institution," said *Time* magazine, adding that his "leavetaking contains a lesson that should not be lost on Kennedy's counterparts in academia, business, and government."[29]

A government auditor and CPA, Paul Biddle, discovered the revelations that put the school in an intense glare of unwanted publicity. He found that payments by the United States to Stanford for research contracts and grants were the university's "second-biggest revenue source after tuition, providing 28 percent of the operating budget."[30] Rep. John Dingell, Michigan Democrat who chaired the House committee concerned with oversight of research contracts, added investigators in the search for documentation.

Found in the probe: charges by Stanford of $184,286 in depreciation on athletic equipment that included a 72-foot luxury yacht; a shared ownership in a retreat facility at Lake Tahoe for the board of trustees; monies spent for furnishings in Kennedy's home; even $17,730 to pay for a reception for his wife. As the crescendo about questionable billings rose, Kennedy also had to contend with the resignation of a prominent female neurosurgeon from the medical school because of "blatant sexism," drug charges leveled against a computer science lecturer, and plagiarism against a business lecturer.

While the school repaid several million dollars to the government and engaged in ethical reconstruction, *The New York Times* noted, "Experts say Stanford is not the only university in need of a housecleaning."[31] Government examinations at other universities substantiated this statement. At the first 13 additional schools investigated, including Yale and Dartmouth, sleuths "found $14,113,746 in unallowable or inappropriate charges." Rutgers, with $4.9 million in inappropriate expenses, had the largest amount.[32]

The *Times* posed questions related to ethics in academia generally to several ethics experts. Commented R. Edward Freeman, director of the University of Virginia's Olsson Center for Applied Ethics: "Academics believe that their pursuit of truth and knowledge is so important that they can bend the rules. After all, it is just government money. Professors must understand that if they take money that was intended for defense research and apply it to cancer research, they have cheated a customer. If universities lived in a fishbowl the way that corporations do, they would manage themselves differently."[33]

For more than 300 years, the nation's institutions of higher learning created a large reservoir of trust and credibility. While there are cracks showing, total collapse can be avoided. Public relations communicators can be part of the preservation process.

POINTS

• Push for the strongest possible audit and other financial controls in your organization so that it is nearly impossible for frauds in money handling to exist.

• You can't check every possible source of plagiarism, but if it's suspected, it may be uncovered through properly directed questions.

• Set aside time for meetings and encourage open discussions on ethics and ethical issues among members of a department and groups convened from different departments. Consider scheduling outside speakers for workshops and seminars.

• Relate ethics to the accomplishment of the goals of your organization, and make use of a variety of communications media for disseminating the message.

NOTES

1. Gilbert M. Gaul, "How Blood, the 'Gift of Life,' Became a Billion-Dollar Business," *The Philadelphia Inquirer*, September 24, 1989, p. A1.
2. Ibid.
3. Ibid.
4. Ibid.
5. Gilbert M. Paul, "Selling Blood: Officials Take a Look at the Ethics," *The Philadelphia Inquirer*, March 4, 1990, p. 5D.
6. Ronald Bayer, Ph.D., "What Should Your Community Know about Resource Sharing?" speech, National Conference spon-

sored by the American Blood Commission and the Council of Community Blood Centers, Clearwater, Fla., February 18, 1990.

7. Paul, "Selling Blood: Officials Take a Look at the Ethics," p. 5D.
8. "How the Series Came to Be Written," *The Philadelphia Inquirer*, reprint edition, p. 24.
9. Felicity Barringer, "United Way Head Is Forced Out in a Furor over His Lavish Style," *The New York Times*, February 28, 1992, p. A1.
10. Felicity Barringer, "Affiliates Fear Bitter Fight by Ex-Head of United Way," *The New York Times*, April 5, 1992, p. A12.
11. Lawrence F. Mihlon, "Sweet & Sour Charity," *California Business*, December 1986, p. 32.
12. Ibid.
13. David Johnston, "United Way Report Cites Management, Funding Problems," *Los Angeles Times*, June 9, 1986, sec. II, p. 1.
14. Mihlon, "Sweet & Sour Charity," p. 32.
15. David Johnston, "United Way Assumed $200,000 in Aides' Loans," *Los Angeles Times*, June 11, 1986, sec. 2, p. 1.
16. David Johnston, "United Way Chief Will Take Leave," *Los Angeles Times*, June 13, 1986, sec. 1, p. 1.
17. Roxane Arnold, "No Dishonesty Found in Loans by United Way," *Los Angeles Times*, September 9, 1986, part 1, p. 1.
18. Mihlon, "Sweet & Sour Charity," p. 32.
19. "Fresh Start," *Los Angeles Times*, September 10, 1986, part 2, p. 4.
20. Roxane Arnold, "United Way Hails County Counsel Report," *Los Angeles Times*, October 7, 1986, part 2, p. 2.
21. John Sanko and Fawn Germer, "Donations Whittled Away," *Rocky Mountain News*, July 23, 1990, p. 7.
22. Fawn Germer and John Sanko, "Some Fund-Raising Companies Keep the Lion's Share," *Rocky Mountain News*, November 24, 1991, p. 6.
23. Sanko and Germer, "Donations Whittled Away," p. 7.
24. Ibid.
25. John Sanko, "Charity Laws not Toothless," *Rocky Mountain News*, July 23, 1990, p. 9.
26. Sanko and Germer, "Donations Whittled Away," p. 7.
27. Fawn Germer, "Hard-Sell Outfit Kept 87% of Funds Raised," *Rocky Mountain News*, July 23, 1990, p. 7.
28. Marguerite T. Smith, "How to Give to Charity without Being Taken," *Money*, December 1989, p. 142.

29. Walter Shapiro, with reporting by Minal Hajartwala/New York and Robert Hollis/San Francisco, "Putting the School First," *Time*, August 12, 1991, p. 57.
30. Eugene Methvin, "He Caught the Campus Chiselers," *Reader's Digest*, January 1992, p. 81.
31. Claudia H. Deutsch, "Academia Fails the Ethics Test," *The New York Times*, November 3, 1991, p. 26.
32. Eugene Methvin, "He Caught the Campus Chiselers," p. 81.
33. Claudia H. Deutsch, "Academia Fails the Ethics Test," p. 26.

Chapter Six

News Media: A Mixed Bag

Public relations communicators depend upon the news media to channel their ideas, plans, and programs to their audiences. The news media depend upon the PR people for a good amount of their news. While this dependency exists, it is by no means a perfect relationship; there may also be friction. The media's handling of a story may anger and upset those whose programs are described and they call foul, asserting that they were victims of unethical acts. Intertwining of the interests of the communicators and the media, and unsettling consequences, are found in the first two segments of this chapter.

Maintaining credibility of readers, listeners, and viewers is at or near the top of the priority list for the news media. They need this to keep circulation and audience ratings as high as possible, factors that in turn influence the amounts and rates of their advertising. The media know it's difficult to present a news story in a way that will suit everyone. Their attempts at accuracy and objectivity please some, irritate others. Ethical problems in public relations faced by the media as they strive for credibility are the subject of the third segment.

CATTLEMEN OBJECT TO COVERAGE BY NBC NEWS "TODAY"

A 10-minute segment on the NBC News "Today" program of January 9, 1990, enraged a portion of the viewers, who gave it this review: "highly inaccurate, misleading, and lacking in objectivity and balance."[1] These were strong charges of unethical tacks against a major member of the mass media. The critics represented the National Cattlemen's Association and the Public Lands Council, whose membership is near 260,000. They leveled the complaints at Paul Ehrlich, controversial ecologist who gave a report during that "Today" show on the impact of cattle-grazing on the western plains. Ehrlich appeared as a guest commentator in his series on "Assignment Earth."

The presidents of the cattlemen's and public lands groups expressed their outrage in a joint letter written January 10 to the executive producer of the program. More than 1,000 other letters and telegrams of complaints from those with interests in grazing cattle on public lands bombarded the "Today" offices.

"Specifically," said the joint letter, "we object to the basic conclusion by Dr. Ehrlich that the only way to improve range conditions in the west is to remove cattle. Experience and studies show that rangelands have improved while supporting cattle-grazing."

The writers went on to list eight points made by Ehrlich they said were "inaccurate." In one instance, Ehrlich was quoted with the claim that "nowhere has the damage from cattle been more severe . . . than on the public lands of the American West." Countering this, they said, was a 1988 report by representatives of two universities that put U.S. rangelands "in the best condition they have been in the past 100 years and, on the average, they are improving."

Ehrlich at another point said the only way "to restore the grasslands and wildlife of the Southwest . . . is to pull cattle off the range." The response to this, using as a reference the Bureau of Land Management and U.S. Forest Service, was that "intelligent and proper use of grazing is a good tool to enrich wildlife habitat, improve water quality, and help regenerate the land."

Disappointment was also expressed at the refusal of the on-location program producer to include information provided by the National and Arizona Cattlemen's associations and the Lands Council. "Obviously, though he appeared interested, he clearly ignored the facts and information we provided him, as we note that most of Ehrlich's reporting of the cattle industry's viewpoints was misleading or taken out of context."

The letter suggested a meeting with "Today" representatives at which those with cattle-grazing interests could "clearly convey the important environmental and economic contribution which cattle and cattle grazing make to the western United States . . . your viewers have the right to be presented with information on both sides of an issue, fairly and accurately."[2]

Phone calls to "Today" to attempt to set up a meeting were unsuccessful. John Lacey, president of the NCA, recounted, in a letter published in *The Wall Street Journal* on March 1, the futile efforts to get a response from "Today". "We then wrote letters, sent letters by courier and even faxed letters to NBC requesting the opportunity to discuss the inaccuracies in the show. Much to our disappointment, there was no response," he said. Where was responsible journalism? you might ask. Lacey gave the answer when he said, "We were treated irresponsibly by one of the country's largest media institutions."[3] To him and his associates in cattle and public lands, the brand of unethical conduct was stamped on the incident.

The January letter was finally answered with one written March 16, by Tom Capra, who had become executive producer of "Today." He expressed "profound apologies" for the delay in responding and blamed it on a change in producer and other shifts. He said NBC realized "that there may be room for interpretation and debate on some of the details in our report. We believe however . . . the assignment was carried out responsibly, fairly, and accurately." Capra said the report was not intended to accuse anyone, "least of all today's responsible cattlemen. It simply tried to shed light on a basic long-term issue of how humans should live in their environment."[4]

This belated reply from NBC led to an even more belated meeting between cattle industry representatives and those of NBC News in June. One of those present, a staff member for NCA, said afterward that the meeting was seen as "fairly productive," though he added that "our expectations were not too high." The cattlemen didn't ask to be put on a program to air their views. They did talk about the cattle industry in the West and the environmental considerations, and also pointed out to NBC that Ehrlich and other environmental advocates have agendas to push. "They listened . . . were impressed with our sincerity," he said.[5]

"Killer Cows" was the heading of an editorial comment of *The Wall Street Journal* about the dispute. "Many people laughed in 1980 when Ronald Reagan suggested that trees contribute to air pollution," said the paper. "Now environmentalists are dredging up the same kind of argument to paint a picture of a world on the brink of ecological disaster." It was noted that the report of Ehrlich, "the man who predicted the population bomb that wasn't," was introduced as one that told "how man is destroying the entire ecological system with something that appears to be completely harmless. Mr. Ehrlich then proceeded to indict the lowly cow . . . but we still have trouble seeing cows as environmental villains."[6]

The fray was joined by Reed Irvine, chairman of Accuracy in Media (AIM), and Joseph C. Goulden, AIM staff writer, in their syndicated newspaper column. They accused NBC News of advocacy in the report, which implies a straying from ethical operation for the news organization, and said, "In failing to respond (at that time) to the cattlemen, NBC is thumbing its nose at those who think that journalists have a duty to be accurate and fair." They further labeled Ehrlich "one of the nation's foremost radical environmentalists" and said he aired a report "that clearly set out to 'lead people into battle' on an environmental issue.'"[7]

Behind the protests of the cattlemen and related groups is the frustration over what they perceive to be stonewalling and lack of fairness by the "Today" folks. Theirs is not a new, or even uncommon, situation. Many other individuals and organizations have reacted similarly when they could find no way to get their points of view expressed to counter what they felt were biased, unfair news accounts. Almost invariably when these situations arise, there is damage of some kind. There are victims. An individual or organization is less than it was before. There may be loss of reputation and credibility; the loss may be financial. Whatever the kind of wound, there has to be a fight back to regain the position or esteem or financial stability that was lost because of what is perceived as an unjust act.

The one who fails to allow for a rebuttal, a counterpoint, to a news story is a participant in unethical public relations as much as those who more overtly deal in fraud or lies in fulfilling business contracts or in other ways.

POINTS

• As a communicator who deals with the news media, you protect your credibility by offering accurate information as complete as you can make it. Be appreciative when your material is used and feel free to ask for an explanation when it isn't. In the explanation, you may learn something that will be useful to you in a future similar instance.

• Let the media know when a story you're involved with that is published or aired is sloppy, inaccurate, or misleading. Sometimes, you'll be thanked for pointing out mistakes. If you think that you or your organization were damaged, tell why and ask for a correction or rebuttal.

• Don't castigate or give up on all of the news media because of one sour experience. You may have been the victim of forces you were unable to confront that were working against you. Bounce back; treat it as a one-time learning phenomenon.

• If you're a communicator on the media side, be an advocate for fairness, for respect for ethical standards, in all programming. You'll help to enhance the credibility of your organization.

WOULD MORE ATTENTION TO ETHICS HAVE MADE THIS SCARE UNNECESSARY?

Thousands of dollars financed a high-powered PR campaign that caused a $100 million loss to growers of apples and fueled expenditures of more than $2 million for public relations efforts to win back public support for the Great American fruit. This was the Alar apple scare.

This "major media event" was instigated by the Natural Resources Defense Council (NRDC).[8] More specifically, it was birthed and nourished by a "carefully-planned media campaign conceived and implemented" by Fenton Communications, a public relations firm hired by NRDC. David Fenton, political publicist and head of the company, said a "sea change in public opinion" took place because of the campaign.[9] What he might well have said is, "Damn the ethics; full speed ahead."

The public reaction, which might better be described as near hysteria, was touched off by a CBS News "60 Minutes" program on February 26, 1989. NRDC had several months before given "60 Minutes" an exclusive for release of a Council report, "Intolerable Risk: Pesticides in Our Children's Food." CBS titled its presentation, "A is for Apple." Shown on the television screen with the words were a skull and crossbones over a bright red apple. Ed Bradley opened the segment for his audience of 50 million viewers with these words: "The most potent cancer-causing agent in our food supply is a substance sprayed on apples to keep them on the trees longer and make them look better. That's the conclusion of a number of scientific experts. And who is most at risk? Children, who may someday develop cancer from this one chemical called daminozide." After a brief interview exchange, he added, "Kids are at high risk because they drink so much apple juice. . . . If those apples were treated with daminozide, the cancer risk is perilously high." One of those interviewed by Bradley, Janet Hathaway, senior attorney for NRDC, claimed, "What we're talking about is a cancer-causing agent used on food that EPA knows is going to cause cancer for thousands of children over their lifetime."[10]

What was the nature of the death agent Bradley and those he interviewed on the program were talking about? Why had the NRDC orchestrated the release of the word about Alar in such a forceful fashion? The Environmental Protection Agency (EPA) had been familiar with Alar for some time. The agency proposed banning use of the pesticide in 1985 because of possible cancer risks, but the science advisory panel that reviews EPA decisions rejected the action. On February 1, 1989, EPA announced that interim test results of Alar indicated a potential cancer risk but said the product could remain on the market pending full-test results expected in 1990. Apple growers who used the worrisome Alar sprayed it on trees several times during a season. However, only about 15 percent of the apple crop was treated with Alar in the year before the NRDC release. The pesticide helped red apples to be redder and have increased firmness and crispness and longer storage life. Alar also was used on Golden Delicious apples, but not on green apples, such as Granny Smith.

The morning following the telecast of "60 Minutes," 70 journalists and 12 camera crews attended an NRDC news conference in Washington for general release of the "Intolerable Risk" report. At the same time, there were news conferences arranged by NRDC in 12 cities around the country to announce the report.

The NRDC's purported risks of eating apples treated with Alar flashed around the nation. The public relations campaign was in motion; the credibility of all apples was falling.

A week later movie actress Meryl Streep was the feature of a Washington news conference to announce NRDC's "Mothers and Others for Pesticide Limits" and to warn moms about Alar. NRDC arranged for Streep and other guests to appear on network television news and talk shows to talk about Alar and additional pesticides that it viewed as harmful. The day after "The Phil Donahue Show" aired a discussion about Alar in early March, the New York City public school system removed apples and apple products from lunch menus. The Los Angeles schools and many other districts around the nation followed this example.

News coverage of the Alar story in the weeks following "60 Minutes" was extensive. Households were running scared. The upsetting news led parents to phone the International Apple Institute to ask if they should dispose of their apple juice at a toxic waste site.[11] Many mothers poured apple juice down kitchen sink drains.[12] The scare, though shortlived, was nearly everywhere.

While families were scared, apple growers were in near panic as they worried about the effect of the Alar publicity on retailers and customers in the supermarkets. The growers saw a "main advantage: The NRDC report was based on weak extrapolations from faulty interpretations of old data from studies that had been discredited years ago by the scientific community."[13] But they also realized that the public's perception of food safety was the real issue being confronted. Apple industry leaders looked to "solid scientific and medical evidence" and to a long-term campaign to assure the public that apple products were safe, and as a counter public relations offensive to the NRDC's public relations bombardment.[14]

The industry found scientists and scientific groups that detected flaws in the NRDC report. There was a question of whether there had been peer review of the NRDC report, although the NRDC insisted that the report was indeed reviewed by what it called a blue-ribbon panel. Bruce Ames, chairman of the department of biochemistry at the University of California, provided information for a comparative index of possible cancer hazards. Peanut butter posed a hazard 300 times higher than Alar, and Diet Coke was considerably higher.[15] He believed the NRDC report "is guilty of overexaggerating the risk associated with synthetic chemicals" and said he places "little faith" in the NRDC's cancer-risk estimates. "I'm going to continue to eat apples and apple products without worry about health risks," Ames explained.[16]

The director of the California Department of Health Service said school officials who removed apples from the lunchrooms out of fear of chemical contamination were running from a "toxic bogeyman." He took bites from a red apple as he talked about the issue with reporters.[17]

The International Apple Institute led the industry effort, which featured a full-page ad with the headline, "Why an Apple a Day Is Still Healthy Advice." The ad ran on March 10 in four major newspapers—USA Today, The New York Times, The Washington Post, and Los Angeles Times— and in the following days in 35 more newspapers in 30 markets. Population of all these markets was about 100 million people. The ad message pointed out that Alar was used sparingly on a "very small portion of the nation's apple crop. What's more, to approach the exposure levels that produce ill effects in the laboratory, a person would have to consume more than 28,000 pounds of Alar-treated apples every day for 70 years."

The U.S. government supported the apple industry. On March 15, John Bode, assistant secretary for food and consumer services of the U.S. Department of Agriculture (USDA), asked regional offices of Food and Nutrition Services to inform all schools that the USDA recommended schools continue serving apples. Apples almost immediately were back on school menus from which they had been removed.

On the following day, the USDA, Environmental Protection Agency (EPA), and Food and Drug Administration (FDA) issued a joint statement that declared apples safe, and encouraged Americans to eat apples, and schools to continue serving them. "Data used by NRDC, which claim cancer risks from Alar are 100 times higher than the Environmental Protection Agency (EPA) estimates, were rejected in 1985 by an independent scientific advisory board created by Congress," said the agencies. The statement said the EPA was continuing to gather data, which would be independently reviewed, and said it would ban Alar if there appeared to be sound scientific reasons to do so.[18] Two days later the then-Surgeon General Everett Koop issued a public health statement reassuring mothers that apples are good for children.

The joint FDA–EPA–USDA statement led *The Wall Street Journal* to say: "When the day arrives that you need three federal agencies to say it's safe to eat apples, it's time for scientists, regulators, and the press in this country to help people understand the difference between environmental health and environmental horror stories." The paper also commented on the Alar and Chilean grape scares, whose news breaks were separated by less than a month. The paper said, "Witchcraft tales have been drummed into the American psyche these last years principally by environmental groups flogging issue after issue as threatening America with an apocalypse of cancer and disease. There has been almost no effort by scientists, government, or news outlets to place these events in a balanced context."[19]

(Chilean grapes were dumped after an anonymous phone call to the U.S. Embassy in Chile on March 2, 1989, reported there was cyanide in some of the country's grapes exported to the

United States. Inspections ordered by the Food and Drug Administration followed and on March 14 the government advised stores to remove Chilean farm products from their shelves. Only two grapes containing the poison were found in a check of 2,000 crates at the Philadelphia port, and none elsewhere. The FDA recommended, however, that all Chilean fruit be held temporarily from market, and hundreds of thousands of pounds of Chilean fruit were detained at U.S. ports. The hold order was in effect only a couple of days, after which the FDA announced that 5 percent of incoming Chilean fruit would be inspected instead of the previous 1 percent. Tons of grapes already delivered to stores and wholesalers were ordered destroyed. In Chile, thousands of workers were temporarily unemployed.)

Columnist William Safire, examining the apple scare, said "Minimal risks were inflated into imminent threats with no thought of unintended consequences. . . . Few paused to ask about the source of the allegations of alarm. We are prone to be terrified of risk, any risk, and malleable media amplify the alarmists' cries."[20]

Apple shipments, which had dropped dramatically by mid-March, returned to normal by May and were at record levels in the summer months of 1989. Despite this highly welcome turnaround for the apple industry, growers suffered losses of more than $100 million. There was a report that the NRDC campaign and the resultant loss of business resulted in "bankrupting dozens of family-owned orchards."[21] In some instances, the bankruptcy cases may have been those of growers with marginal operations for whom the Alar hit was the last straw.

Even though customer purchases of apples rebounded, concern about customer confidence continued to bother apple growers and processors. There was that worry about public perception. Their trade groups called on Uniroyal Chemical Co., the producer of Alar, to remove the product from the market to help restore confidence and credibility. Uniroyal in early June announced it was voluntarily halting sales of Alar in the United States, though James A. Wylie, Uniroyal vice president said, "We continue to believe in the safety of the product."[22] Three months later, Uniroyal said it was ending the sale of Alar in other countries, pointing out that the company found it uneconomical to produce only for overseas shipments. Sales of Alar were about one half a percent of Uniroyal's total annual revenues.[23]

Blame for unethical conduct in NRDC/"60 Minutes" versus apple growers must be laid at the door of the Natural Resources Defense Council. The group was irresponsible and manipulative to create a PR monster that begat unwarranted fears and high financial costs. It was insensitive to do this without concern for the losses inflicted on innocent parties, particularly the 85 percent of growers who did not use Alar. Those who used Alar might also be counted with the innocent, as their use of the pesticide conformed with laws and regulations. There is also an ethical issue surrounding the tests that were the basis for the NRDC report, viewed as flawed by many in the scientific community. NRDC knew that the EPA had Alar under study. If the group sought to turn up the spotlight on Alar, wouldn't its effort have been better directed against the EPA? Another question, posed by the Josephson Institute for the Advancement of Ethics: "We wonder if there should not be a further definition of standards for reports which carry such a potentially powerful economic effect?"[24]

The final scenes in the Alar story may be played in the courtrooms. A group of Washington state apple growers on November 28, 1990, filed a class-action lawsuit in Yakima superior court against the NRDC, CBS, and Fenton Communications asking multimillion-dollar damages as compensation for reduced sales during the Alar scare. The growers also formed Farmers for Responsible Media. With the acronym FARM, this is a registered trade association that will raise funds for what's expected to be a costly legal battle.

A footnote of interest to all this came from Albert Heier of the EPA Press Office in Washington. On two announcements of what EPA deemed to be major significance in the summer of 1990, there was little coverage by the news media, much less than was expected by those in the agency, "It's like those in the media feel they were burned by the Alar incident, and now they're afraid of overplaying a story to the point they give little attention," he said. One announcement regarded restrictive actions to be followed in the use of a group of pesticides and fungicides with "much greater risk than Alar was ever thought to be"; the other was a warning on risks of mercury in indoor paint, an ingredient since eliminated in paint manufacture.[25]

Sidelight: Prompted by damages he suffered during the Alar scare, a Colorado apple grower and legislator, Republican Rep. Steve Acquafresca, introduced a bill in the 1990 session of the legislature to allow lawsuits against persons who made critical remarks about the state's agricultural products. Columnists and editorial writers of some of the nation's media poked fun at the proposal. *The New York Times* cautioned travelers to Colorado, "If you have something bad to say about peas or carrots or for that matter T-bones, you had better have a good explanation."[26] The House and Senate both passed the measure, but Gov. Roy Romer vetoed it.

POINTS

• In planning an announcement or event, consider the ripples and waves it may generate, the individuals or organizations beyond the target audience that may be affected, and in what ways and to what degree.

• Make sure of scientific information you distribute; have it checked by reputable experts who satisfy you that the correctness cannot be successfully contested.

• Be particularly careful when engaged in a PR program that will affect people's emotions or safety and public health, even more particularly when it will affect children.

• If you or your organization are attacked in ways you believe unfair or ill-informed, respond quickly. Bring together all affected parties to act in concert in a counter-attack of potent thrusts.

NEWS MEDIA WORRY ABOUT CREDIBILITY AS THEY WRESTLE WITH ETHICS

On the one hand, the news media flay at the disregard for ethics in the public relations they find in individuals and in other institutions of U.S. society. On the other, the media are constantly looking inward to determine how well they perform on the ethics stage. They worry about how the public judges the credibility of their news products.

Ethical dilemmas, often with public relations and credibility ramifications, abound among those in the media. Some of the ethical crossroads are formed by the nature of the business, the work of reporters, photographers, and editors always with deadlines in covering, reporting, and commenting on the continuous stream and unending assortment of news developments. Newspapers publish a new product every day, most with two or more editions; radio and television change their news broadcasts several times a day and move quickly with coverage of breaking news. The dilemmas are inevitable. For example, journalists may sometimes think it's necessary to be deceitful or to lie to obtain information for a story. Can such unethical conduct be condoned? When? How? By whom? Or, they may invade someone's privacy or damage another's reputation in the publishing or broadcast of news. Is this fair? Is it the-news-at-any-cost, without regard to injuries that may be inflicted? Or do the media compromise themselves? Do they print or broadcast only a partial coverage of a happening, tell only part of a story, to reduce the amount of injury? What standards are considered in making these decisions? Do media public relations suffer in the public perception?

Invasion of Privacy

What about invasion of privacy by the news media? Who has a right to privacy? Media invasion of the privacy of the public takes many forms. Something as relatively minor as the publishing of a person's age is protested by the one so identified. Likewise, there may be anger at the publishing of another's address or phone number. Taking and publishing or televising unauthorized photographs of people in the news may be considered an invasion of their privacy. For instance, camera coverage of victims of an accident or their grief-stricken relatives may seem to some as simply too personal to be released to public view. Similarly, the attempts to elicit comments from relatives or accident survivors at such moments may seem, at the least, to violate good taste.

What about the privacy of those in the public eye? Certainly the president has almost none; and high-ranking elected and appointed government officials and high-profile entertainers and athletes and leaders in business and other fields have little more. What about Arthur Ashe, who became a public figure as the only black person to win the United States Open, Australian Open, and Wimbledon—first black man inducted into the International Tennis Hall of Fame? He learned in 1988 that he had AIDS, the result of infection with the HIV virus in a blood transfusion during double bypass heart surgery in 1983. He wanted to keep the information private, told only a few close friends. On April 7, 1992, Doug Smith, tennis writer, and Gene Policinski, managing editor/sports, of *USA Today*, acting on a news tip, asked Ashe if he had the disease. Ashe did not give a direct answer and the paper decided that without on-the-record confirmation it would not publish a story.[27] The next morning Ashe scheduled a news conference for later in the day, at which, angry that he felt pressured to do so, he announced his illness.

"I am sorry that I have been forced to make this revelation now," said Ashe. "I didn't commit any crime. I am not running for office."[28] Questions among journalists and the public arose over whether Ashe was a figure of such prominence that he had no personal privacy in this instance. Ashe expressed concern about how the news would affect his five-year-old daughter. *USA Today* said that through the following evening it received 481 phone calls from readers about the Ashe story, most of them critical of the paper.[29] Policinski and Editor Peter S. Prichard handled most of the calls. "You have to answer people's questions," said Prichard. "I think people have a legitimate interest in why we did what we did."[30]

David Lawrence, Jr., then president of the American Society of Newspaper Editors (ASNE) and publisher of *The Miami Herald,* said he could not find "one reason whatsoever to quarrel with how that story was handled. It was handled with care and fairness and decency and, yes, compassion."[31] Most editors attending the ASNE annual meeting in Washington at the time the story broke said they would have pursued the story if they'd had it first. "The real villainy," commented *The New York Times,* "lies in the cruel and benighted public attitudes that compelled Mr. Ashe to keep his disease secret for three years. What a sad day for America when even an icon like Arthur Ashe can't reveal his AIDS affliction for fear that he or his family will suffer adverse consequences."[32]

On the privacy issue, a storm of divergent views centers around identification by the media of victims of rape. Should the rape victim be given the protection of anonymity? Does release of the name attach a stigma to the victim? If the victim's name and address are published, does that lead the offender to further intimidate, threaten, harass, or harm the victim?

Negative answers to all of these questions were supplied in a column by Geneva Overholser, editor of *The Des Moines Register*, which led to a series published by the *Register* that won the 1991 Pulitzer prize for public service reporting. Overholser, writing in mid-1989, stated her belief that only through printing the names of the victims would the stigma disappear; that by failing to identify the victims to protect their privacy, the press compounded the stigma. She urged victims to speak out, to let their identity be known. "As long as rape is deemed unspeakable—and is therefore not fully and honestly spoken of—the public outrage will be muted as well," she said.[33]

One of the readers of Overholser's column was Nancy Ziegenmeyer of Grinnell, who had been raped nine months earlier. Ziegenmeyer was in her car outside Grand View College in Des Moines reviewing notes for a real estate license exam she was to take, when the rapist entered her car. He shoved her aside and drove to a deserted area where the rape occurred. The wife of a mechanic and mother of three children, Ziegenmeyer was impressed by the viewpoint of the column. She phoned Overholser and said she'd like to tell her story.

Ziegenmeyer met with a reporter for the paper, Jane Schorer. Together they went over the victim's experience from the day of the rape to the day of the rapist's conviction—14 months and 12 days. Schorer's account was published as a five-part series on page one of the paper. "What followed, "said *The New York Times*, "was an extraordinary personal and journalistic enterprise, which held tens of thousands of Iowans transfixed for a week and still sparks debates about rape and journalistic propriety."[34]

Michael Gartner, a former editor of *The Des Moines Register* and president of NBC News, said, "Iowa will never be the same. Women started talking about their own rapes—rapes they have hidden in the deep corners of their minds for decades. Men began to understand the enormity of the crime. Classes began discussing the stories and the crime. The series became the talk of the state, and, judging from letters to the editor and conversations in the cafes, Iowans overwhelmingly approved of the stories—and deemed Nancy Ziegenmeyer, Geneva Overholser, and Jane Schorer heroes."[35]

Despite the highly positive reader response, Ziegenmeyer thinks the press should name rape victims only with their consent. "Rape victims need a great deal of healing before they can talk about the crime," she thinks.[36] Overholser appears to concur. She said the paper will continue its policy of not identifying rape victims—though it may ask if they're willing to have their names published.

The controversy over whether to identify or not will continue for some time, with well-meaning individuals on each side of the issue. The writer of a letter that appeared in *The Wall Street Journal* said, "My view is that the media do not have a right to all the information about everyone; rather, that everyone has a right to privacy. A person suffering from rape might not want to share that experience with everyone in the world." Another letter writer said, "Victims who come forward with their stories chose to do so, and more power to them. Those who choose to remain silent are no less heroic . . . the healing process varies from victim to victim."[37]

The publication of the series in the Des Moines newspaper prompted Karen Jurgensen, senior editor of *USA Today*, to write for publication the story of her rape 15 years earlier. She said she had talked with friends about her experience, but she hadn't been publicly identified. After she read the series, she thought: "If we all spoke up, you would know victims are all around you. . . . We need your help to put a stop to rape."[38]

Another kind of media invasion of privacy, and the newsroom ethics responsible for the invasion, was the topic of a column in 1990 by Fred Friendly, former president of CBS News and professor emeritus at the Columbia University Graduate School of Journalism. He wrote of the media treatment of Oliver Sipple, who jarred the arm of a would-be assassin of President Ford in San Francisco on September 22, 1975, and perhaps saved the life of our country's chief executive. Friendly said he was nudged to write after a reporter called "to inquire if I had any reaction to the new press dilemma presented by the recent gay rights tactic called 'outing'; that is, the involuntary unmasking of prominent citizens who are secretly gay." He said he knew how Sipple, who had died a year earlier, would have responded to outing, and he was "compelled to write about his (Sipple's) ordeal by press fire."

Gay groups wanted Sipple to receive all the credit they thought he deserved for deflecting the bullet aimed at the president and they asked the newspapers and radio-television stations in San Francisco to tell of the heroism of "one of us." Sipple, said Friendly, saw it differently. He tried to prevent publicity. "He begged the news media to leave him alone and protect his privacy, pleading that neither his employer nor his mother and family in Michigan understood that he was gay. . . . 'My sexual orientation has nothing at all to do with saving the president's life.' " The uncooperative newspapers published all the details. Sipple, an ex-Marine who was wounded in Vietnam, sued the press for invasion of privacy, but lost. His mother, who lived in Detroit, was so harassed by neighbors, according to Friendly, she stopped speaking to her son.

Friendly was bitterly critical of the media handling of the Sipple story. He quoted a remark to him by the late Supreme Court Justice Potter Stewart, "The trouble with you journalists is that you are all mixed up between what the Constitution gives you a right to publish and the right thing to do." After 15 years reflection, Friendly said he had concluded that "the press had a legal license but no ethical justification to rip away the harmless mask that protected his sexual orientation. Total objectivity may occasionally elude us, but the need to be fair is as essential as the obligation to be accurate.

"Whatever the cause, do we journalists have the ethical or moral prerogative to strip away anyone's privacy, unless there is an overriding and prevailing justification?"[39]

Deception

What about deception in journalism? It's been used by reporters. One of the classic cases of journalistic deception occurred in Chicago in 1978. The object of the deception, created by two reporters of the *Chicago Sun-Times,* was to uncover corruption among the city's building and electrical inspectors. They were thought to have been soliciting bribes from small businessmen as incentives to overlook code violations in business buildings.

The reporters devised a full-blown scam. They bought a tavern, named it the Mirage, and then prepared to do some remodeling. They secretly taped conversations and shot photographs of meetings with inspectors about the work to be done, and the "cooperation" of the inspectors to assure it would be codeworthy. Of course, the discussions included the price for the cooperation. The reporters played their parts well, and the newspaper had a series of articles on the improper and unethical conduct of the inspectors that ran several weeks. Indictments of many Chicago inspectors followed. A Pulitzer jury recommended the *Sun-Times* for a Pulitzer prize in 1979, but the board that made the final selections turned down the nomination on the ground that the reporters should have operated in the open.

Is it OK to lie to get a story? Two doctors who performed abortions on unpregnant women were put out of business through deception planned by editors of *The Virginian-Pilot* and *The Ledger-Star* of Norfolk, Virginia, in 1984. There were what were believed to be well-founded rumors in the city that the doctors at a local clinic told women they were pregnant, when they were not, and performed abortion procedures on unpregnant women. The editors decided to conduct their own investigation after concluding the authorities did not plan one.

Women from the newspaper staff and from a women's organization went to the clinic for free pregnancy tests. Most of them, including one who took a man's sample of urine for analysis, were told they were pregnant. A woman reporter who lied in saying she was pregnant was being prepared for an abortion before she said she'd rather make an appointment for another day. In the course of writing an expose of the clinic, a reporter who called the prosecutor's office with a question about the state law on pregnancy tests was asked to hold publication of the story pending arrests. The paper cooperated.

Three policewomen then went to the clinic and collected evidence for arrests of the two physicians. One doctor's license to practice medicine was revoked. The other left the country before his trial. The phony clinic operation was put out of business.

When are deception and lying justified in investigative journalism? For an answer, we turn to Louis Hodges, professor and director of Society and the Professions: Studies in Applied Ethics at Washington & Lee University. He proposes three tests, each of which must be passed to justify deceptive tactics. The first has to do with the importance of the information sought. He says the information should be such that "readers need to know in order to achieve important goals or to avoid serious harm."

The next test revolves around accuracy. "There must be no reasonable likelihood that comparably accurate and reliable information could be obtained as efficiently through conventional investigative techniques." Safety is the key word in the third test. Hodges thinks the contemplated deception must not place innocent people at serious risk. It would be a failure of the safety test in his view for a reporter to pose as a fireman, a police officer, or a doctor, a role for which the journalist is unqualified and could cost life or injury to another.[40]

Under Hodges' rating system, the reporters in Chicago and Norfolk were engaged in justifiable deceit. He does add a caveat: "Once we have applied the threefold test to a particular case and have completed the masquerade, we owe it to readers to explain exactly what our methods of investigation were and why we used deceptive tactics."

Conflict of Interest

Reporters face many kinds of conflict-of-interest situations. What do their consciences say is the ethical thing to do? Tom Goldstein posed several questions that bear on this issue: "Should a reporter work for the Central Intelligence Agency? What about serving on a local school board? Can a reporter make known strongly held views? What happens when a reporter has a close personal friendship with a source?"

Let's look first at an example of the ethical problem posed in the last question. This vignette from Goldstein is about Laura Foreman, a political reporter for *The Philadelphia Inquirer*, who became romantically involved with a source, Pennsylvania State Sen. Henry J. "Buddy" Cianfrani, in the 1970s. Since he was a source for news, she wrote stories about him, and about others for which he gave her information. Foreman left the paper for a job in the Washington bureau of *The New York Times* in 1977. Her attachment to Cianfrani continued, but she no longer wrote stories about him.

After Foreman was in Washington, in August of 1977, her relationship with Cianfrani became public. Readers of the *Inquirer* found a page-one story in which Foreman was reported to have told the agents of the Federal Bureau of Investigation of her involvement with Cianfrani and of his gifts to her with a value of more than $10,000. Shortly thereafter, Cianfrani was indicted and later convicted on charges of mail fraud and racketeering and sent to prison.

Foreman resigned from the *Times* at the request of A. M. Rosenthal, executive editor, who said, "She committed a major journalistic offense." At the time, the paper was investigating possible conflict-of-interest charges against Bert Lance, who was prominent then as a friend of President Carter as well as director of the administration's Office of Management and Budget. "We investigated Bert Lance not for what he did as budget director, but for what he did in Georgia," said Rosenthal. "How could we apply different standards to Laura Foreman?"[41]

Back at the *Inquirer*, the expose of Foreman prompted the writing of a code of ethics for the staff. "We wanted to be sure everyone was on notice that something like that wasn't acceptable," said Gene Foreman (no relation), the managing editor. "Staff members have an obligation to disclose conflicts."[42]

Writing of her experience in *The Washington Monthly* magazine, Foreman said: "Reporters should try to walk the narrow line of friendship with politicians they cover if it will help them write better stories. I don't think they should fall in love with them—that makes honest reporting well-nigh impossible."[43] She and Cianfrani were married in 1980 after his release from prison.

What about a reporter being a member of a school board? Goldstein offers another example. Jacquelyn Brown McClary was a general assignment reporter for *The Knoxville News-Sentinel* in 1983. She did not cover events in Alcoa, about 25 miles from Knoxville, where she and her family lived. Interested in improving the quality of education, McClary ran for and was elected to a vacancy on the school board. The paper fired her, charging she violated its guideline against "participation of an employee in any political activity that could raise questions as to the newspaper's objectivity."[44]

After her dismissal, McClary said she was asked to run for the nonpartisan school board position and "saw no conflict between my job and my civic responsibility." While she was losing her job, her editor, Ralph L. Millett, Jr., was serving as chairman of the Knoxville Parking Authority, whose members were appointed by the mayor. Meetings of this body were covered by reporters. Millett said, "I see no valid comparison between this and an elected, legislative office." An arbitrator, to whom the case of McClary's firing was submitted, decided in her favor, and she returned to her job at the paper. Another sequel: The editor turned in his resignation to the parking authority.

Objectivity

The debate among journalists about their ability to maintain objectivity in reporting news events may never end. There are loud voices who say simply that there is no such thing as objectivity; that each reporter brings to the coverage of news his or her feelings of prejudice and bias that weaken, if not bar, objectivity. Opposing this view are those who declare they attempt to subdue their beliefs or persuasions that interfere with objectivity and strive—some think with a degree of success—to present balanced accounts of happenings.

Search for objectivity in reporting of the abortion debate and what do you find? David Shaw, media critic for the *Los Angeles Times*, wrote in 1990 that media bias against opponents of abortion exists. His report reflected the findings of a Los Angeles study of major newspaper, television, and news magazine coverage over 18 months. The study included interviews with more than 100 journalists and activists on both sides of the abortion controversy.

"Examination of stories published and broadcast does reveal scores of examples, large and small, that can only be characterized as unfair to the opponents of abortion," said Shaw, "either in content, tone, choice of language, or prominence of play."

He said television coverage "probably was more vulnerable" to the bias charges than newspapers and magazines. Shaw also cited major media studies that found 80 to 90 percent of U.S. journalists "personally favor abortion rights."[45]

Among examples of ways the news media have used language to favor advocates of abortion rights, Shaw pointed to the reporting of the U.S. Supreme Court decision in the Webster case in 1989, which handed states more leeway in regulating abortion. "Many media stories termed the decision 'a major setback for abortion rights,' " he said. "Couldn't it also have been called 'a major victory for abortion opponents?' " His answer: "Yes. But most reporters don't identify with abortion opponents."

"The culture in the newsrooms just assumes that abortion is right," argued John Buckley, quoted in Shaw's story. Buckley, a corporate consultant, has been a media spokesman for conservative politicians.

"Abortion," Buckley went on, "is the first issue since the Vietnam War, in which some journalists' instinctive allegiance to their own 'social class and generational world view is stronger than their professional allegiance to objectivity.' "[46]

Journalists are concerned about the kinds of ethics that go into the forming of their products and about the public perception of their ethics. Such media organizations as the Society of Professional Journalists, American Society of Newspaper Editors, Associated Press Managing Editors, Radio-Television News Directors Association, and National Association of Broadcasters publish codes or statements of ethics. Committees of these groups delve into applied ethics and they publish reports to attract the attention of members. One matter of concern for the 1990–91 ethics committee of the American Society of Newspaper Editors was the disclosure of honoraria, speaking fees, and other outside income by editors and reporters. Ted M. Natt, editor and publisher of The (Longview, Washington) Daily News and chair of the committee, pointed out that papers routinely report outside earnings of congressmen and other public officials in the news columns and asked, "Are we as diligent and concerned about reporting our own? Does the public have a right to know who or what might be influencing what is reported or commented upon in newspapers?

"Some argue that there is a difference between an elected official and someone who works for a private company. Yet both seek the public's trust—one in the form of votes, the other in the form of readership, and believability. If disclosure of outside income enhances public trust in the one instance, doesn't it do the same in the other?"[47]

By a three-to-one ratio, editors responding to a questionnaire of the committee said no reports of outside income were required of editors or reporters. Editors favored the reporting of outside income by syndicated columnists by almost two to one. When they were asked whether a columnist's refusal to disclose would lead an editor to cancel the column, however, the response was negative, by the same margin. The committee report noted that syndicated columnists drew as much as $18,000 for a single speech.[48]

Constantly looming in the background during a discussion of media ethics is the First Amendment of the Constitution and its guarantee of freedom of the press. What is this right? How is it to be used? What happens to media credibility when it is abused? The public mind is not favorably impressed by the right of a free press, according to a survey released at the annual ASNE meeting in April, 1991. "If American voters were asked to ratify the Bill of Rights today, freedom of the press would not likely be included," said a report of the study. The survey found about two thirds or more of all citizens "fail to give unqualified support for certain basic press rights, including: editorially endorsing candidates, criticizing politicians or the military, reporting past mistakes of public figures, running graphic photographs of violent events, or reporting about the sexual habits of public figures."[49]

Yet the First Amendment is the protection that assures the public will be informed about what goes on in government, at all levels, and in other institutions surrounding the lives of citizens. Newspapers have failed to inform citizens adequately about the role of free expression in a democracy, said Burl Osborne, then ASNE president and president of the *Dallas Morning News.* "We have a great deal of work to explain to people what we do and why it is being done," added Osborne, arguing that newspapers must "cause people to understand the First Amendment is not a license for some people but has applications for everyone."[50]

POINTS

• For communications managers who work with the news media: Among priority concerns of the news media are First Amendment issues, freedom of information, higher literacy rates for those in their audiences, more women and minorities on their staffs. Look for opportunities to develop mutually sponsored programs in your communities that take up these and related subjects. Such activities can include talks, small group and larger town meetings, workshops and seminars, to which diverse community groups are invited. You'll find that sincere participation in such ventures can build your credibility with the news media.

• For communications managers in the news media: Take advantage of the communications talents of those in business, education, and other organizations, and in counseling firms in your community. Talk to them about goals you wish to accomplish, those related to ethical coverage of the news as well as commercial success, among your audience. Invite them to participate with you, to share their expertise with you, in planning and presenting programs that will help meet these goals. Look for areas of mutual interest and build on these.

• Yes, it can work both ways. Public relations experts and news media executives can successfully work together on community agendas.

NOTES

1. Bob Josserand, president, National Cattlemen's Association, and Jim Magagna, president, Public Lands Council, letter of January 10, 1990, to Marty Ryan, executive producer, "Today."
2. Ibid.
3. John Lacey, "NBC Branded Us, Then High-Tailed It," letter to editor, *The Wall Street Journal*, March 1, 1990, p. A17.
4. Tom Capra, executive producer, "Today," letter to Bob Josserand, president, National Cattlemen's Association, March 16, 1990.
5. Phone conversation of the author with Kendal Frazier, National Cattlemen's Association, October 8, 1990.
6. "Asides," *The Wall Street Journal*, February 9, 1990, p. A10.
7. Reed Irvine and Joe Goulden, "Environmental Tilt at NBC," *Washington Times*, February 16, 1990, p. F4.
8. Doug Haddix, "Alar as a Media Event," *CJR*, March/April 1990, p. 44.
9. Excerpts from David Fenton Memo, "How a PR Firm Executed the Alar Scare," *The Wall Street Journal*, October 3, 1989, p. A22.
10. "A Is for Apple," CBS News "60 Minutes," transcript, February 26, 1989.
11. Derl I. Derr, "Alar/Food Safety," statement, at press conference during Ohio Fruit and Vegetable Growers Congress, Cleveland, Ohio, February 6, 1990.
12. Donna S. Shimskey, "Cracking under Scrutiny," *Fruit Grower*, May 1989, p. 6.
13. "The Alar Scare: Rebuilding Apple Consumption during the Alar Crisis," report of the Washington Apple Commission, undated.
14. Donna Shimskey, "Industry Fights Back," *Fruit Grower*, April 1989, p. 15.

15. Gary Acuff, "Media Sensationalism Creates Pesticide Panic," *Fruit Grower*, April 1989, p. 6.

16. Shimskey, "Cracking under Scrutiny," p. 6.

17. "Health Official Rebukes Schools over Apple Bans," *The New York Times*, March 16, 1989, p. B10.

18. News release, Environmental Protection Agency, March 16, 1989.

19. "Fruit Frights," *The Wall Street Journal*, March 17, 1989, p. A14.

20. William Safire, "Madness of Crowds," *The New York Times*, March 23, 1989, p. A29.

21. Robert James Bidinotto, "The Great Apple Scare," *Reader's Digest*, October 1990, p. 53.

22. Barbara Rosewicz, "Avery's Uniroyal Ends Alar Sales in U.S.; Apple Product Imports Still Worry Critics," *The Wall Street Journal*, June 5, 1989, p. B3.

23. "Company Ends Use of Apple Chemical," *The New York Times*, October 18, 1989, p. A18.

24. "The Side Effects from Taking Aim at Apples," *Ethics: Easier Said than Done* 2, no. 2 (1989), p. 31.

25. Phone conversation of author with Albert Heier, Press Office, Environmental Protection Agency, July 20, 1990.

26. Dirk Johnson, "Meant for the Stomach, Really Taken to Heart," *The New York Times*, February 17, 1991, p. A30.

27. Gene Policinski, "Sports Editor: It's a News Story," *USA Today*, April 9, 1992, p. 2A.

28. Rachel Shuster, "Star Wanted His News to Stay Private," *USA Today*, April 9, 1992, p. 1A.

29. James Cox, "Pursuit of Ashe Story Brings Mixed Reviews," *USA Today*, April 10, 1992, p. 6B.

30. Stacy L. Hawkins and Elliott Peppers, "When the Media Itself Becomes the News," *The ASNE Reporter*, April 10, 1992, p. 5.

31. James Cox, "Pursuit of Ashe Story Brings Mixed Reviews," p. 6B.

32. "Why Arthur Ashe Kept It Secret," *The New York Times*, April 10, 1992, p. A36.

33. David Margolick, "A Name, a Face and a Rape: Iowa Victim Tells Her Story," *The New York Times*, March 25, 1990, p. 1A.

34. Ibid.

35. Michael Gartner, "The Scarlet Letter of Rape: A Courageous Victim Fights Back," *The Wall Street Journal*, March 15, 1990, p. A15.

36. Ibid.

37. Letters to the Editor, "Allow Rape Victims to Choose Silence," *The Wall Street Journal*, April 17, 1990, p. A17.

38. Karen Jurgensen, "I Was Another Nameless Victim," *USA Today*, April 4, 1990, p. 8A.

39. Fred W. Friendly, "Gays, Privacy, and a Free Press," *The Washington Post*, April 8, 1990, p. B7.

40. Louis W. Hodges, "When Is Lying and Deception Justified?" *Journal of Mass Media Ethics*, Fall 1988, p. 26.

41. Tom Goldstein, *The News at Any Cost*, (New York: Simon and Schuster, 1985), pp. 27, 36–37.

42. Carolyne Rittinger, "The Pros and Cons of Drafting a Code," Newspaper Ethics Report, Associated Press Managing Editors, 1990, p. 6.

43. Goldstein, *The News at Any Cost*, p. 37.

44. Ibid., p. 40.

45. David Shaw, *Los Angeles Times*, reported in *The Denver Post*, July 1, 1990, p. 4A.

46. Ibid.

47. Ted M. Natt, "Red Light Ethics vs. Green Light Ethics," *The Bulletin*, American Society of Newspaper Editors, April, 1991, p. 14.

48. Report of the Ethics Committee, 1990–91, American Society of Newspaper Editors, undated.

49. "If Voted on Today, First Amendment Might Exclude Press," news release, American Society of Newspaper Editors, April 12, 1991.

50. George Garneau, "Press Freedom in Deep Trouble," *Editor & Publisher*, April 20, 1991, p. 11.

Chapter Seven

How the Credibility Factor Affects Politics and Government

The pilings of credibility have been weakened by the actions of those in numerous sections of the executive and legislative branches of the federal government in recent years. Laws and regulations affecting ethical conduct did little to reinforce them. These examples of deceit, cover-up, and manipulation contain lessons for all who plan and manage public relations communications.

On the executive side, we've witnessed the news media pummel the U.S. Defense Department for restricting coverage of the Gulf War in 1991, and heard from the Pentagon revised versions that reduced the degree of success earlier claimed for U.S. forces in that brief conflict. The coverage complaints were similar to those voiced after the invasions of Panama in December 1989, and Grenada in October 1983. The U.S. Navy took its punishment for allowing information about a homosexual relationship of two sailors to taint its investigation into the explosion of the U.S.S. *Iowa* in April 1989; and a probe reported in November 1990 exposed scandals of waste and unethical operations in the Department of Housing and Urban Development.

Over in Congress, there were the stories of overdrafts in accounts at the House bank by at least 325 current and former representatives and illegal practices in operation of the House post office; the resignations of former House Speaker Jim Wright of Texas for alleged violations of House ethics rules and of Majority Whip Tony Coelho of California, who left to head off investigations by the House ethics committee and the Justice Department; the cozy relationship between Charles H. Keating, Jr., savings and loan executive, and senators known as the Keating Five that existed during the collapse of the S&L business; and in both houses of Congress the failure to regulate contributions through political action committees, a force that undermines ethics in election campaigns.

THE HOUSE BANK AND POST OFFICE

Disclosure in mid–1991 about check-bouncing at the House bank by U.S. representatives brought calls from the public for names of the check writers and amounts. The House Ethics Committee released on April 1, 1992, a preliminary list of 22 abusers who together had written 11,000 bad checks, and on April 16 announced the names of another 303, whose check tally was 13,000. Leading the list of worst abusers were former Arkansas Rep. Tommy Robinson, a Republican, with 996 overdrafts, overdrawn in 16 months of a 33-month period; New York Rep. Robert Mrazek, Democrat, 920 overdrafts, overdrawn in 23 months during a 39-month period; and Michigan Rep. Robert Davis, Republican, 878 overdrafts, overdrawn 23 months during a 39-month period. Ahead of the release of the names, the House Sergeant-at-Arms, Jack Russ, who ran the bank, resigned after the Ethics Committee decided he had misused his office.

There were grumblings from constituents that the April announcements failed to include the amounts of checks. At least they could breathe a sigh of relief that the House closed the bank. Still, as Iowa Rep. Fred Grandy, Republican, noted, ''Say that two members each overdrew one check. But one member wrote a bad check for $10,000 just days before a key election. The other member wrote one check for $50 to a gasoline credit card company . . . disclosure won't distinguish between the two." *The Wall Street Journal* commented, "The puffed-up men and women of Congress created the atmosphere that made this cheap spectacle inevitable. Their self-made world is one of per- quisites, exemptions from the land's most burdensome laws, gaudy committee inquisitions, and the comforts of incumbent entrenchments that have deterred more serious men and women from serving in Congress."[1]

At the House post office, three former employees pleaded guilty to embezzlement charges. A grand jury charged a fourth with selling cocaine at the post office and conspiring with fellow employees to conceal thefts of postal funds. While a task force of the House Administration Committee was probing allega- tions of mismanagement at the post office, the House postmas- ter, Robert Rota, resigned on March 19. The two resignations reinforced the belief that the House was poorly managed.

FORMER SPEAKER JIM WRIGHT AND MAJORITY WHIP TONY COELHO

These two long-time members of the House resigned their seats under fire in June 1989. Wright, a Texas Democrat, member of the House since 1954 and speaker since 1987, quit in the wake of an investigation that brought six charges against him for alleged violations of House ethics rules. Coelho, Democrat of California, who had served there since 1978 and moved to majority whip in 1986, left to turn off probes by the House Ethics Committee as well as the Justice Department.

Their alleged and, to some degree, admitted acts touched off deep introspection and subjective examinations among their peers. It was much more than "there but for the grace of God go I," or "we call it constituent service," or "doesn't everybody do it? Isn't that what we're here for?" However, there was some of that.

House members should have been at least somewhat ac-
quainted with the manual on ethics provided for their guidance.
But, said *U.S. News & World Report*, the rules were "porous as
a tennis net." So, to some extent, the concern of the representatives was in knowing how to keep within bounds, or, stated
another way, how much they could get by with without over-
stepping the boundaries and attracting the attention of those
who would criticize. They worried about the appearance of impropriety, particularly among voters in the homes and offices
back home. The alleged trespasses of Wright "have raised uncomfortable questions about the ways in which all members do
their jobs," said the magazine. The investigation of his activities
"makes it clear that Congress operates in a way that not many
beyond the Capitol either understand or approve."[2]

Special Counsel Richard J. Phelan headed a 10-month investigation of the speaker and found evidence upon which he concluded that Wright had violated House rules in six instances.
After receiving the report, though, the House Ethics Committee
in April 1989, voted 8 to 4—two Democrats joining the six Republicans—in finding that Wright contravened the rules on only two
of the six counts. Phelan devoted nearly one third of his report
to support one of the counts that the committee dropped:
charges that Wright breached House rules in attempts to influence savings and loan regulators in behalf of officials of troubled
S&L associations.

One portion of Phelan's report said: "During the period that
the recapitalization bill [to provide funds for the nearly insolvent
Federal Savings and Loan Insurance Corporation] was pending,
Wright interceded with the Federal Home Loan Bank Board on
behalf of four individuals. . . . The bank board officials ada-
mantly believe that Wright coerced them—or attempted to co-
erce them—into changing regulatory responses for three of the
four. They believe that Wright sought specific regulatory results.
Moreover, they believe that Wright had placed a 'hold' on the

FSLIC recapitalization bill until the bank board complied with his demands.''

Phelan also told of a phone call to then-Chairman Edwin Gray of the bank board, in which Wright said ''that he understood [an official of the Federal Home Loan Bank in Dallas] was a homosexual. And he understood from people that he believed . . . [he] had established a ring of homosexual lawyers in Texas at various law firms and that in order for people to deal with the Federal Home Loan Bank supervision people, they would have to deal with this ring. . . . He said to me [Gray], 'Isn't there anything you can do to get rid of Selby or ask him to leave or something?' '' Phelan said Wright's request ''greatly exceeded'' the bounds of proper congressional conduct and cited the appropriate House rules.[3] The committee didn't think Wright was using undue influence.

This committee view of Wright's overture to the bank board led *The Wall Street Journal* to say, ''All present and future members of Congress have just been instructed as follows: It's entirely ethical to block needed legislation until a regulatory agency does favors for your friends. It's also ethical to try to get agencies to fire employees who are tough with your political contributors, even if that means spreading accusations of homosexuality. Similarly, it's ethical for you or your staff to demand that regulators be fired under suspicion of having told the press unflattering things about you.

''Such interventions with regulators are ethical though they are on behalf of insolvent institutions, perhaps on behalf of crooks. It is also ethical even though it costs the taxpayer $100 billion.''[4]

The two counts that the committee held against Wright had to do with his business relationship with a Fort Worth developer and bulk sales of and the income Wright received from a slim paperback he wrote called *Reflections of a Public Man*. The publisher gave Wright an abnormally high author's royalty of 55 percent and Wright was free to peddle the books wherever he could. There were 76 bulk sales in quantities reaching to several thousand each that earned Wright some $55,000 in one year. The committee looked upon the book deal as a ruse for Wright to circumvent the limit on honoria income from speaking engagements, as groups could buy books in lieu of payments for talks.

The Ethics Committee voted unanimously to hold hearings on the two charges, and the first day was just ahead of the 1989 Memorial Day weekend holiday. Before they resumed, Wright on May 31 announced to the House his resignation as speaker. In a speech packed with emotion, he defended his conduct, attacked the committee, and called for an end to "this period of mindless cannibalism."[5] He also indicated he would resign as a representative by the end of June. He was the first speaker of the House to resign for alleged misconduct.

The New York Times reported Wright made his farewell speech "to a House beset with fear, where every rumor, every phone call from a reporter, every partisan spat could be the beginning of the end of a career." Members were "angry at him . . . for edging so close to the ethical line that he has brought down the wrath of ethical righteousness on all of them."[6]

The accusations against Wright were at white heat when Rep. Tony Coelho came under fire. He had been a successful fundraiser for the party and chaired the Democratic Congressional Campaign Committee. Among businessmen he solicited were officials of Drexel Burnham Lambert, the investment firm. Newspaper accounts accused him of getting an inside deal in the purchase of a $100,000 junk bond from Drexel Burnham Lambert, sold to him by Michael Milken, the firm's junk bond king and convicted trader. There were reports that the Justice Department and the Securities and Exchange Commission were readying probes. Common Cause asked the Ethics Committee to take a look at Coelho's financial maneuverings.

Coelho avoided the public ethical pummeling he'd seen administered to Wright. Before the investigative wheels began to turn against him, Coelho said he was leaving his House leadership post and that he would resign from the House on June 15, his 47th birthday. He made the announcement five days ahead of the day Wright took to the House floor to announce his decision to resign as a speaker. Coelho chose to make known his plans in a quieter manner, in an interview with two reporters of *The New York Times*. In six terms he had risen to the number 3 post in the House. "I don't intend to put my party through any more turmoil," he said.[7]

THE KEATING FIVE

Chairman Gray of the Federal Home Loan Bank Board also figures prominently in the manipulative attempts of Charles H. Keating, Jr. A Los Angeles superior court judge on April 10, 1992, sentenced Keating, 68, who became a symbol in the financial crisis of the savings and loan industry, to 10 years in prison and fined him $250,000 on California securities fraud charges. He had been convicted on 17 counts of defrauding buyers of about $250 million in unsecured bonds of American Continental Corp., which were sold at or near branches of a subsidiary, Lincoln Savings & Loan Association. American Continental filed for bankruptcy in April 1989, and the government declared Lincoln Savings insolvent and took over the operations. The failure, among the costliest of the thrift insolvencies, will cost taxpayers $2.5 billion. Keating still was to be tried under federal criminal and bankruptcy-fraud indictments.

The name, the Keating Five, was applied to five U.S. senators in 1989 after it became known that they had received large election campaign contributions—$1.35 million in total—from Keating, his family, and associates. The five were Democrats Alan Cranston of California; Dennis DeConcini of Arizona; John Glenn of Ohio; Donald Riegle, Jr., of Michigan, chair of the Banking, Housing, and Urban Affairs Committee; and Republican John McCain of Arizona. News accounts told of their meeting with S&L regulators in 1987 on behalf of Keating and Lincoln Savings. The degree to which they tried to influence the regulators to take actions favorable to Lincoln Savings became a matter of ethical discussion and of great controversy.

Cranston received nearly two thirds of the contributions, $885,000 for a voter-registration program in California he was pushing, and $35,000 in direct campaign contributions. Glenn's share was $34,000 for his 1986 campaign and $200,000 for a political action committee he controlled. There were $112,000 to McCain for his 1986 campaign, $76,100 to Riegle for his 1988 campaign, and $48,000 to DeConcini for his 1988 campaign. Riegle returned the contribution to Keating in 1988. However, he still ranked second among senators who received money from savings and loan interests in the 1980s, accepting $200,900.[8] DeConcini returned his money in September 1989 after the probe into these relationships with Keating grew.

According to information gleaned from news sources and congressional hearings, four of the senators, all but Riegle, met with Chairman Gray in early April 1987 in DeConcini's Washington office. The meeting was arranged by Reigle, according to testimony presented later at the Senate Ethics Committee hearing. Gray testified that the senators tried to get him to drop a regulation that would make Lincoln Savings divest itself of large real estate holdings and, in exchange, the senators would talk Keating into making more home loans. "I was appalled," said Gray. "These men controlled my budget, and they asked me to kill a regulation for their friend."[9] He suggested they talk with staff members of the San Francisco regional office, which had responsibility for examining Lincoln Savings.

A week later all of the five met again in DeConcini's office with four staff members from the San Francisco office. The senators learned Lincoln Savings was operating in violation of the law and regulations. DiConcini and McCain talked about problems Lincoln Savings was having with bank board appraisals of its assets. Others joined in the discussion but Cranston attended only briefly, then left to give attention to a bill on the Senate floor. The San Francisco office recommended in May that the government seize Lincoln Savings to prevent further losses. M. Danny Wall, who succeeded Gray in June, put aside the closure recommendation and the losses piled up until the takeover.

Keating, his relationship with the senators, and their part in the affair were in the news for more than two years—from the spring of 1989 to the summer of 1991. A House Banking Committee hearing in the fall of 1989 heard from examiners in the San Francisco office who wanted the government to take control of Lincoln Savings earlier. Wall testified that he blocked the takeover because he believed such an act would be challenged in court, as Keating had threatened. Keating refused to answer questions, but issued a statement blaming the regulators for the demise of Lincoln Savings.

A complaint filed by Common Cause with the Senate Ethics Committee in October led to the committee appointment of Robert Bennett as special counsel to head an investigation into the propriety of the actions of the Keating Five. He conducted a year-long investigation, whose results he unfolded at a hearing of the committee, which began in November 1990. Bennett recommended that Senators Glenn and McCain be dropped from the probe, because they ceased contact with Keating after learning in the meeting with the San Francisco regulators that they planned to start criminal proceedings against the S&L. The committee turned down the recommendation, preferring to hear testimony on the roles of all.

The Wall Street Journal greeted readers editorially the day the hearing began by saying that commentary on the ethics hearings that speculates on the fate of the five senators "misses the larger issue: how concepts such as 'constituent service' and 'legislative courtesy' have been twisted into a form of crass influence-peddling on behalf of special interests whose failures are now the burden of all taxpayers. If the hearings prompt the American people to realize the extent to which their government has become unaccountable and focused on the interests of a Beltway ruling class, then they will have served a larger purpose."[10]

Gray repeated his earlier charges that in the 1987 meeting, Senator DeConcini offered him a deal that would favor Keating. He also said the participation of himself and other regulators in the two 1987 meetings "capped years of private threats and public vilification designed not just to change particular decisions by the bank board but to render us unable to carry out our central responsibilities."[11]

"Let's talk about the most important defense that's been raised throughout this case," said Special Counsel Bennett in his closing presentation to the committee on January 15–16, 1991. "It comes back time and time again. It's the 'everybody does it' defense. If everybody does do what was done here, then that means this place doesn't have an infection that can be cured, it means that you're terminal.

"Everybody does not do it, and you know it."

Bennett also talked about "constituent service . . . [which] we've heard a lot about . . . in this case. You're United States senators, and your constituents are the whole country. The people that Charles Keating destroyed are your constituents. The taxpayers who have to pay for the Lincoln disaster are your constituents. The ultimate constituent service . . . is for you to finally nourish the American people's need to know that this is indeed a temple of honor and a temple of integrity and a temple of high ethical standards."[12]

The committee's preliminary report issued in late February 1991 said there was substantial evidence of ethical misconduct on the part of Senator Cranston and recommended that investigation of him continue. (Cranston had announced he suffered from prostate cancer and would not run for reelection.) There were only reprimands for the other four. The report led *The Wall Street Journal* to say, "All but the most crass kinds of influence peddling and interference with regulators is permitted as 'constituent service.' "[13]

The hearings and testimony may have made all members of Congress more aware of the need for concern about the appearance of impropriety and about their credibility. But isn't it the impropriety itself, not the appearance of it, that should be the greater consideration? And shouldn't the unethical public relations on the part of Keating and the Keating Five, and others involved and concerned, have alerted them to both?

POLITICAL ACTION COMMITTEES

For the first century and a half of this nation, contributions to political campaigns—at national, state, and local levels—went unregulated. Opportunities for corruption in the process were almost unlimited. Unrecorded cash contributions could appear from anybody, from anywhere. Sometimes they were "stuffed in paper bags or rolled up in bandanas."[14] Even though there were more contributors of modest incomes and fewer who were wealthy, the latter provided a disproportionate amount of funds.

It was 1925 before Congress passed a law that required candidates to disclose their campaign financing. This turned out to be a feeble attempt: it was vague and inconclusive, and enforcement was difficult. Faring better was the Federal Election Campaign Act of 1971, which called for reports on expenditures by candidates for federal offices and by national political committees. As part of several amendments in the 1970s, there was established the Federal Election Commission, as well as limits on political contributions.

From small beginnings, the political action committee, or PAC, crept into the election process. Labor unions set up the first PACs in the 1940s. Federal law prohibited them from supporting candidates with money collected from members as dues. There was, however, no bar to such use of voluntary contributions from members. So the unions created political action committees to collect and contribute such funds, and the PACs numbered some 600 by the mid-1970s. Corporations meanwhile had generally been unable to organize PACs because of the Hatch Act, which barred a business selling to the federal government from contributing to candidates for national offices. Legislation in 1974 gave PACs to corporations, even though they could not contribute directly, and the boom began. The FEC counted 4,681 PACs in 1990.

A PAC represents a pooling of money from those with shared interests in legislation, from managers and other employees in a particular industry or people in a common vocation or profession. Their interest may be in legislation they would like to see introduced and passed, or in laws already on the books that they favor and want retained or that they find distasteful and want repealed. The donations go, of course, to those candidates whom, the donors hope, will share their legislative interests.

A natural partner in the growth of the sources and amount of campaign funds has been the sizable escalation in the cost of campaigns. In 1990, incumbent candidates seeking election to the House spent, on average, $363,986 and to the Senate $4,491,802. This meant that to win a Senate seat, a candidate had to raise almost $12,000 per week for every week of a six-year senate term.

What do PACs have to do with ethics in public relations? A PAC is one kind of a public relations organization, one that utilizes public relations tools and techniques to gain its objectives. A PAC appeals to members of its group for funds and apportions the money to candidates. It takes on some of the characteristics of a lobbyist as it communicates with successful candidates who received its election funds on self-interest legislation and works to influence them to act in that interest.

Are PACs open, straightforward, and honest in what they say and do? Or do they exhibit some of the faults of overzealous lobbyists and move with ease and without qualms from buying access to influence-peddling, or influence-buying? And as they move in these latter ways, do they create conflict-of-interest headaches for congressmen and congresswomen?

Comments from others respond to these questions:

- *Forbes* magazines put the headline, "Influence for Sale," over an article that spoke of those who use PAC money to buy influence, and of "some brave business people" who are rebelling.[15]
- "Seats in Congress have been placed on the auction block and their price is going through the roof with no end in sight. . . . Our decision-making process is being held hostage to the special interests that PACs represent," claimed Sen. David Boren, Oklahoma Democrat, in an article that called for reform in the financing of election campaigns.[16]
- Campaign consultant Eddie Mahe said, "They're [PACs] payoffs pure and simple," according to writers Rowland Evans and Robert Novak. They added that PACs "grossly distort the electoral process."[17]
- Common Cause, a citizens' lobbying organization, after the 1988 congressional elections, invited prospective members to "join our campaign effort to take the 'For Sale' sign off of Congress." Fred Wertheimer, president of Common Cause, wrote to solicit assistance "to help stem the flood of special-interest Political Action Committee (PAC) money that is corrupting the United States Congress and threatening our representative form of government." Wertheimer's letter said, "No one is mincing words any more about the dangerous influence of PAC money in Congress," and

added quotes from three newspapers: "The power of PAC money threatens increasingly to turn members of Congress into legalized political prostitutes." (*Dallas Times Herald*); "Disguised bribery has grown like a cancer in Congress, corrupting the lawmaking process, making 'bag men' of most senators and representatives." (*The Charleston, West Virginia Gazette*); "The present congressional campaign financing system 'is fundamentally corrupt. Every citizen knows that. So does every legislator.' " (*The Washington Post*)[18]

Another fault charged against PACs is that their financial clout serves to protect incumbents in Congress and shut out challengers. In the words of *Forbes*, business PACs have become "a powerful instrument for keeping congressional incumbents safe in their seats . . . [and] remain an equally powerful barrier to political newcomers."[19] In the 1988 elections, 98 percent of the members of Congress seeking reelection won their seats; only seven House incumbents lost. Why was this so? One good reason is that in most instances PACs enabled the incumbents to outspend their opposition. The effect of this is to make ineffective, if not pointless and useless, the election process. Aren't PR acts that produce this result unethical?

For examples of comparative spending, offered by Common Cause, look at the 1990 election campaigns for congressional seats:

In the Senate races:

- Overall, incumbent senators in the election outraised challengers by nearly 3 to 1.
- Campaign spending by incumbents increased by 12 percent in 1990 compared to 1988; spending by challengers decreased by 5 percent in this comparison.
- Incumbents raised $32.8 million from PACs; challengers raised $8.3 million from PACs.[20]

In the House races:

- House incumbents seeking reelection had six and one-half times more campaign funds available than challengers.

- Campaign spending by incumbents increased by 5 percent in 1990 compared to 1988; spending by challengers decreased by 5 percent in this comparison.
- PAC contributions received by incumbents were 13 times more than those by challengers.[21]

Who are the big PAC contributors to candidates for federal offices? How much do they give? The Realtors Political Action Committee, affiliated with the National Association of Realtors, was the number one contributor in the 1989–90 election cycle, passing out $3.09 million. Closely bunched, the next three were the American Medical Association PAC with $2.37 million; the Democratic Republican Independent Voter Education Committee, affiliated with the Teamsters' union, $2.35 million; and the National Education Association PAC, $2.32 million. The remainder of the top 10 contributors were, in descending order, UAW Voluntary Community Action Program, Committee on Letter Carriers Political Education, American Federation of State County & Municipal Employees, National Association of Retired Federal Employees PAC, Association of Trial Lawyers of America PAC, and Carpenters Legislative Improvement Committee, United Brotherhood of Carpenters & Joiners. Their contributions ranged from $1.79 to $1.49 million. Six of those 10 are affiliated with labor unions.

You might have expected to find PACs of American business corporations among the top 10. The AT&T PAC almost made it—landing 13th and in first place for corporate PACs with $1.45 million. Following in the corporate group were Federal Express Corporation PAC, RJR PAC, UPSPAC, Philip Morris PAC, Union Pacific Fund for Effective Government, Barnett People for Better Government, a PAC of Barnett Banks, American Family Corporation PAC, Lockheed Employees' PAC, and Northrop Employees PAC. Contributions for these PACs ranged from $757 to $411 thousand.[22]

Who received the largest amount of these political contributions? During the 1985–90 Senate election cycle, 18 Senate candidates raised more than $1 million each from PACs. Sen. Phil Gramm, Texas Republican, obtained $1.845 million from PACs and led the list of those with such income. Sen. Tom Harkin, Iowa Democrat, was in second place and close on his heels with $1.815 million.[23] For the House in the 1989–90 election cycle, 10 winning incumbent candidates raised more than $500,000 from PACs. The leaders were Missouri Democrat Representative Richard Gephardt, with PAC receipts of $764,687, and Michigan Democrat David Bonior, with $728,056.[24]

A senator's or representative's membership on a strategic committee seems to affect the amount of his or her PAC income. There are 52 members on the House Banking Committee. They were drafting a banking reform bill in 1991. "For the moneyed interests affected . . . the stakes are huge," said *The Wall Street Journal*. The paper then pointed out that, according to the Center for Responsive Politics, "banking, insurance, real estate, and other interests gave panel members $3,254,040" in PAC contributions in the 1989–90 election cycle. The center also noted that half of the top 10 House recipients of PAC funds served on the committee.[25]

Cries for reform have come from members of Congress, defeated challenger candidates, the White House, public interest groups, the public, and the media. President Bush signed an ethics reform law in November 1989 that moved a step toward clean-up. Its provisions applied mostly to those in Congress, but it does not target campaign financing, though the bill brought momentum on that point.

In 1990, the Senate and House failed to agree on a bill that would ban PACs and end other election-financing abuses. Prospects for a law brightened in the new Congress, but not in the White House. After the Senate and House agreed on comprehensive campaign reform legislation that put restrictions on PAC contributions and had other controls, President Bush found the proposal unacceptable and vetoed it in May 1992.

THE PERSIAN GULF WAR; INVASIONS OF PANAMA AND GRENADA

Shreds of tattered credibility dotted the landscape after each of these U.S. military excursions. In Panama and Grenada, there were severe restrictions on coverage by journalists in the early days. In Desert Storm, news reporters in pools created by the Defense Department did not have free coverage access, and there were management of interviews with servicemen and women and censorship of stories and videotape. While the news media complained of their handling, the public sided with the military and was thrilled at the purported accuracy of U.S. nighttime air attacks on Iraq and the progress of the allied nations. Following each of the three actions, however, there were revised reports on troop activities; the U.S. public learned the earlier accounts had factual faults.

In the days of U.S. air and ground attacks against Iraq in January–February 1991, the military in its briefings reported a series of successful encounters. Versions of what was happening as released by the Defense Department gave the government's viewpoint. The press, having little choice, accepted and distributed these to keep Americans informed. Reporters and their bosses, however, objected strongly to the tightly controlled press pools and security reviews of their dispatches. "Journalists understandably have chafed under these restrictions, which are unprecedented—even in times of war," said Bruce W. Sanford, First Amendment counsel to the Society of Professional Journalists.[26] Three separate lawsuits challenged the military's restrictions on the press to no avail.

Some shine faded from the glowing Defense Department reports after Pentagon officers more fully digested earlier reports. For instance, claims about the Patriot missile's effectiveness against Iraqi Scuds turned out to be grossly inflated and were steadily reduced. In April 1992, the army told the House Government Operations Committee "it successfully destroyed or di-

verted only 40 percent of the Scuds fired at Israel and only 70
percent of those over Saudi Arabia." After the committee questioned these figures, the army said it "had succeeded in destroying about 24 Scuds fired at Israel and Saudi Arabia." And it
further conceded that it had high confidence about only 10 of
those kills. While the army had originally said that Patriots "in-
tercepted 45 of 47 incoming Scuds, "all it meant," said *The New
York Times,* in reporting testimony of Brig. Gen. Robert Drolet
of the Army's Missile Command, is that "a Patriot and a Scud
passed in the sky." The General Accounting Office said that,
using data from the army, it couldn't substantiate claims of Scud
damage. The Congressional Research Service told the committee that "it could find conclusive evidence for only one warhead
kill."[27]

The Defense Department's post–Gulf War figures on the
number of American deaths by friendly fire, soldiers killed by
their fellow combatants, rose 218 percent after several months.
The number of these victims was 35, compared with 16 who died
as a result of contact with the enemy.

Talks between the media and the military on press coverage in
battlefield operations continued a year after the conflict ended.
Representatives of major news organizations and Pete Williams,
assistant secretary of defense/public affairs, met over six months
on a 10-point statement of principles. They reached agreement
on all but one on prior review of news stories and film.

Coverage was one of the issues that clouded the government's
credibility in the dispatch of troops to Panama and Grenada.
When the United States invaded Panama on December 20, 1989,
the Bush administration insisted the action was hurriedly
planned after provocation—the killing of a U.S. soldier at a military checkpoint on the Saturday preceding the arrival of soldiers
and marines at 1 A.M. the following Wednesday. Countering
this was information that "the plans to invade were set in motion
much earlier, and the sheer momentum of preparation—along

with President Bush's desire to get Noriega—made the invasion inevitable."[28]

If there was questionable use of spin control by the administration in its explanation, there was further manipulation in its control of the news coverage of the invasion. This was the failure of Defense Department officials to adequately implement the arrangement for a news pool to accompany the troops. By the time members of the pool arrived in Panama, "the fighting was all but over."[29] To activate the 16-person pool, the Defense Department sent word to its members at various locations in Washington at 7:30 P.M. on December 19. This timing "guaranteed that the pool would reach Panama hours after the operation began."[30] Once those in the pool landed in Panama, there was a host of complaints about ways they were rebuffed by the U.S. military in attempts to cover the fighting.

As for the invasion itself, one U.S. general said, "The invasion went so well that 'there were no lessons learned.' " Perhaps he overlooked the word that "as many as 60 percent of the 347 American casualties may have been due to 'friendly fire,' " according to results of an investigation by *Newsweek*, published the following June.[31] Counter reports also dealt with the number of Panamanian casualties, said to be several times the official U.S. count.

If there was *deja vu* among those in the Panama news pool, it was because they recalled the Pentagon's denial of reporting access to the fighting on the tiny Caribbean island of Grenada after troops landed on October 25, 1983. The Reagan administration ordered an unprecedented 48-hour news blackout. The reported reason for this was that Pentagon officials needed secrecy in launching the invasion, and they were concerned about the safety of reporters and camera people. With the media shut out, the public too was shut out and will never know for sure what happened in the first hours of the invasion.

The possibility of cover-up by the United States of developments during this time in Grenada came to light in an article more than six years later in *The Wall Street Journal*: "Grenada, even partly disclosed, turns out to be an account of how the most powerful nation on earth nearly came a cropper in its bungled efforts to topple a little Marxist island." The paper said the picture formed in "dribs and dabs, in heavily censored documents and in obscure military writings . . . is a grim one." It quoted a military analyst who said the government "used security to cover up what happened. They've got a lot to hide."[32]

Cover-up, manipulation, and deceit practiced by the U.S. government in the handling of information about our fighting forces means the public is shortchanged, is less able to make a qualified judgment about how well the executive branch conducts its business. Unwittingly or otherwise, the government axes its credibility.

U.S. DEPARTMENT OF HOUSING AND URBAN DEVELOPMENT (HUD)

For HUD, another executive department of the government, waste, fraud, and abuse were among words used to describe its operation during the eight-year Reagan administration. One news publication fumed that "the HUD ripoff . . . [was] a rampant case of influence peddling, favoritism, and lust for power" and went on, "in terms of breathtaking cynicism and hypocrisy it's hard to match."[33] A huge public relations operation that failed to observe ethical conduct was responsible for further weakening of government credibility.

HUD Secretary Samuel Pierce, the agency head who should have been the chief PR officer and communicator, testified at only one hearing of the House Government Operations Committee in 1989 through 90. Thereafter, he invoked the Fifth Amendment when questioned and otherwise was silent. Pierce was the first former cabinet official to refuse to testify before Congress on the grounds of the Fifth since 1924. Then, the scandal was the Teapot Dome mess and Albert Fall, President Harding's secretary of the interior, pleaded the Fifth.

HUD was an agency with a $20 billion budget and $650 billion in loan and mortgage guarantees. Behind its doors were portfolios of the Federal Housing Administration, the Government National Mortgage Association, and smaller guarantee funds. Months of hearings by the House committee drew testimony with details of the disgraces and revealed estimates that the cost to taxpayers might be as much as $8 billion. In its report released in November 1990, the committee said taxpayers lost $2 billion because of "widespread abuses, influence peddling, blatant favoritism, monumental waste, and gross mismanagement." Committee Chairman Rep. Tom Lantos, California Democrat, said the sworn testimony and records found Pierce "was directly and intimately involved in the abuses and favoritism in HUD funding decisions."[34]

In the theft of funds, the most spectacular thief was known as "Robin HUD." This was Marilyn Harrell, a private escrow agent who was entrusted with HUD funds. She was indicted by a federal grand jury in Baltimore and charged with making false statements and embezzling $5.6 million from the department. She admitted to taking the money and said she gave some to projects that helped the poor. Ms. Harrell was sentenced in June 1990 to a 46-month prison term plus three years of probation and ordered to pay $600,000 in restitution and complete 624 hours of community service.

Pierce's executive assistant, Deborah Gore Dean, was a key player. Pierce delegated to her control of the rent subsidy program, known as Section 8 Moderate Rehabilitation, or mod rehab. She allowed an altered system in the application to HUD for federal grants, permitting local developers to work through high-priced consultants, some of whom were former HUD officials and Republicans with influence. The consultants made a few phone calls or wrote a few letters, and the desired contracts rolled from HUD headquarters. The consultants' fees were built into the government's costs. Sometimes the local housing authorities first learned of a contract after it was awarded to a developer.

One consultant was James Watt, former secretary of the interior. His aid was enlisted in 1986 by a Rhode Island developer, Judith Siegel, after HUD rejected her 312-unit project in Maryland. Watt made eight phone calls to the department, had a 30-minute meeting with Pierce, and the project was approved. Watt collected a fee of $300,000. Ironic in Watts' participation was that while heading the Department of Interior he was strong for less government, one that was leaner and smaller. *Newsweek* said, "Local ethicists distinguish between a lobbyist who gets paid to advocate something he may or may not believe in and a 'crass influence peddler' who gets paid to advocate something he may or may not know anything about. His [Watt's] offense was not what he sought but how—using contacts instead of persuasion."

Another biggie among the consultants was Paul Manafort, of the PR-lobbying firm of Black, Manafort, Stone, and Kelly, and a political consultant to Presidents Reagan and Bush. His pull enabled a developer to obtain a project in Upper Deerfield Township, New Jersey, which *Newsweek* said was opposed as unnecessary and wasteful by the mayor.[35] For his trouble, Manafort's firm received a consulting fee of $326,000 in late 1987. Other consultants were John Mitchell, attorney general under President Nixon, who earned $75,000 while lobbying for a Miami developer; Richard D. Selby, a White House personnel officer under President Reagan, who consulted on several HUD projects and grabbed $445,000; and the Winn Group, named for Philip E. Winn, former assistant secretary for housing at HUD and U.S. ambassador to Switzerland, when the committee took a look at the activities of him and his associates.

As an attempt to control the unsavory events in mod rehab and other sections of HUD, President Bush appointed Jack Kemp as HUD secretary to succeed Pierce. Kemp, former challenger of Bush for the Republican presidential nomination and former U.S. senator, fired 126 political appointees in his first week on the job and promised reforms.

Congress, in December 1989, passed the HUD Reform Act, which included ethics provisions. These were intended to move HUD decision making into the open by requiring that awards of housing assistance and waivers for most program requirements be made in a well-documented manner. Successful full reform of HUD, if or when it comes, will not remove the ethical blotches and loss of credibility left by the profiteers during Pierce's time.

U.S. NAVY INVESTIGATION OF THE U.S.S. *IOWA* EXPLOSION

A few lives were damaged by the U.S. Navy during its inquiry into the cause of an explosion on board the battleship U.S.S. *Iowa*, a tragic accident that also killed 47 sailors on April 19, 1989. From the inquiry floated bits of information disguised as news that put the ethical practices of the navy at question. The navy report of its investigation, released on September 7, 1989, raised such doubt and disbelief that on May 24, 1990, the department reopened its search for the cause of the blast and gave a changed version on October 17, 1991.

The navy's first explanation, based on thousands of tests, hundreds of interviews, and examinations of many documents, placed the blame on one of the ship's enlisted men, Gunner's Mate 2nd Class Clayton Hartwig. He was the center gun captain in the number-two turret of the ship at the time, and one of those killed. A rumor that floated during the four-month Navy investigation linked Hartwig in a homosexual relationship with another sailor aboard the *Iowa*, Kendall Truitt, who survived.

Leaking of the Hartwig-Truitt rumor to the news media began a month after the explosion. Adm. William Shachte of the Naval Investigative Service (NIS) said in an interview on "60 Minutes" that "the leaks were unfortunate," but he didn't know where they came from. On the same program, Bill Arkin, author of a study of naval accidents, said people in the "investigative bureaucracy" in the navy, people he knew, said there was "a homosexual love triangle, that this was a guy trying to commit suicide," that the information came from individuals in the NIS and elsewhere in the Navy Department.[36] Even though the first navy report didn't mention the homosexuality hearsay, damage was done.

There was discussion as to what degree the news media assisted the navy in spreading the innuendo. "Neither the Navy nor the press can take much pride in what happened [to Truitt]," said David Offer, editor of *The Newport* (Rhode Island) *News*, in a commentary written for his paper and published later by the Society of Professional Journalists. The Truitt-Hartwig story was first printed by newspapers in Virginia and Washington, D.C., according to Offer; then NBC News broadcast it nationally and "added details—again from unnamed Navy sources."

Offer said, "Secret Navy sources, for reasons that are not clear, hung Truitt out to dry . . . these same sources found willing listeners in newspapers and television stations that passed on these assertions." Offer pointed out that his paper and others have a policy of not publishing the name of a criminal suspect until he or she has been arrested. "If the explosion had been in Newport, we would have used all our resources to report what happened, but we would not have named an unarrested, uncharged Kendall Truitt, no matter who had leaked his identity."[37]

Doubts about the navy's conclusions in its first report were not long in coming. Rep. Nicholas Mavroules, Massachusetts Democrat and chairman of the House Armed Services investigative subcommittee, in October claimed an FBI analysis failed to support the navy assertion that the explosion was deliberately set. His subcommittee and another on defense policy found fault with the navy's probe and conclusions in a report issued in March 1990. The Senate Armed Forces Committee scheduled testimony by officials from Sandia Laboratories and the General Accounting Office for the day after the navy reopened its inquiry, on May 24, 1990.

The skipper of the *Iowa*, Capt. Fred P. Moossally, blasted the navy for bungling its investigation in his first public comments on the matter at the time of his retirement in May 1990. Moossally said the navy paid too much attention to its image, that the investigation was handled by "people more concerned with 'getting it over with,' " and the navy used "facts and opinions based on unsubstantiated third-party information, unsubstantiated reports, and supposition."[38]

When the navy reported on its second look at the explosion, it absolved Hartwig of blame—sort of. In an announcement on October 17, 1991, Adm. Frank B. Kelso, chief of naval operations, said, "There is no certain answer to the question of what caused the tragedy," and added that the navy couldn't find, or rule out, "an intentional act nor an accidental cause." He did say there was no "clear and convincing proof" that Hartwig was to blame and, extending "sincere regrets" to Hartwig's family, said, "We're sorry Clayton Hartwig was accused of this."[39] The U.S.S. *Iowa* incident will go down in navy history as a poorly handled ethical dilemma in public relations with a negative affect on the navy's credibility.

POINTS

• Never underestimate the value of oversight and monitoring of the activities of you and your associates. Test what you find against ethical conduct.

• Don't accept past practices in your office and elsewhere in the organization without question. Time may have changed their validity or need for or application to the overall operation. Reexamine from time to time how things get done.

• Be careful about how you use the power of your position or authority as pressure on others to fulfill your demands. In pressuring, are you seeking benefit for yourself, department, or organization that can't be justified on ethical grounds?

• Decide for yourself what your ethical standards and conduct will be rather than accepting or copying, uncritically and without question, the acts of others.

• Avoid defaming or unjustly accusing another person in the interest of acquiring your goals.

• If you're pressured to act in ways you know are unethical or illegal, take time to analyze what's happening, and plan to react in a manner that puts ethics first and maintains your credibility.

• Analyze what you're trying to buy when you make a political contribution. Differentiate between seeking a decision based on facts and a personal favor, between access and influence-peddling. Question a system in which dollars buy laws and regulations.

• Embellishing reports of your programs for personal aggrandizement can be dangerous, may damage credibility.

• Don't use power or authority to impose restrictions that result in cover-up or deceit.

• When you delegate authority to another, provide for sufficient supervision to assure ethical and other proper procedures are observed.

• Examine the example you set for those whom you manage; talk with them about what they may perceive as ethical missteps.

NOTES

1. "Full Disclosure . . . Not!" *The Wall Street Journal*, March 16, 1992, p. A8.

2. Gloria Borger, "The Last Stand of Speaker Jim Wright," *U.S. News & World Report*, April 24, 1989, p. 27.

3. "Ethics Committee: No Problem Here," excerpts from report of Special Outside Counsel Richard J. Phelan, *The Wall Street Journal*, April 19, 1989, p. A20.

4. "Ethical Interference," *The Wall Street Journal*, April 19, 1989, p. A20.

5. Robin Toner, "Wright Resigning as Speaker; Defends His Ethics and Urges End of 'Mindless Cannibalism,' " *The New York Times*, June 1, 1989, p. A1.

6. Michael Oreskes, "An 'Evil Wind' of Fear Is Felt in House," *The New York Times*, June 1, 1989, p. A1.

7. Nancy Traver, "How Many Will Fall?" *Time*, June 5, 1989, p. 34.

8. News release, Common Cause, June 29, 1990.

9. "Senatorial Shills," *The Wall Street Journal*, June 13, 1989, p. A18.

10. "Keating's Senators," *The Wall Street Journal*, November 15, 1990, p. A18.

11. Associated Press, "Former S&L Chief Primed for Shootout with Senators," *Rocky Mountain News*, November 28, 1990, p. 2.

12. Robert Bennett, "Everybody Does Not Do It, and You Know It," *The Wall Street Journal*, January 31, 1991, p. A14.

13. "Sham and Shame," *The Wall Street Journal*, March 4, 1991, p. A10.

14. "Campaign Financing," *World Almanac of U.S. Politics* (New York: Pharos Books, 1989), p. 38.

15. Janet Novack, "Influence for Sale," *Forbes*, February 20, 1989, p. 108.

16. Sen. David Boren, "Congress on the Auction Block," *USA Today*, May 1990, p. 10.

17. Rowland Evans and Robert Novak, "Congressmen for Life: The Incumbency Scandal," *Reader's Digest*, June 1989, p. 79.

18. Letters and attachments from Archibald Cox and Fred Wertheimer, Common Cause, undated.

19. Novack, "Influence for Sale," p. 108.
20. News release, Common Cause, February 28, 1991.
21. News release, Common Cause, March 26, 1991.
22. News release, Federal Election Commission, March 31, 1991.
23. News release, Common Cause, February 28, 1991.
24. News release, Common Cause, March 26, 1991.
25. Kenneth H. Bacon, "For Financial Firms, Banking Reform Involves Huge Stakes—and Big Donations to Lawmakers," *The Wall Street Journal*, May 25, 1991, p. A24.
26. Bruce W. Sanford, "SPJ Pushing for Pentagon Flexibility," *The Quill*, March 1991, p. 11.
27. "Patriot Games," *The New York Times*, April 9, 1992, p. A24.
28. Jon Meyersohn, "Letters," *Harper's*, May 1990, p. 4.
29. William Boot, "Wading around in the Panama Pool," *CJR*, March/April 1990, p. 18.
30. Fred S. Hoffman, "Review of Panama Pool Deployment," prepared by the U.S. Department of Defense, March 1990, p. 7.
31. Douglas Waller and other staff members, "Inside the Invasion," *Newsweek*, June 25, 1990, p. 28.
32. James P. Perry and John J. Fialka, "As Panama Outcome Is Praised, Details Emerge of Bungling during the 1983 Grenada Invasion," *The Wall Street Journal*, January 15, 1990, p. A14.
33. Steven Waldman with Bob Cohn and Rich Thomas, "The HUD Ripoff," *Newsweek*, August 7, 1989, p. 16.
34. Craig Flournoy, "House Report Faults Pierce in HUD Scandal," *The Dallas Morning News*, November 2, 1990, p. 3A.
35. Newsweek, "The HUD Ripoff," p. 16.
36. "U.S.S. *Iowa*," CBS News "60 Minutes," May 27, 1990.
37. David Offer, "Use the Story, but Not the Name," *The Quill*, December 1989/January 1990, p. 14.
38. Associated Press, "*Iowa* Skipper Blasts Navy at Retirement," *Rocky Mountain News*, May 5, 1990, p. 2.
39. Associated Press, "Navy Apologizes for Accusing Sailor in *Iowa* Blast," *Rocky Mountain News*, October 18, 1991, p. 42.

Chapter Eight

Implementing the Credibility Factor, Part I

As you put ethics in public relations to work to achieve credibility, you will discover it's not always easy to do. You may run into personal dilemmas, discover pressures applied on you to take an unethical course that is not compatible with your values and your conscience. How do you react? This chapter offers advice from those who have learned from their own experiences and by observation of others in resolving dilemmas. Their comments will help you recognize and understand the forces of a dilemma that challenges you and to prepare in advance your reactions to such a situation. This chapter also presents observations of executives in business and public relations, who place a premium on the qualities of credibility and integrity that will fortify reasons for you to have credibility as a goal.

ETHICS IN SOCIETY—AND IN PUBLIC RELATIONS

There's been a megaexplosion of concern in recent years about ethics by those in many occupations. Among reasons for the extreme interest in the subject are said to be the higher stresses and pressures in our lives. As people react to, and sometimes yield to, the demands put upon them, they try to find what is basic in their lives and separate that from the fluff, and they become more questioning of values.

Another reason is said to be public reaction to, and, for some, revulsion by the sleaze, deceit, falsification, conflicts of interest, personal greed at other's expense, borderline illegal, and truly illegal doings they see in both the private and public sectors. Not only do people see the enlarged nature of the unethical environment, but also apparent acceptance—even admiration or perhaps lack of condemnation—of the individuals and organizations involved.

To say this is to oversimplify. There are more complicated reasons, best left to discussions by sociologists and those of allied professions in another forum.

How do we think about and evaluate ethics in the PR communications directed toward us or that we observe about us daily? How do we judge those individuals and organizations whose public gestures seem based on truth, fairness, candor, and integrity? Or those who appear deceitful, misleading, even downright dishonest? How do we react as we witness the unfolding and resolution of their ethical dilemmas?

Let's think first about ethics in a broad societal context, then narrow the focus to its role and effect on the many-faceted activities that qualify for the public relations stamp.

The basic tenet of individual moral conduct, which is a foundation for ethical precepts, can be found in the Old Testament of the Bible, in the Ten Commandments and the Golden Rule; also, in older maxims of ancient civilizations. Citizens of the Egyptian city of Alexandria heard these rules:

Act with a kind heart and love what is good.
Be of help to all.
Learn to love truth.
To do what is right is difficult.

Confucius, the Chinese philosopher and teacher, expressed the sentiment of the Golden Rule, but in a quite negative way. When he was asked, ''Is there any one word that can serve as a principle for the conduct of life?'' he replied, ''Perhaps . . .

'reciprocity.' Do not do to others what you would not want others to do to you.''

These examples illustrate a point made by Michael Josephson, an ethicist and founder of the Josephson Institute for the Advancement of Ethics: Every civilization has had a sense of right and wrong, and secular philosophers as well as religious leaders have expressed these ethical beliefs. He says the essence of ethics is "some level of caring," which is expressed in the quotations.

Josephson brings us to the present with insightful comments. Asked if the people who are teaching us ethics are more ethical than the rest of us, he responds: "First of all, the people who are really teaching us ethics aren't even thinking about ethics. We don't learn ethics from people who sermonize or moralize or try to preach to us about ethics; we learn ethics from the people whom we admire and respect, who have power over us. They're the real teachers of ethics."

He's saying we get our ethics from parents, from teachers, from peer groups, from role models. The latter, such persons as politicians, corporate executives, and athletes, have a responsibility. The way they behave influences many other lives.

Josephson talks of two levels in ethical decision making: "The first is to distinguish the clearly unethical decisions from the ethical ones. It's usually unethical to lie, to steal, to injure others. There's a second level of decision where you're choosing between ethical values, truth and fairness, truth and loyalty, where no one answer is absolutely right or absolutely wrong. Here you just have to analyze the situation as clearly as possible and be sensitive to what your values are."

The role of former Lt. Col. Oliver North in the Iran-Contra affair during the Reagan administration "is one of the toughest issues for me to analyze ethically," says Josephson. "Unlike most of these cases, where people were acting out of self-indulgence or self-protection, which are obvious motives, North appeared to be acting out of a different and nobler (to him) kind of motive. People judge him only on his motives. But self-righteousness can be as much a cause of unethical conduct as anything else. North was so certain he was right that everything he allegedly was fighting for—a democratic society, making the world safe for democracy—he violated. I think Oliver North violated the law, and he did so in order to impose his view of the world on everyone else. He denied people their input."[1]

Speaking from the viewpoint of business corporations, Alden Lank says that "ethics is concerned with values and ensuring that decisions reflect and support the values of each society that has mandated corporations to act on its behalf in the wealth-creation process. One of the acid tests for what is 'good' or 'evil' resides in societal values." He adds the unfortunate note that in too few instances business decisions lend themselves "to a simple 'yes/no' answer to the good/evil question."

In the final analysis, he says, "The ultimate arbiter of what is good or evil can only be ourselves. Therefore, it is we who must take moral responsibility for all our acts—be they in the personal or business spheres of our lives."

As a test for the ethical issue, Lank gives one that the chief executive officer of a major Scandinavian multinational company presented to his managers: "Assume that the decision you are about to make in Timbuktu becomes public knowledge in our home country, the host country, and significant third countries where our company is operating. Assume further that you, as the decision maker, are called upon to defend the decision on television both at home and abroad. If you think you can defend it successfully in these public forums, the probability is high that your decision is ethical."[2]

Professor Mel Sharpe takes the view that "what is ethical is directly related to what appears at the time to be in the interest of a social group." In support of this point, he asks you to reflect on U.S. history. Slavery, he contends, was considered ethical, as was racial discrimination. Through the years, he adds, it was ethical to drive back the American Indian from his land; to put workers, including children, in conditions that endangered their health and welfare; to pay women substandard wages; to remove Japanese-Americans from their homes and move them into camps where they were held without due process. Getting more up to date, he declares "dirty tricks" were considered part of the game of politics until Watergate.[3]

Certainly, there were indicators of a steadily growing interest in ethics in public and private lives during the last half of the 1980s and into the 1990s:

- "An ethics boomlet" is the tag put on the vigorous interest in the subject by Arthur L. Caplan, director of the Center for Biomedical Ethics at the University of Minnesota in Minneapolis. He says the activity is characterized "by new expectations concerning the private behavior of politicians, new concerns about the invasion of privacy by computer databases and the media, and new interests in the rights of animals, children, minorities, the handicapped, the elderly, and the ill."[4]

- Sissela Bok, ethicist and author, has noted in the years that she's been teaching and writing about ethics that "people are much more in agreement that we need to talk about ethics—that there's nothing sissyish about it."[5]

- Don Fry, associate director of the Poynter Institute for Media Studies, St. Petersburg, Florida, points to an "escalating interest" in the programs on ethics and the media that the institute presents.[6]

Moving from society in general to the public relations arena, what better person to turn to than Edward L. Bernays, a pioneer in the field. Ethical standards of conduct concerned Bernays when he wrote the book *Crystallizing Public Opinion*, published in 1923. "Ethical Relations," is the title of the final section where he states, "The standards of the public relations counsel are his own standards, and he will not accept a client whose standards do not come up to them. While he is not called upon to judge the merits of his case any more than a lawyer is called upon to judge his client's case, nevertheless he must judge the results which his work would accomplish from an ethical point of view.''[7]

Nearly 70 years later, in a conversation about ethics in public relations, Bernays said, ''If you ask me about ethical conduct, I would say that every decent human being who isn't going to let money affect him more than morals affects him is going to utilize the Judeao-Christian ethic in carrying out his work.

''He isn't going to lie, he isn't going to take money under false pretenses, he isn't going to cheat, and he is going to follow the moral code of behavior which decent people follow in their everyday actions. And, if that is practiced, he'll get a better reputation, or she will, than carrying out devious actions which other people will hear about or recognize and very often exaggerate to validate their own integrity.''[8]

Is one voice representative of a larger chorus? What about those thousands in the practice of public relations who counsel clients and serve employers? They're working and coping daily. Ethics are a vital concern to them, according to a survey by the International Association of Business Communicators of those attendings its annual conference in 1989.

Results of the poll, as reported by *PR News*: ''A whopping 85% of the 600 respondents believe that ethics affect a company's bottom line; 63% feel that ethics can harm or enhance an organization's public reputation, and 21% stated that ethical issues can lead to costly regulation.'' Asked what they had done to improve ethical conduct, 49 percent said they had discussed this with senior management; 26 percent said they had ''participated in or organized an internal audit to monitor compliance'' with ethical conduct; and nearly the same percentage had published a code of ethics and helped organized ethics discussions or training.

The report said, "Another significant finding is that 60 percent of top executives are personally involved in improving ethical conduct in their companies."[9]

There are public relations practitioners who say they run into pressures to act unethically or condone acts that are unethical.[10] What do they do if, for instance, they are asked to issue a news release or supervise publication of information that is false, or misleading and deceitful? What are their choices?

To some degree, perhaps, the answer relates to their relative position in the structure. If their voice commands sufficient attention and they state their beliefs with conviction, they may be able to counsel successfully for another more ethical course. They may convince others that the less-than-forthright course is fraught with more risks that a candid, open route.

What if their counsel goes unheeded? What if the course of action is not changed, and they find their ethical standards ignored? Then what? They may give in to the pressure and act in the way they've been requested, even though they can barely stand a minute of it! At the same time, they may vow that if a similar situation arises again, they will speak even more loudly for acting ethically and, meanwhile, freshen their resumes. And there's the more extreme alternative, which may be the only satisfying one. That's to immediately walk away, leaving the organization or resigning the client.

The counseling approach, as illustrated in the first alternative above, is recommended by Pat Jackson, a fellow as well as past president of the Public Relations Society of America.

"When asked to violate ethics by a boss or client, I don't take the arbitrary position that a practitioner should immediately quit, or threaten to. That is bad negotiating technique. Moreover, it implies that ethical issues are black and white.

"My feeling is that an ethical practitioner can do more good in the short run by making an issue of the situation, gathering allies, supplying the offending executive with cases and literature from third parties—and generally trying to persuade this person that such tactics are self-defeating, both in the instant and as a practice.

"It is far more righteous to convert a sinner, or even sensitize one, than to avoid them as impure. Obviously, if one is repeatedly asked to be unethical, leaving may be inevitable."[11]

Backing up Jackson's point on converting is a comment that comes from Jerry terHorst while serving as White House press secretary under President Ford. He said there were several deceptions or "covers" about pending actions given to him by other aides in the White House. He cites one in connection with developments surrounding Ford's pardon of former President Nixon.

A Ford emissary, Benton Becker, had returned from San Clemente, California, with a tentative draft of a Nixon statement to be issued as a response to the pardon announcement. TerHorst said that one member of the Washington press corps had "smoked out Becker's work on the Nixon pardon." The deception cloak handed to terHorst meant that he told the reporter Becker was in San Clemente to discuss the disposition of Watergate tapes and documents with Nixon. On the basis of terHorst's "erroneous description" of the purpose of Becker's trip, the reporter did not write the story.

TerHorst did not see this kind of deception and dilemma as a reason to resign (by comparison, it was nowhere near as monumental a matter as the pardon, which did cause him to resign) any more than a reporter has reason to resign when a news source gives less than a complete story.

While not liking the situation, terHorst saw himself in a position to bring improvement. "I had felt . . . ," he said, "that half-truths by my White House colleagues could eventually be eliminated by convincing them that the President's reputation is harmed whenever his spokesman is misled."[12]

TerHorst has been in the business of transmitting information as a journalist, a government press chief, and a corporate public affairs head. "I don't think there's a different set of ethics, whether you're in one of these fields or another," he said. "Everybody has his moral bottom line, his ethical bottom line. And that travels with you from job to job—at least I think it should.[13]

"What happens when a client/employer insists that we do something that is deceptive or dishonest?" asks PR Counselor Joe Epley, 1991 president of PRSA. "We must have the courage to stand by our principles and if need be, to walk away from the client. Two wrongs do not make a right. Sacrificing one's principles is just as wrong as the principle being sacrificed.

"Now, how does an individual with two children in college, a mortgage, a $3,000 orthodontist bill, and a wife thinking about divorce walk away from a high-paying job on a matter of principle? That's true courage. Yet, that's what we must be prepared to do if we as individuals are to maintain credibility, professionalism, and self-esteem.

"If the profession is to maintain the prestige it wants to enjoy in the marketplace, its members must be above reproach."[14]

Frank W. Wylie, a fellow and past president of PRSA with public relations experience in business and education, says, "I've known people who have resigned an account that they could not handle ethically. They didn't do it for formal reasons, but for practical ones. If they lied on one account, the media would think they lied on all."[15]

Coauthors Sam Black and Melvin L. Sharpe are quite blunt about the proper course for a responsible person who discovers the policy of the organization is contrary to law or his/her conscience. ''Resign immediately.'' In a less extreme example, in which there may be actions of doubtful honesty or possible conflict, ''it is essential and in the best interest of society to try to get these policies reversed, and if this proves unsuccessful then resignation must follow.'' They acknowledge that ''these are deep waters'' and add: ''It takes courage to resign from a good position, especially if one has family responsibilities, but there can be no compromise with one's conscience under such circumstances.'' Black and Sharpe pose specific situations. For example, they believe ''it would probably be generally accepted as unethical'' for a confirmed teetotaler to work for producers of alcoholic beverages.[16]

Another view about public relations people who terminate positions ''that forced them to compromise their ethical standards'' comes from Donald K. Wright, educator, researcher, and author on ethics in public relations. ''Managements and clients probably would have little difficulty replacing them with other communicators who had lower standards of morality. Perhaps . . . it would be best to . . . compromise the ethical idealism slightly, and see to it that the communication process is carried out in a more ethical manner than otherwise might be the case.''[17]

In his book *Power and Influence*, Robert L. Dilenschneider, former CEO of Hill & Knowlton, the nation's largest public relations firm, said one way his company has come to know ethical dilemmas, ''I'm sad to say, is through a very small number of clients.''

''Sometimes, clients have asked us to help them do something wrong. I think that this situation arises with all kinds of professional services firms. For example, a client will ask us to pay for a set of luggage, an air ticket to Hawaii, or even a hooker, and pad the amount of their firm's bill. For some people, an appeal to ethics just will not work. In this case, we have a strong, standard answer: 'If you were ever caught, this would be terribly embarrassing for you . . . and we just couldn't allow you to put yourself in such a position.' "

"Bad ethics is bad for business," asserted Dilenschneider. He recommends that firms "make high ethical standards evident in everyday business decisions"; also, "give employees clear ideas and symbols for what ethical behavior means."[18]

He said he had discussed ethics with managers of the firm. In a letter to all of them sent in August 1989, Dilenschneider said, "We have always maintained that a high ethical standard of conduct is the first principle of good public relations . . . the only conduct we can control is our own, and it is imperative that it be—and be seen to be—always in the high end of the ethical scale. And it is our responsibility to urge the same conduct on our clients."

Dilenschneider concluded by quoting the founder of the company, John W. Hill, who wrote: "It is my firm conviction that under no foreseeable circumstances will the demands for good public relations services diminish. I stress the word *good* because that is going to be the criterion of the future. My idea of good is being effective, combined with high standards of ethics and sound judgment."[19]

Heads of organizations, businesses particularly, can cause their own ethical dilemmas, and may not recognize that they do so. They may allow competitive pressures to thrust aside good judgment; and they may communicate in a way that wasn't intended, and the wrong message moves down the line.

Josephson makes the point about competitive pressures that put executives at risk. They're the ones who make decisions, he says, and "ethics is all about decision making."[20] The competitive atmosphere can create lax moral standards, he charges, even a corrupt atmosphere that can sweep through those in all departments.

A similar dilemma is caused by the unintended communication, by signals from an organization that it didn't intend. According to Gary Edward, executive director of the Ethics Resource Center in Washington, "They [employees] look around for signals about what to do. And the organization gives signals that it doesn't intend to give . . . what they see is that people who meet quarterly profit performance objectives go up the ladder. And people who don't get plateaued or they're gone." Edwards says these are "people who are down in the guts of the organization, who come to believe that in order to keep their job and do their job, they have to do what it takes."[21] Ethical sensibilities get pushed aside.

Barbara Ley Toffler calls such signals the "move it" syndrome. Toffler, a founding partner of Resources for Responsible Management, a consulting firm, says that's when the boss tells the subordinate to "move it . . . just get it done, meet the deadline, don't ask for more money, time, or people, just do it." She cites examples in which unethical actions followed such orders, and warns, "If a process takes four weeks with all operations at capacity, management must realize that a message to accomplish it in two weeks is likely to produce unethical behavior."[22]

Implicit in all the previous discussion is the point that ethics in PR and in all fields is a highly personal matter, that one's personal values and standards of conduct determine that person's ethics. Since an ethical decision is an individual decision, one's ethical behavior is not something one can turn over to someone else.

How does one rate the qualities of fairness, honesty, openness, and truth on a scale of 1 to 10? Are those qualities placed in the 9–10 range, or in the 1–2 range? Or do these figures shift depending upon the situation and circumstances? As Raymond Simon points out, those in every walk of life and vocational endeavor "face ethical dilemmas in which their personal ideas of right and wrong may clash with the practical demands of their working lives."[23]

Persons sometimes try to rationalize their way out of ethical dilemmas. The Josephson Institute puts forth "the most common rationalizations which tend to justify unethical conduct:"

"If it's necessary, it's ethical."
"If it's legal and permissible, it's proper."
"I was just doing it for you."
"I'm just fighting fire with fire."
"It doesn't hurt anyone."
"It can't be wrong; everyone's doing it."
"It's OK if I don't gain personally."
"I've got it coming."
"I can still be objective."[24]

One test has been suggested for the individual whose values collide as he or she strives to determine just what the conscience is saying. That test: How would you like an account of what you're planning to be published in tomorrow's issue of *The New York Times*, or on the front page of your local newspaper? This is a simplified form of the more reasoned view of the Roman statesman and philosopher, Seneca, who said, "I am content if you only act, in whatever you do, as you would act if anyone at all were looking on; because solitude prompts us to all kinds of evil."

Bernays, recognized as the father and early practitioner of public relations, might direct you to this descriptive quotation of his: "I wouldn't want it on my superego that I did for money what I wouldn't do without money." These words were part of a sketch of Bernays as one of the "100 Most Important Americans of the 20th Century," published in 1990 by *Life* magazine. This philosophy guided him in turning down some prospective clients, including Adolf Hitler and General Francisco Franco, notorious former rulers of Germany and Spain, respectively.[25]

CREDIBILITY—INTEGRITY—TRUST:
PERSONAL AND CORPORATE

Credibility, a nice, wholesome word that some might link with apple pie and motherhood, does have a deep and real meaning for most in the PR world. Too bad we can't say *all* instead of *most*. But it's readily apparent from examples in this book, and the much wider file available in newspapers, magazines, and corporate records, that some individuals and institutions are willing to sacrifice credibility in exchange for certain desired gains.

It's fair to say, though, that the majority of individuals and institutions do want credibility in the eyes of their publics. Whatever their PR goals, they want to demonstrate and establish their credibility and integrity. They want to create trust.

The corporate business world has concerns about credibility, and has had for some time. The restoration of business credibility—"the number one issue in the minds of most executives"—was the theme of a meeting presented for executives and consultants by The Conference Board as long ago as January 1976. The edited transcript was made available afterward "because we believe that the information exchanged during the discussion is of continuing relevance for corporate executives responsible for public relations, public affairs and external relations . . . should also be valuable to senior management, which is ultimately accountable for the company's external relations posture and efforts."[26]

The introduction to that report said, "Many senior executives believe that the need for improved communication is at the heart of the problem of the public's distrust of business. In a recent speech, one business leader outlined his estimation of the causes of this erosion of public confidence, citing two general causes: business' failure to communicate, and business' failure to be responsive.

The keynote speaker, Katharine Graham, then publisher of *The Washington Post*, urged greater disclosure by business and spoke about the "gaps between words and actions and standards." There was talk about the media and about PR, which, as one participant, Ralph F. Lewis, then of *Harvard Business Review*, said, "are not only parts of the problem but also potential solutions." He added that "all too frequently the PR person's worst enemy is the boss or the client . . . management gives the PR people the 'mushroom treatment'—they are kept in the dark and told nothing except that they are to improve the image of the company."[27]

Another participant, Opinion Pollster Daniel Yankelovich, said the post–World War II peak of credibility probably was in 1967 to 68, when more than 7 out of 10 people thought business was doing a good job. Erosion of that standing began a couple of years later, and in the 1970s fell to 19 percent—"one of the most massive declines in credibility we have ever seen." He stated that the matter of business credibility had become increasingly vital as the amount of government regulation of business increased.

"The lack of business credibility is not only a driving force behind creating regulations and legislation," he said, "but it also means that the regulation and legislation will tend to be biased against business and will tend to be one-sided and punitive, as long as the lack of credibility and the mistrust exist."[28]

While this meeting aired views of a common concern, the problem was not solved. Credibility worries still plagued business as we entered the 1990s. C. J. Silas, Chairman and CEO of Phillips Petroleum Company, began an article in *Public Relations Journal* with these words: "Our nation's industry is facing a must-win situation. . . . We're fighting to restore our credibility with the public and demonstrate that we can carry out our activities without harm to the environment. Right now, I don't believe the American people trust industry to be responsible with our country's air, water and land.

"To win their trust, we must have the attitude of champions, not runners-up. . . . Champions constantly improve on their performance, while runners-up struggle to maintain theirs."[29]

Veteran PR man John F. Budd, Jr., wrote that "one lesson the 1980s should have taught American business leaders is the pivotal importance of corporate credibility." He went on, however, to find that "abstracts like integrity and values generally have little agenda space as business copes with quantitative issues—competition, costs, quality, legal headaches, etc." He asks, then answers, why these issues are considered more important. "Trade is a tangible problem; trust, an intangible."[30]

For another expression on this topic, turn to Chester Burger, for many years a PR executive before he became a management consultant to PR firms. "Isn't credibility our biggest problem? I believe the basic factor in public opinion today is fundamental public distrust of government leaders, corporations, unions, religious leaders. All have lost public trust."[31]

Burger fortified his statement with a quote from Lee Atwater, then chairman of the Republican National Committee. "If you want to look at a solid trend for the last 15 or 20 years," said Atwater, "it is that the American people are cynical and turned off about all the institutions, and politics is one. It's only one of them.

"Bull permeates everything. In other words, my theory is that the American people think politics and politicians are full of baloney. They think the media and journalists are full of baloney. They think organized religion is full of baloney. They think big business is full of baloney. They think big labor is full of baloney."[32]

Certainly, there is cynicism. And that is not all bad. Surely a portion is healthy. Atwater's categorical statements do emphasize his point, even if they extend beyond what many would call an accurate description.

Besides business' concern about credibility with the general public, they prize the quality in dealings with other firms. We find the factors that comprise credibility come to the fore when we hear the responses from companies asked to describe what they expect from their public relations firm.

"Character and integrity" were listed first by Glenn H. Parson, vice president for corporate communications, Entergy Corporation; "integrity" was named first by Richard P. Gulla, public relations director of *The Boston Globe*. Naming qualities that make a client-agency relationship succeed, "trust, candor" led the list for David A. Fausch, vice president, corporate public relations, The Gillette Company.[33]

To narrow the focus of this subject, and hear a view on individual credibility, listen now to terHorst in his position as director, national affairs, Ford Motor Company, in Washington, after leaving the post of White House press secretary.

"In any job," according to terHorst, "your credibility and your integrity are your only marketable qualities—marketable not only in terms of your work but in terms of being believable. With these qualities, you demonstrate you put a high value on being truthful and having a high standard of morality and ethical behavior.

"Those are the only commodities I have. My believability and my personal integrity create a climate of credibility that serves not only me well but also my employer."[34] A strong personal endorsement of this valued personal asset.

Suspicion and skepticism were expressed by long-time public relations counsel Bernays when asked if the need for public relations people to maintain credibility and a favorable reputation was not sufficient to guide their ethical performance. "People don't hear much about individual conduct," he said, "unless he or she breaks the law and is arrested and gets negative publicity.

"I would say the adherence to ethics is more the desire not to take a chance of getting negative publicity than it is a conscious effort of behavior patterns."[35]

A further skeptical tack was expressed by Wylie: "One problem about ethics is that most people address it from the side of morality. Perhaps I'm a pessimist but I believe that moralism reaches about 10 percent of the population (max) and that the others pooh-pooh anyone who tries to bring morality into the world of modern business enterprise. What is needed is an approach that avoids morality, and the divisiveness of its issue and presents ethics as the simple, bottom-line orientation to success."[36]

POINTS

• If you're the object of pressure from a boss or client to be part of an unethical conspiracy, speak out for what you believe is right and fair. Portray the folly of the unethical way and the credibility benefit of the alternative.

• Always protest the deceitful course. Only *you* can decide to what degree you want to compromise on an ethical issue. Remember that your credibility is on the line and that you must decide how your reputation will fare in the decision you are part of.

- Avoid applying pressure on others that may be misunderstood: for example, setting unrealistic deadlines if completion of the assignment can mean cutting ethical corners. Be sure that your demands can be fulfilled in an ethical way.

- Be a salesman for earned credibility in your organization, or with clients. Explain the trust it can create among those publics whose opinions affect the success of the enterprise.

NOTES

1. Bill Moyers, *A World of Ideas* (New York: Doubleday, 1989), pp. 15–25.
2. Alden G. Lank, "Business Ethics: A Moral Imperative," *Public Relations Journal*, November, 1988, p. 20.
3. Melvin L. Sharpe, "The Professional Need: Standards for the Performance of Public Relations," *International Public Relations Review*, November 1986, p. 11.
4. Rushworth M. Kidder, "Public Concern for Ethics Rises," *The Christian Science Monitor*, January 2, 1990, p. 13.
5. Ibid.
6. Ibid.
7. Edward L. Bernays, *Crystallizing Public Opinion* (New York: Boni and Liveright), p. 215.
8. Conversation with the author in Bernay's office, April 9, 1991.
9. "Ethics Are a Vital Concern to PR Execs," *PR News*, July 10, 1989, p. 2.
10. Reported in surveys conducted by author, 1989 and 1990; see Chapter 15.
11. Correspondence with Pat Jackson, March 8, 1990.
12. Jerald F. terHorst, *Gerald Ford and the Future of the Presidency* (New York: The Third Press, 1974), p. 235.
13. Conversation with the author in terHorst's office, April 2, 1990.

14. Correspondence with Joe Eply, April 24, 1991.

15. Correspondence with Frank Wylie, October 26,1989.

16. Sam Black and Melvin L. Sharpe, *Practical Public Relations* (Englewood Cliffs, N.J.: Prentice-Hall, Inc. 1983), pp. 16–17.

17. Donald K. Wright, "Ethics in Public Relations," *Public Relations Journal*, December 1982, p. 12.

18. Robert L. Dilenschneider, *Power and Influence* (New York: Prentice Hall Press, 1990), p. 34.

19. Ibid., pp. xxvi, xxvii.

20. Warren Kalbacker, "Doing the Right Thing," *M* magazine, July 1990, p. 48.

21. Dilenschneider, *Power and Influence*, p. 41.

22. Barbara Ley Toffler, "When the Signal Is 'Move It or Lose It,' " *The New York Times*, November 17, 1991, p. F13.

23. Raymond Simon, *Public Relations: Concepts and Practices*, 3rd ed. (New York: Macmillan Publishing Co., 1984), p. 378.

24. "Common Rationalizations," *Ethics in Action*, January–February 1991, p. 2.

25. "The 100 Most Important Americans of the 20th Century," Special Issue, *Life*, Fall 1990, p. 52.

26. "Business Credibility: The Critical Factors," January 15, 1976, Conference proceeding, The Conference Board, edited by Phyllis S. McGrath, p. iv.

27. Ibid., p. 1.

28. Ibid., p. 4.

29. C. J. Silas, "The Environment: Playing to Win," *Public Relations Journal*, January 1990, p. 10.

30. John F. Budd, Jr., "Wanted: A Corporate Champion," *Manager's Journal, The Wall Street Journal*, April 16, 1990, p. A12.

31. Chester Burger, speech given at the Indiana Public Relations Conference, Indianapolis, April 19, 1990.

32. Michael Oreskes, "America's Politics Loses Way as Its Vision Changes World," *New York Times*, March 18,1990, p. 1.

33. Eugene P. Ritchie, APR, and Shelley J. Spector, "Making a Marriage Last—What Qualities Strengthen Client–Firm Bonds," *Public Relations Journal*, October 1990, p. 20.

34. Conversation with the author in terHorst's office, April 2, 1990.

35. Conversation with the author in Bernay's office, April 9, 1990.

36. Correspondence with Frank Wylie, October 26, 1989.

Chapter Nine

Implementing the Credibility Factor, Part 2

There is advice in this chapter on what to do and what not to do, the positive and negative in putting ethics to work in public relations. Being truthful and honest are on the positive side. The credibility that results when communications contain the truth is illustrated and urged by PR professionals. You are warned about the dangers of conflicts of interest, the credibility problem they can create; and there are ideas for handling conflict-of-interest situations. Problems with the misuse of the term *PR* and the resultant diminishing of credibility are also addressed.

THE CASE FOR TRUTH IN ETHICAL PUBLIC RELATIONS

"Ye shall know the truth and the truth shall make you free."

Tell the truth. How many ways can you say it? How many ways do you need to say it? Isn't it a simple statement, easy to understand? Can there be disagreement and an argument about its meaning? Why do interpretations of its meaning lead to public relations dilemmas? Do those who issue public statements, who write and print special interest publications, who edit film and videotape—or who cook up strategies or explain tragedies—need a seminar on the meaning of those three words, "Tell the truth"?

Would that it were that simple. Yes, there can be and often is disagreement about what constitutes the truth. Is it "the truth, the whole truth, nothing but the truth,'' as witnesses are called to swear in courtrooms? Or can it be the truth, meaning the absence of anything false, but something less than the whole truth? As we shall shortly see, there are supporters of both lines of thinking.

More than one PR expert (at least self-styled) have said that the truth could have been President Nixon's salvation. Had he declared early in the Watergate revelations that the burglary was wrong, named and punished the culprits, and voiced his outrage, they contend, others would have suffered disgraces while he remained in the public's good graces.

Many who practice PR say the truth can be less than the whole truth, perhaps much less. When the press calls with questions, they say, you can and should answer each truthfully, but tell no more than you are asked. So, you tell less than the whole story, or the whole truth. "Respond to the questions with the facts as requested, but nothing more," is their policy. "There's no reason to volunteer additional information."

How much to disclose? Joe Epley, a PR counselor, says you have to look at the circumstances and raise additional questions: How much needs to be disclosed? How much should the public know? What is proprietary? "As counselors," he says, "our role is to argue those issues with the attorneys and client management to ensure that the client meets the spirit as well as the law of openness required. We have an obligation to be advocates for our clients. It is . . . unethical to be reckless in our decision making.

"I don't think that the spirit of openness in public relations is like a confessional at a Baptist revival, where one gets up and spills his guts to everyone to cleanse his soul. Where is the line that says enough is enough? That's one of the biggest challenges we as practitioners have to find; and, when we come to that line, and there is still a question, we should err on the side of more disclosure. There can . . . be no compromise with honesty.''[1]

In the short-lived war between allied forces and Iraq in early 1991, U.S. television watchers were in awe at the visuals of precision bombing released by the military. The accuracy pictured was, indeed, unprecedented. Viewers were led to believe through the news briefings by officers and the videotapes they showed the journalists that the pinpoint shelling with the "smart" bombs was typical of the air war.

A few weeks after the fighting ended, Air Force Gen. Merrill A. McPeak disclosed to the news media that precision-guided bombs amounted to only about 7 percent of the tonnage dropped on Iraqi targets. In the story reporting this information from General McPeak, *The Washington Post* said it had learned from another senior Pentagon official that 70 percent of the bombs released over Iraq, mostly unguided or dumb bombs, missed their targets.

The partial truth had been that the accuracy rate of the bombing was exceptionally high; the whole truth was that, as the paper said, far more unguided bombs were dropped, and the unguided bombs were far less accurate. "The portrait that emerged . . . contrasted sharply with the high-tech, never-miss image that the Pentagon carefully cultivated during the war," said the *Post*.[2]

A missionary for the "whole truth" is Frank Wylie, former director of public relations for Chrysler Corporation, who left the business world to become a PR educator. "Tell the truth because it is the smartest thing to do, and people will begin to believe you," he advocates. "Keep telling the truth, all of it, and people *will* believe you.

"Some will say that you can't tell the whole truth. That's hogwash. If two people know something, it's public and all of it will be told sooner or later. Tell it yourself and you get first shot at the news. Tell it all and you surprise and make believers out of people. Honesty is so rare it's perhaps the most effective weapon available.

"Tell it all, and tell it first and you get the best shot at the world. Hold it back, any of it, and you'll be trying to play 'catch up' and you'll never really make it."[3]

Another distinguished PR counselor, Chester Burger, said, "I believe the best communicators will be those who, to the very limit of their ability and in good conscience, tell not half-truths for their employers or clients, but the truth, as best as they can see it. That's the only way to justify our professional and personal existence."[4]

Fred Alexander, a corporate communications manager, tells it more personally. "During my initial interview with the president of the small power company I now work for, I said, 'Please don't offer me a job if you expect me to lie, steal, or cheat for the company.' I haven't been asked to do any of those things in the nearly 10 years with [the company.]" He goes on: "I have the same inner struggles from time to time that others do. Sometimes I fail. But, I decided early in my career that a clear conscience was worth more than some kinds of work and their rewards.

"My Christian beliefs help keep me straighter than I would otherwise be. And, I remember a line from an old Maverick TV show: 'Always tell the truth—that way you don't have to remember what you said.' "[5]

Followers of the advice of these three would avoid the consequence found by Irving Kristol, writer, editor, and educator: "One of the reasons the large corporations find it so difficult to persuade the public of anything is that the public always suspects them of engaging in clever public relations instead of simply telling the truth."[6]

Truth is "the real hallmark of our profession," observes Paul A. Dowd, director of public relations at St. Anselm College. He believes that "telling the truth is one strategy which in the long run will never come back to haunt you or your client." He admits, though, that the short-term consequences may seem "too damaging." He nominates truth as the basis for all PR objectives and the anchor of any disaster plan.

Why, asks Dowd, is the PR profession almost invariably identified in the media with the tools of deceit? Writing in 1987 when interest in the U.S. sale of weapons to Iran and the alleged diversion of the proceeds to the Nicaraguan Contras was at its height, he said, "Every ploy except the truth is being tried, and 'public relations' is getting a big share of the blame." A collective opinion of columnists, he added, was that "the president's 'public relations experts' have tried every strategy possible to package and manage Irangate, all to no avail." Those whose course is to tell the truth and to operate ethically suffered, he found, "as a result of the Iran-Contra scandal and the media's invariable use of the term 'public relations' to describe public deception."[7]

James V. O'Connor, partner in a public relations counseling firm, echoes Dowd's comments. He thinks those who practice public relations "have done a poor job of developing respect for their own craft. The general public seems convinced that half-truths, cover-ups and deception are tools of the trade." Life in the real world is not like that, goes on O'Connor. "A PR person who proves to be dishonest loses credibility, and future information coming from him and his company will be viewed with skepticism."[8]

In the same philosophic camp is Epley. He believes PR people "should have the backbone" to tell their clients or employers if a message is dishonest or deceitful, and should not be used. He said on the occasion when a client asked him to do something of this nature, he has pointed out that what was requested was unethical and "they backed off." "Our role," he added, "is to help them realize that their credibility is on the line with every public statement . . . our job is to help them find an effective alternative course."[9]

Coauthors Sam Black and Melvin L. Sharpe plead the case for truth in drawing a distinction between public relations and propaganda. For a description of propaganda, they turn to a qualified source, Nazi Propaganda Minister Joseph Goebbels, who termed it "an instrument of politics, a power for social control" and added, "The function of propaganda is not essentially to convert; rather its function is to attract followers and to keep them in line."

On the other hand, say Black and Sharpe, public relations "recognizes a long-term responsibility and seeks to persuade and to achieve mutual understanding by securing the willing acceptance of attitudes and ideas." They then add: "It can succeed only when the basic policy is ethical and the means used are truthful. In public relations the ends can never justify the use of false, harmful, or questionable means."[10]

Denny Griswold, founder and editor-at-large of *PR News*, links ethics and truth when she says, "I have observed a spectacular rise in the ethical behavior of public relations practitioners. This is in large measure due to the growing recognition that public relations policy must be based on truth."[11]

One who looks back and wonders about what now seem to him as questionable reasons for deceit or cover-up is Ron Nessen, press secretary under President Ford. He remembers a time when the president wanted to play golf in Florida with former Congressman Tip O'Neill and others in a Pro–Am tournament. He says he couldn't "bring myself to look the press corps in the eye and say, 'He wants to play golf and he's going to Florida to play golf.' '' So, instead, Nessen said there had to be a meeting found that the president could attend and address in order to legitimatize the trip. Now he asks, "Why in the world didn't I just come out and tell the truth?

"It's silly little things like that where I found myself shading the truth and where, looking back on it, I think it was just a damn fool thing to do."[12]

Another former press secretary, Pierre Salinger, who served under President Kennedy, has talked about dealing with truth when national security is involved. He said that during the Cuban missile crisis there were things the United States was doing that the White House did not want to reveal to the press. The press sensed there was a hold-back of information. There was, according to Salinger, a good reason for putting restrictions on what was told the press. Whatever was told to the media was also being told to the Soviet military, he points out, and, in view of the U.S.–Russian confrontation, withholding information was necessary.[13]

LYING—ALWAYS WITH US?

"When I was a White House press secretary, I thought often of the line, 'I am not a professional liar, and I'm surprised at the extent to which in my infirmity I'm an amateur one.' I kept being surprised at the extent to which I could be an amateur liar."—Bill Moyers[14]

The man who occupied the White House in 1990 found he was the target of more than one arrow labeled *liar*. The charges came after President Bush reversed his position and announced he was ready to consider higher tax revenues as part of a budget deficit reduction plan. His critics said he lied in 1988 when he made his campaign promise of "no new taxes." His defenders, wrote columnist Garry Wills, "might say he did not lie, since he thought he was telling the truth" when he spoke the famous words in his acceptance speech at the Republican national convention, and during the contest to defeat Democratic candidate Michael Dukakis.

"Yes," continued Wills," he probably did believe. Politicians are willing to believe the most outrageous things if they happen to be saying them. But believing whatever one wants, without bothering to take in the evidence that would warrant an assertion, is a way of avoiding the truth. And that is a lie."[15]

According to a Gallup poll, 74 percent of the public didn't think Bush would keep the campaign promise.[16] In a *USA Today* poll, only 12 percent had "a great deal" of confidence in members of Congress.[17]

This loss of confidence in government did not just happen. Philosopher Sissela Bok noted that in 1975, after the public was rocked by Vietnam and Watergate, 69 percent of those responding to a national poll agreed that "over the last ten years, this country's leaders have consistently lied to the people."[18]

Two former White House press secretaries have told of instances when they lied to reporters. One did so knowingly and the other did so based on information he was given that he assumed to be factual.

Jody Powell tells of the time in 1980 when President Carter and his staff were preparing in deepest secrecy for the mission to rescue American hostages being held in Iran. Powell was informed about the project. Less than a week before the helicopters were to take off to pick up the hostages, a reporter asked him in a direct question if the government had such plans. Powell not only replied, "No," but went on to explain why there would not be such an attempt, drawing on an earlier prepared story to be used in such an event. It was a convincing lie.[19]

Larry Speakes, on the other hand, didn't know in advance about the invasion of Grenada planned by the Reagan administration in October 1983. A reporter from CBS News questioned him, "Are we going to invade Grenada today?" Speakes said he went to the National Security Council and asked Admiral Poindexter about the invasion and the reply was, "Preposterous." Speakes used the same word to answer the reporter. The next morning, U.S. troops went ashore in Grenada. A lie, unwittingly.[20] Powell, commenting on this incident in his book, supported the White House decision to deceive or lie to the journalists rather than risk the possibility of disclosure of the invasion plans. He called the deception "eminently defensible."[21]

Marvin N. Olasky, educator and former PR executive, found quite a blasé attitude where lying is concerned in interviews with members of the public relations department of one of the 10 largest corporations in the United States. He quotes an upper-level department manager: "Does the word 'lie' actually mean anything anymore? In one sense, everyone lies, but in another sense, no one does, because no one knows what's true—it's whatever makes you look good. Everybody does it. You know everyone's doing it. Like you know all those girls getting married aren't virgins, but you don't tell them to leave the white dresses home, do you?"

"To talk of lying is to live in the past," another manager said to Olasky. "I doubt if the word will even be in our everyday vocabularies in a couple of decades. There are no lies any more, just interests waiting to be served."[22]

The position that "PR can lie without lying" is offered by authors Jeff and Marie Blyskal. Their example to support this is the PR for the Cabbage Patch Kids of Coleco in 1983, "one of the greatest product PR campaigns to come along," the work of Robert S. Wiener, formerly executive vice president of Richard Wiener. Cabbage Patch Kids were, of course, the hot item of the 1983 Christmas season. Riots that bordered on violence took place in toy stores as customers jostled for what became a scarce item.

Expressing regard for public safety, Coleco announced it would reduce the demand for Cabbage Patch Kids by canceling all ads. Left unsaid was that the PR campaign continued. The PR, which had been extensive, was credited with creating the demand to a much greater extent than the modest ad program. Did Coleco lie? "Well, no," say the Blyskals. "The press simply never asked about the PR effort." They also added that Coleco found all the dolls it needed for PR promotion in major markets even though it couldn't supply enough to stores.[23]

For those who have to cope with the consequences of deception, and certainly those who are lied to by PR communicators are among those who must, the problem can be real and burdensome. "For them, to be given false information about important choices in their lives is to be rendered powerless," writes Sissella Bok. "For them, their very autonomy may be at stake."[24]

Similarly, Ethicist Michael Josephson decries the loss of autonomy even when "little white lies" are spoken, adding they "deny people . . . their ability to decide for themselves on the basis of facts." He finds lies a means of coercion.[25]

Yet, lying does have its advocates. One is Nancy Reagan, who advised that course when she was First Lady. Mrs. Reagan in 1988 asked Joan Quigley, her astrologer, not to talk to reporters. Quigley asked what she should do if questioned about a sensitive matter. Mrs. Reagan's reply, "Lie if you have to. If you have to, lie."[26]

Bok sees a "casual approach" by professionals to deception and the truth. She found this first in medicine, she writes, and then came to realize the condition existed in other professional contexts: "In law and in journalism, in government and in the social sciences, deception is taken for granted when it is felt to be excusable by those who tell the lies and who tend also to make the rules.

"Government officials and those who run for elections often deceive when they can get away with it and when they assume that the true state of affairs is beyond the comprehension of citizens. Social scientists condone deceptive experimentation on the ground that the knowledge gained will be worth having. Lawyers manipulate the truth in court on behalf of their clients. Those in selling, advertising, or any form of advocacy may mislead the public and their competitors in order to achieve their goals. Psychiatrists may distort information about their former patients to preserve confidentiality or to keep them out of military service. And journalists, police investigators, and so-called intelligence operators often have little compunction in using falsehoods to gain the knowledge they seek."[27]

Figures to lend support to Bok's statements are from a study of 211 physicians. The results: 70 percent of the doctors said they would "misrepresent a screening test" to help a patient receive coverage for a mammogram; and, a majority also would allow a male patient who had caught gonorrhea from a prostitute to deceive his wife "to preserve a marriage."[28] A form of the word *lie* can be substituted here for misrepresent and deceive.

Another supporting example, from the arena of politics and government: Republican Sen. Conrad Burns of Montana sent out a fund-raising letter that had as the opening line, "Please excuse my handwriting." There was the appearance of a personally written letter. Later, Burns confessed, "That's not my handwriting."[29]

CONFLICTS OF INTEREST

Ethics in public relations has no room for conflicts of interest. Real, actual conflicts are the worst kind, of course, but the wise

PR men and women know that perceived conflicts can also do them in, or at least subject their programs to suspicion and put their campaigns at risk. Ramifications of conflicts of interests are best seen through examples, such as those that follow.

Congressman Lights Conflict Fire with Peripheral Pursuit

Questions of conflict of interest cloud a PR activity of U.S. Representative Les Aspin of Wisconsin. Aspin, a Democrat and member of the House since 1970, started the Aspin Procurement Institute in 1986 to help bring more defense dollars to his state. A worthy purpose. Too bad that fuzzy ethical dilemma lines appear because of the conflict.

Congressman Aspin cited the success of the institute, located in Racine, Wisconsin, in television ads beamed to his district during his campaign for reelection in 1988. In a 15-month period, he said, 77 Wisconsin firms obtained $500 million in federal contracts and these orders were stimulus for 5,000 new jobs.

There was much that the ad left out, as reported by *The Milwaukee Journal*:

The Defense Department gave a grant of $150,000 of taxpayers' money to the institute. Aspin chaired the House Armed Services Committees, which reviewed the then $290 billion budget of the department.

Some of the Wisconsin firms "probably would have received the contracts without the help" of the institute.

Companies that had worked with the institute gave at least $32,000 in contributions to Aspin's campaign between the summer of 1987 and fall of 1988.

"In the politics of procurement," said the newspaper, "the line between hype and hope can be blurred."[30]

There is good reason for questions—the relationship between Aspin and his influential role as head of the Armed Services Committee, and the Defense Department; the government's annual funding for the program that operates under his name; the contributions to Aspin's campaigns from those who have worked with or been assisted by the institute.

One critic quoted by the *Journal* was David Isenberg, with the Project on Military Procurement, a Washington-based organization that checks on defense spending. "It furthers the appearance, whether justified or not, of a conflict of interest," he said.

Ralph Nader, self-appointed protector for consumers and taxpayers, said he was "astonished" to learn that Aspin's institute received Defense Department financing. Because of Aspin's committee chairmanship, said Nader, "he must have maximum independence from any appearance or reality of being obligated to the Defense Department that he is overseeing.

"The separation of powers principle is based on such an assumption."

The paper reported Aspin as saying the institute was named after him "because of his chairmanship" of the committee. "The reason it's called the Aspin Procurement Institute, frankly, is to get the attention of the Pentagon and the big defense contractors," said Aspin. "If it's called XYZ Corp. and you call over to Northrop to get them to come to a defense workshop in Wisconsin, why should they come?"[31]

At the time, according to a defense department spokesman, there were 60 similar agencies around the country receiving money from the department. None of the others, however, bore the name of a U.S. congressman.

The defense department money is less than half of the institute's operating budget. Corporate sponsors from Wisconsin match those funds. The institute is a nonprofit organization named after the congressman, who receives no income from it. He does give talks at workshops and seminars that the institute sponsors around the state. These programs present speakers from the defense department and from major contractors.

The institute gives technical assistance through staff members in Racine and Milwaukee to state firms that seek contracts with the defense department or other federal agencies. It helps businesses to meet requirements as contractors and assists them in contracting the appropriate offices.[32]

Regarding the companies that have been assisted by the institute and the contracts they've obtained, Aspin said: "There's no question that a number of them would have gotten them (contracts) on their own, and a number of them were ones we had a hand in, and others we were very influential in."

The links between companies that worked with Aspin and the institute and those that made contributions to his political campaign are not all clear, but the *Journal* gave some examples of ties. The Oshkosh Truck Co., Oshkosh, located outside Aspin's district, had received $466 million in military contracts. From July 1987 to October 1988, executives of the firm gave $3,250 to his campaign. Those at Marinette Corp., Marinette, also outside the district, which gained a $52 million contract while working with the institute, made a campaign contribution of $3,500.

The paper also reported large political contributions from companies outside Wisconsin that do business with the military. There was, for example, a total of $21,000 from five aircraft manufacturers.

Aspin's comment regarding the campaign contributions: "I guess what these people are doing is they want to make sure you hear their side of the story. It doesn't mean necessarily that you are going to do anything about it or that you believe them . . . .

"They are interested in members of the committee and then they are more interested in subcommittee chairmen and they are more interested in the chairman than the subcommittee chairmen."[33] That tells it like it is!

And here's a final comment from a different point of view. According to *Common Cause* magazine, Aspin came under fire for his insistence that the Army okay a $750 million purchase from Oshkosh Truck Co. "His demand was for 3,849 more trucks, costing an additional $500 million, than the Army wanted." Oshkosh Truck moved in to help Aspin, and to get the business it wanted. "Just two hours before the armed services procurement subcommittee voted on the amendment, Oshkosh paid six members of the subcommittee $2,000 each for attending a breakfast. Over the Army's objections, the subcommittee passed the amendment."[34]

Related conflict of interest note: Aspin, "who is leading efforts for more M-1 tanks," was reported dating a steel company executive whose firm obtained more than $6 million in M-1 contracts, according to the Associated Press. The woman, Sharon Sarton, was plant manager for Scot Forge Co., Clinton, Wisconsin, which made a mechanism related to the firing of the M-1. The report said the Aspin Institute was helping her firm compete for more defense department work. Sarton said contracts between her company and the department were won by competitive bidding.[35]

PR Firm Protects Interests of Clients, Avoids Conflict

It took more than a bit of doing at Carl Byoir & Associates, national PR firm, when counselors found themselves with a totally unexpected dilemma caused by a conflict of interest that they must resolve. As told by authors Norman R. Nager and Richard Truitt, "The firm had no way of avoiding and no way of reporting to two client companies, Honeywell and Eastman Kodak."[36] The problem: "Within a period of about seven weeks, executives of both clients called on top management supervisors at Byoir to report that each company shortly would be announcing a new product that had been in development for some time and that would represent a major advancement in consumer photography. In each case, the product was identified as the first practical, consumer-oriented, auto-focus camera lens."

Byoir executives were members of the Public Relations Society of America and committed to be guided in this instance by the society's Code of Professional Standards, which in part declares, "A member shall not represent conflicting or competing interests without the express consent of those involved, given after a full disclosure of the facts. . . ." That language tells one to avoid conflicts, but doesn't tell how.

Byoir developed the answer to "how," and in doing so illustrated several of what Nager-Truitt call "conflict management approaches." Here's what happened:

The Byoir supervisor for each account safeguarded the significant trade secrets while moving ahead with plans for the announcements.

Each brought essential Byoir personnel into the loop, with clients' permission, and the problem surfaced.

Neither client was told of the other's secrets, as it would be unethical for a supervisor to tell one client of the other's competing development.

Byoir asked the clients to obtain help for this assignment from another public relations company "because of a product conflict that exists within the firm." Neither Honeywell nor Eastman

Kodak accepted the suggestion, each professing its faith in Byoir's ability to keep its project confidential.

The two groups within Byoir proceeded "with remarkably little leakage." Each announcement received good media coverage, and Byoir demonstrated that, at least for a short time, it could separate two competing projects.

This example can serve as an object lesson for other PR people who find themselves facing similar conflict situations. While they can accept guidance in this, they will need the sensitivity and the dedication shown by those at Byoir.

Speaking in a more general way, Joe Epley, who heads a PR counseling firm in Charlotte, North Carolina, said that a potential client approaching the firm is informed if there may be a conflict of interest with an existing client. He said there had been times when the clients determined there was no conflict—but they made the decision. At times, obvious conflicts arose in attempting to serve two clients, and the relationship with one was ended immediately. "We err on the side of caution to ensure that there will be no misunderstanding later," he added.[37]

Financial Interests Lead to Conflicts for Doctors

There is a growing trend for physicians to own laboratories and other health-care facilities to which they can refer patients. Sometimes the ownership is open and known, an overt operation with appropriate public relations; other times, the interest is undisclosed.

Regardless of whether the financial interest of the doctor is known, these developments, although bona fide business ventures, have generated concern about conflicts of interests. Is the ability of the doctor to exercise independent professional judgment influenced by personal considerations, such as financial gain? The answer is in the affirmative, according to a report of the Inspector General of the Department of Health and Human Services. This report claims that doctors with these interests prescribed 45 percent more clinical services for Medicare patients than did other physicians. The cost of these services to the Medicare program was $28 million in 1987.[38]

How to eliminate these conflicts of interest and reduce health-care costs? Legislation was thought to be the way. A bill introduced by Rep. Fortney Stark, California Democrat, in 1989 would have prohibited doctors from referring patients to facilities in which they held financial interests. The bill was opposed by the American Medical Association until it died in Congress. This public relations conflict continued into 1991, when there were these related developments. The government issued regulations that curtailed referrals of Medicare and Medicaid patients by doctors to medical labs and other facilities in which they have an interest. A Florida State University report indicated labs in which physicians had ownership charged more and tended to receive more referrals from doctor-investors than other such facilities. On the heels of these two announcements, the AMA took a different position. It told doctors they must tell patients when they are referred to a medical facility in which the physician has a financial stake. AMA General Counsel Kirk Johnson said there was no study that "conclusively" showed physician abuse, "but [the studies] do shift the burden on the profession to either explain itself or better communicate what the ethical issues are."[39]

In December 1991, the association's house of delegates adopted even tougher guidelines. These prohibited members from referring patients to a healthcare facility at which they did not practice but in which they had an investment interest, unless "there is a demonstrated need in the community for the facility and alternative financing is not available." The AMA said that in such situations persons outside the medical profession should have opportunity to invest, and the return on physicians' investments should relate to their equity in the facility.[40]

Journalists March for Cause and Step into Conflict

Journalists traditionally have avoided taking sides publicly on political and most other issues. How, for example, can a reporter be involved as an activist for a particular issue, then maintain objectivity while covering and writing about it? Clearly, a conflict of interest.

Journalists from *The New York Times* and *The Washington Post* ignored the conflict-of-interest policies of their papers when they marched to support abortion rights in Washington in 1989. Editors at the papers said that "they believed the breaches were unwitting errors that stemmed from confusion over what was allowed and what was prohibited." The editors added that they would increase efforts to broaden understanding of their policies.[41]

The incident generated discussion among editors as to what constitutes conflict. A reporter who covered abortion issues would not be allowed to participate in an abortion demonstration. But what if the reporter covers banking or agriculture? The concern of the media is to protect their credibility. Even perception of conflict can lessen this protection.

MISUSE AND ABUSE OF PR TERM

People use *PR* and *public relations* interchangeably, but neither has a common meaning to all—and more's the pity. The lack of a generally accepted definition by all who use the term clouds understanding and credibility. Why is this so? How did it happen? Why isn't there a neat, compact sense of the term that means the same to all? One answer comes from PR Counselor John Budd, who says, "Public relations as a term has been debased by misuse, overuse, and abuse."[42]

Edward Bernays, who in 1920 adopted the term *public relations counsel*, its first use, found there are 51 different titles used to designate a person who practices public relations. He described an incident in which a young lady phoned him at his home in Cambridge, Massachusetts, and asked if she could meet with him. He asked her, "What do you do?" She replied that she was in public relations. "And what do you do?" asked Bernays again. "I'm in public relations," was her answer. I understand what you said, Bernays replied, but tried once more, "What do you really do" The response: "I give out circulars in Harvard Square."[43]

What can you expect when you find such newspaper headlines as:

"Dear Japan, save the PR and just send the cash."
"Games may be PR coup for China."
"Army loses PR battle."
"Bush cranks up PR push for Coloradan, others."
"Cuomo's Real Race: Seeking a Victory in Public Relations, Too."

Or references such as the following in newspaper and magazine articles?

"It is about Power and Recognition, which, when looked at together, is Washington's way of saying 'PR.' "
"It follows other instances of bad judgment. You have a public relations problem."
"It's as if the business conducted in City Hall is day-by-day public relations instead of sober management of the politics of scarcity."
"Some have tried to block the reports from public view to prevent 'bad P.R.' "
"Is government in this nation just another permutation of the insidious art of P.R.?"
"In the past, scientific conferences have usually been forums for the expression of different opinions, but the asbestos partisans have turned them into public relations vehicles."[44]

Not only are the terms applied in different contexts of meanings, but notice there is lack of agreement on the use of periods after the *PR* letters. And, incidentally, how do you drive a public relations vehicle?

Pollsters contribute to the problem. *The Wall Street Journal/ NBC News* poll reported on December 13, 1990, a few weeks before the allied forces began air attacks on Iraq after its invasion of Kuwait, the following question put to 1,002 registered voters:

"Do you think (the release of the hostages) is a real and sincere effort to find a peaceful solution to the situation in the Persian Gulf . . . or just a public-relations gesture to put pressure on the U.S. not to attack Iraq?"

The survey disclosed, incidentally, that 78 percent viewed the hostage release as a public relations gesture.[45]

And television makes a contribution to the confusion. One example is the words spoken by a soap opera actress: "I'll bet money this is a PR manipulation."

These quotes lead us to an apropos comment from coauthors Allen Center and Pat Jackson: "The term *public relations* is often confusing because it is used inaccurately. Used correctly, public relations describes the *processes* of practice—the techniques, strategies, structures, and tactics of the field. As such, the term is analogous to law, medicine, nursing, etc.

"To often, public relations is also used to describe the *outcomes* of effective practice—so we hear of good public relations, which technically means good techniques or strategies. The proper term for the desired outcomes of public relations practices is public *relationships*. An organization with effective public relations will attain positive public relationships."[46]

POINTS

- You may worry that you'll sound like a moralist if you constantly advocate for the truth in the public relations activities of the organization you're involved with. So be sure to point out the practical side, the earned credibility that will result.

* As a step to ascertain that plans and programs are honest and straightforward, ask questions. Don't be satisfied with elusive answers.

* Don't deal in degrees of lying. It's a kind of deceit regardless of how it is used, or regardless of the scope of the lie. And remember that an exposed lie in a public relations action damages not only the credibility of the project it relates to but casts a cloud over those involved long after.

* Conflicts of interest are not hard to spot, except when they're covered up. If you find yourself in a conflict situation, be open about it and talk to the parties affected about a practical way to end it. Be wary too when the conflict is more perceived than real; you may need to clear up the perception to avoid undermining of credibility.

* Take care that you and those you work with treat *PR* as a term with respect. Object to detractors who use it in derogatory ways.

NOTES

1. Correspondence with Joe Epley, April 24, 1991.
2. Barton Gellman, "U.S. Bombs Missed 70% of Time," *The Washington Post*, March 16, 1991, p. A1.
3. Correspondence with Frank Wylie, October 26, 1989.
4. Chester Burger, speech given at the Indiana Public Relations Conference, Indianapolis, April 19, 1990.
5. Correspondence with Fred Alexander, June 25, 1990.
6. Marvin N. Olasky, "Ministers or Panderers: Issues Raised by the Public Relations Society Code of Standards," *Journal of Mass Media Ethics*, 1, no. 1 (1985–86).

7. Paul A. Dowd, "On the Record," *Public Relations Journal*, July, 1987, p. 22.

8. James V. O'Connor, "The Whole Truth and Nothing But," *The Rotarian*, October, 1989, p. 15.

9. Correspondence with Joe Epley, April 24, 1991.

10. Sam Black and Melvin L. Sharpe, *Practical Public Relations*, (Englewood Cliffs, N.J.: Prentice Hall, 1983), p. 7.

11. Correspondence with Denny Griswold, March 19, 1992.

12. "The Presidency, the Press & the People," coproduction of KPBS-TV and University of California, San Diego, taped January 5, 1990.

13. Ibid.

14. Bill Moyers, *A World of Ideas* (New York: Doubleday, 1989), p. 236.

15. Garry Wills, "Bush Proves Reckless with the Truth," *Rocky Mountain News*, July 5, 1990, p. 45.

16. The *Gallup Poll Monthly*, May, 1990, p. 24.

17. Bob Minzesheimer, "Poll: Many Say Congress 'Corrupt,' " *USA Today*, June 2, 1989, p. 1A.

18. Sissela Bok, *Lying* (New York: Vintage Books, 1978), p. xviii.

19. "The Presidency, the Press & the People."

20. Ibid.

21. Jody Powell, *The Other Side of the Story* (New York: William Morrow, 1984), p. 233.

22. Marvin N. Olasky, "Inside the Amoral World of Public Relations: Truth Molded for Corporate Gain," *Business and Society Review*, Winter 1985, pp. 43–44.

23. Jeff and Marie Blyskal, *PR—How the Public Relations Industry Writes the News* (New York: William Morrow, 1985), pp. 120–24.

24. Bok, *Lying*, p. xvii.

25. Moyers, *A World of Ideas*, p. 25.

26. "Intelligence Report," *Parade*, April 1, 1990, p. 6.

27. Bok, *Lying*, p. xvii.

28. Dennis H. Novack, M.D.; Barbara J. Detering, M.D.; Robert Arnold, M.D.; Lachlan Forrow, M.D.; Morrissa Ladinsky; John C. Pezzullo, Ph.D., "Physicians' Attitudes toward Using Deception to Resolve Difficult Ethical Problems," *JAMA*, May 26, 1989, p. 2980.

29. "Minor Memos," *The Wall Street Journal*, October 20, 1989, p. A1.

30. John Fauber and James Rowen, "The Aspin Institute: Politics of Defense," *The Milwaukee Journal*, December 4, 1988, p. 26A.

31. Ibid.

32. Statement of Susan Greenfield, communication specialist in Racine, Wis., office of institute, March 26, 1992.

33. "Defense Industry Aids Aspin," *The Milwaukee Journal*, December 4, 1988, p. 26A.

34. Jean Cobb, "Top Brass," *Common Cause*, May/June 1989, p. 23.

35. Associated Press, "Aspin Push for More Tanks Helps Girlfriend, Paper Says," *Rocky Mountain News*, June 2, 1991, p. 44.

36. Norman R. Nager and Richard Truitt, *Strategic PR Counseling* (New York: Longman, Inc., 1987), pp. 231–33.

37. Correspondence with Joe Epley, April 24, 1991.

38. Kenneth H. Bacon, "Physicians Who Own Labs Prescribed 45% More Tests on Medicare Patients," *The Wall Street Journal*, May 1, 1989, p. B4.

39. "Patients Must Be Told of MD's Lab Investment," *Rocky Mountain News*, September 7, 1991, p. 4.

40. "AMA Adopts Tough Rules on Doctors' 'Self Referrals,' " *The Wall Street Journal*, December 11, 1991, p. B3.

41. Alex S. Jones, "Demonstration Renews Question of Conflict for Newspapers," *The New York Times*, April 16, 1989, p. A28.

42. John F. Budd, Jr., Schranz Lecture, Ball State University, November 30, 1989.

43. Conversation with author in Bernay's office, April 9, 1991.

44. Headlines and excerpts of articles are from various issues of the *Rocky Mountain News*, *The Denver Post*, *The New York Times*, and *Harper's* magazine.

45. Gerald F. Seib and Michel McQueen, "Poll Finds Americans Feel Hawkish toward Iraq but Would Grant Some Concessions to Avoid War," *The Wall Street Journal*, December 13, 1990, p. A16.

46. Allen H. Center and Patrick Jackson, *Public Relations Practice: Managerial Case Studies and Problems*, 4th ed., (Englewood Cliffs, N.J.: Prentice Hall, 1990), p. 2.

Chapter Ten

Beyond the Credibility Factor

Those who criticize PR communicators for failing to level, to tell the truth, even to lie, also charge them with the more subtle forms of unethical conduct—manipulation, influence peddling, deceit and subterfuge, cheating, even forms of bribery. These are broad attacks, indeed. Are they justified? Are these the intent of the words and actions of those whose goals are to affect the minds of others, to sway and persuade them to change their opinions and habits?

There are in the world of PR those who deserve such criticism. Yet, these are in the minority, a small minority. The brush that paints these judgmental words has a broad stroke and tars many of ethical standing. Yet, because there are those so charged by their critics, and they do exist, we acknowledge their existence and present examples of these behaviors and their effect on credibility.

MANIPULATION

Manipulators is one of the less flattering words used to label PR communicators. To repeat the point for emphasis—most of the time it's not deserved; sometimes it is. The word is used often enough in this association, though, that many among the public find this a fitting adjective for PR people.

Spin Control: Twisting What Was Said to Mean Something Else

Looking into the White House during the administration of former President Reagan, we see what is alleged to be "controlling the political agenda by controlling the media," an example of manipulation.

This account comes from Mark Hertsgaard, on the basis of interviews with former deputy White House press secretary Leslie Janka and former deputy chief of staff Michael Deaver, who both served in the Reagan administration: "The Reagan White House 'came to the conclusion that the media will take what we feed them,' explained Janka. 'They've got to write their own story every day. You give them their story, they'll go away. The phrase is "manipulation by inundation."

'You give them the line of the day, you give them press briefings, you give them facts, access to people who will speak on the record. . . And you do that long enough, they're going to stop bringing their own stories, stop being investigative reporters of any kind, even modestly so.'

" 'I think that's true,' added Deaver. 'The only day I worried about was Friday, because it's a slow news day. That was the day that bothered me most, because if you didn't have anything, they'd go find something.' "[1]

Spin control is a name for a special kind of manipulation, managing the news, most often found in the political arena. It's an attempt to apply to words already spoken, say by a candidate for office or an official in the White House or other administrative post, a different meaning from what they at first seemed to say— to put what was said in a perspective that is more favorable to the speaker, or more palatable to the audience, or both.

Columnist Marty Schram provided an example of applying spin in mid-1990 when President Bush departed from his "read my lips . . . no new taxes" position—a campaign promise of 1988—and declared himself willing to support "tax revenue increases." These words were in a typewritten statement of three paragraphs tacked onto the bulletin board in the White House press room. "The White House then lapsed into a three-pronged effort at spin control," said Schram.

One prong had then–Chief of Staff John Sununu dashing to Capitol Hill "to assure apoplectic conservatives that the president really hadn't said anything new." Another had Press Secretary Marlin Fitzwater summoning reporters "to explain that the president had decided to issue this statement as a new and significant assurance for Democrats." Each applied a particular brand of spin to suit the audience. For the third, Schram said, the president hid behind his desk for days so he wouldn't have to reply to questions from the media "asking if he'd meant to say something new or something old."

The furor on the Hill and elsewhere on what the president meant, or meant to say, didn't subside. When Bush finally emerged for a press conference, wrote Schram, he gave what "turned out to be his weakest and least-convincing performance as president." There were ineffective comparisons with times of travail for President Lincoln and "Repeatedly, Bush fuzzed and fudged, ducked and dodged."[2] You can't always manipulate, or win them all, with spin control.

It's a Service—"Highly Manipulative" Is the Charge

We find another kind of manipulation introduced by a marketing professor, Donald E. Vinson. He founded (in 1979) and is chairman of Litigation Sciences, Inc., which has been credited with, or blamed for, "quietly but inexorably reshaping the world of law."

Self-described as a full-service behavioral trial consulting firm, Litigation Sciences modestly proclaims to lawyers, "We can help you win your case," and adds, "When it comes to predicting jury verdicts, we've been right 96% of the time." According to *The Wall Street Journal*, "The firm provides pretrial opinion polls, creates profiles of 'ideal' jurors, sets up mock trials and 'shadow' juries, coaches lawyers and witnesses, and designs courtroom graphics."[3]

How do you make this happen? You gather, as Litigation Sciences has, a group of psychologists, sociologists, communications experts, mathematicians, graphics artists, and technicians numbering more than 100. Twenty-one of these specialists have Ph.D. degrees. They form a team of experts in behavioral sciences.

Writing in 1982 under the headline "Psychological Anchors: Influencing the Jury," Vinson pointed out that lawyers persuade juries, or try to, just as advertisers persuade the public, or try to. Advertisers, he said, have generally accepted and put to work the results of extensive research into the techniques of persuasion, but "lawyers have been less willing to learn from social science." He claimed that in an appropriate case, adding a social scientist to the litigation team could "make the difference between success and failure."[4]

Vinson entered the world of litigation consulting in 1977, when he was hired by International Business Machines Corp. (IBM) to help defend a complex $300 million antitrust suit in a federal district court in California. The plaintiff was California Computer Products of Anaheim. At the time, Vinson was a marketing professor at the University of Southern California.

This was a case with highly technical aspects. IBM trial lawyers wanted to make the puzzling details as understandable as possible to the jurors. They also sought a way to learn if they were getting through to the jurors, and whether the jurors were keeping up with them, as they presented their case.

The IBM counsel had conceived the idea of engaging an expert in behavioral science to recruit a jury that would mirror the demographic and psychological traits of the actual jurors, according to Vinson. Through this "shadow jury," the corporate lawyers hoped to evaluate the extent to which jurors, without understanding of the technical issues, would understand what was going on in court.

Vinson was selected to recruit the shadow jury and supervise the project. He hired six people who demographically would closely match members of the jury. "Our hypothesis was that if we could get inside the mind of a juror while the plaintiff presented its case," said Vinson, "the attorneys for the defense could learn much that would be useful in the development of their own tactics and strategy and assist them in communicating with the jury."[5]

Vinson taught the surrogate jurors to assume psychologically the role of jurors. They acted and reacted in all ways as nearly as possible like the real jurors. They observed everything the actual jurors observed, heard everything they heard, and respected the same admonitions of the court. They even left the courtroom whenever the actual jurors did.

Vinson's role was that of an independent, objective researcher. He did not enter the courtroom during the trial. The shadow jurors reported to him by phone each evening. He asked them questions structured to elicit their feelings about the courtroom proceedings, the lawyers, the witnesses, the exhibits, even their general reactions to the case. From their answers he made notes that were used to prepare memos for the IBM attorneys. IBM won the case and Vinson decided to set up his firm. A large number of its clients have been defendants in product-liability cases.

Research services of Vinson and his staff may include simulated jury deliberation groups and full-scale trial simulation. In the former, individuals who are demographically similar to those who would be on the actual jury are presented with plaintiff and defense testimony and then observed while they are deliberating. Trial simulations may find jurors focusing on issues that attorneys had not considered to be important. They enable an attorney to see how jurors react to the issues of the case as well as to the personal style, body language, and mannerisms of the attorney and those of the witnesses. Jurors in the simulation trial may complete questionnaires that make it possible to compile juror profiles to identify attitudinal and demographic factors that characterize people who are likely to vote for the defense, or the plaintiff—or likely to award exorbitant damages.

Through pretrial surveys, trial simulations, and post-trial interviews, LSI has found that 80 to 90 percent of all jurors come to their decisions during or immediately after the opening statements. They then watch, as the case progresses, for facts to support their view. Drawing on such findings, the firm's consultants suggest numerous tactics to their clients/attorneys. Litigation Sciences strongly emphasizes that lawyers must understand how jurors think. The firm says its jury research "gives you the competitive edge."

An important asset of the firm is a database of interviews with 35,000 surrogate and actual jurors. From these, the staff has prepared basic concepts of juror psychology that can be valuable to lawyers in preparing for trials. The firm also conducts opinion surveys, phone calls to several hundred persons selected on the basis of characteristics of the venue, to gather data on attitudes regarding key issues in a case.

Litigation Sciences introduced a system for presenting visuals in the courtroom based on laser disc technology in 1989. With this, attorneys can have access to 54,000 electronic images: documents, charts, combinations of videotape and graphics, animated graphics, and taped verbal testimony from witnesses or experts. Through testing with jury simulations, a lawyer can make final selections of visuals/images for trial use.

Litigation counseling has grown and Litigation Sciences, now a unit of Saatchi & Saatchi PLC, Great Britain's advertising giant, has competition—some 300 other firms, many with only one or two members. Annual gross income for the industry was estimated at near $200 million in 1989.

While you might find litigation counseling on one side or both of a high-stakes court case, you'll also find its critics.

"Highly manipulative," is the censorious comment of Donald Zoeller, a New York trial attorney. "The notion they try to sell is that juries don't make decisions rationally," he said. "But the effort is also being made to try and cause jurors not to decide things rationally. I find it troubling." Zoeller does admit litigation consultants can be effective and thinks things may have gotten to the point where, if a case is large enough, it's almost malpractice not to use them.[6]

Among lawyers who question the use and the need for the consultants, some say successful trial lawyers have intuitively employed such tactics, in a less formal manner. "The essence of being a trial lawyer is understanding how people of diverse backgrounds react to you and your presentations," according to Barry Ostrager, of Simpson Thacher & Bartlett, who was victorious in a case of insurers against Shell Oil Co.[7]

Another critic is Amitai Etzioni, a sociologist at George Washington University. One of his concerns is the cost, which gives the advantage to litigants with the wherewithal to afford the services. He says, "The affluent people and the corporations can buy it, the poor radicals (in political cases) get it free, and everybody in between is at a disadvantage, and that's not the kind of system we want."

Etzioni has other concerns. One is what has been called the "skillful massage" of the jury system by the litigation consultants. "There's no reason to believe that juries rule inappropriately," he avers. "But the last thing you want to do is manipulate the subconscious to make them think better. What you then do is you make them think inappropriately."

He has suggestions that would reduce the effectiveness of the litigation consultants. One is to more severely limit the number of challenges lawyers have in jury selection, a step that would reduce the number they can remove from the jury panel. Another is to prohibit the gathering of background information about jurors, which can lead to intensive investigations of their personal lives. As the situation now is, what are the litigant experts doing—helping the client to pick prejudiced jurors?[8]

"If the trend in the use of these consultants continues to grow," according to Judith Dancoff, Los Angeles journalist, "there will be more issues to confront than simply ethical ones.

"While many states do not at present ban background investigations of jurors, and no cases have yet been filed for invasion of privacy, such events are conceivable if juror investigations become more widespread, or their techniques more invasive."[9]

We're talking here about a service barely a dozen years old, and enjoying an expanding market. Obviously, there is a clash of opinions. On the one hand are those in the business who feel what they do is legitimate and helps decide justice. "We're an extension of your team," boasts Litigation Sciences. On the other hand are those who see all this as a manipulation of the justice system. They see tampering that corrupts the outcome of legal disputes.

There's a lot of public relations and communication here. What we have for some is an ethical dilemma based on manipulation. For others, there's nothing to get upset about.

Some Say It's Manipulation. Even So, the News Media Eat It Up.

Is it a stunt? Is it manipulation? Is it ethical? What you know for sure is that it's a TV ad created with the expectation that the television networks will find it unacceptable and valuable publicity will be created in the turndown. And the product will benefit from the exceptional exposure.

Case in point: No Excuses jeans and its ad agency, Lois/GGK. In 1990, this agency filmed a commercial starring a notorious celebrity, Marla Maples, the companion of entrepreneur Donald Trump, as a "spokes-celebrity." In the commercial, she urged the audience to clean up the environment as she did her part by trashing two of the weekly tabloids, *National Enquirer* and *Star*, which gave generously of their space to talk not always in flattering words about her affair with Trump. Network TV officials thought this was namecalling and unacceptable, and refused to air it.

Horrors, screamed George Lois, agency head. He lost no time transmitting news releases of complaint to the media. And he sat back to enjoy a blitz of publicity every bit as great as he'd hoped for. He hadn't bought any network time. No Excuses really didn't have that kind of money. As *The Wall Street Journal* said, "The stunt was a textbook case of advertising flackery, of media manipulation."

"No Excuses started with an impossibly puny ad budget, created a controversial commercial that it couldn't afford to air with any frequency on the major networks . . . then used the shock value of the network's rejection to get free publicity."[10]

Television stations across the country aired the story. In New York City, *Newsday* ran an illustration from the commercial in full color on the front page. Gloating over the wide exposure, Lois claimed that without running their ad once "it still looks like we spent $50 million." He said he didn't consider this kind of deceit to be manipulative. Not everyone would agree.

There are similar cases to point to, also reported by *The Wall Street Journal*. "Several ad agencies," according to the paper, "have made a living out of creating scandalous commercials almost purely for their publicity value." In one instance, another ad agency, Della Femina McNamee, with its eye on the network-rejection value, produced an ad campaign for Lifestyles condoms with the message, "I enjoy sex, but I'm not ready to die for it." Success again. There was network turndown, and the media loved the story.

Jerry Della Femina, then chairman of the agency, said he held his breath almost literally until he heard such a commercial has been censored. "What if they said yes?" he asked. "What would I do then? I wouldn't have the money to run it. The networks don't understand that the way they can kill us is to give us our way."[11]

There seems little likelihood that the network censors will change, at least as long as the agencies take care to be sure their creations are on the unacceptable side. What at first looks like a lot of unproductive thrashing around by the agencies really isn't, when you realize that, after all, they do reach their goal. The setting of such a goal can be questioned, however. For in achieving the goal, the agencies surely utilize a practice that is unethical in public relations and business.

INFLUENCE PEDDLING

The New York Times headline cried "Japan's Loud Voice in Washington," and the story quoted a study by the U.S. State Department that claimed "Japanese influence peddling at every level."[12]

Targeted in the article was the Toshiba Corporation of Japan. Two years earlier Congress had condemned the firm for illegal sales of high technology equipment to Russia and there was talk of the United States getting tough with sanctions. There was "little more than a slap on the wrist" for Toshiba in the trade legislation that passed later in Congress. The more favorable treatment was said to have come through assistance given to Toshiba by its high-powered group of lobbyists—former Congressmen and senior administration officials.

The campaign of Toshiba to influence the political climate cost some $30 million. This included fees, whose recipients included James R. Jones, a former Democratic representative from Oklahoma who was chairman of the House Budget Committee and at the time of the article the chairman of the American Stock Exchange; Michael D. Barnes, former Democratic representative from Maryland; former officials in the Nixon White House, Leonard Garment and Stanton D. Anderson; and William N. Walker, former deputy U.S. trade representative.

The focus on Toshiba was to make a point. The state department study, prepared by its Center for Study of Foreign Affairs, saw the broader scale and growing trend and said, "The U.S. has been penetrated—not only by Japanese autos and VCRs, but by Japanese influence peddling at every level."

Is it ethical for former senior officials of the United States to work for the Japanese? The response to this question from Nobutoshi Akao, an economics minister at the Japanese Embassy in Washington, was, "If the American legal system allows it, we are not in a position to say anything against it." He also pointed out that while Japanese companies may have influence, so do those of other foreign countries.

There are some differences he didn't mention. There were lobbyists in the capital employed by more than 250 Japanese government agencies, industry associations, and companies, according to the 1989 directory of Washington representatives—a figure that easily qualified the country for first place. Next was Canada, with 90.

Cost estimates for this Japanese "influence" representation in Washington vary. Sixty million dollars was the figure for 1989, four times that of 1984, according to some congressional aides. Pat Choate, vice president of policy analysis for TRW, was said to put the number at closer to $100 million.

The figure is just for direct lobbying. *Business Week* magazine told of further amounts spent by the Japanese to win friends and influence people: $45 million in public relations, $140 million on corporate philanthropy, and $30 million on academic research grants.

What's the payoff for these expenditures? The *Times* said, "Because of the ubiquitous and amorphous nature of Washington lobbying, which takes place at dinner parties, receptions, trade association meetings, congressional hearings, or simply on the telephone, it is often difficult, if not impossible, to assess a lobbyist's influence.

"Yet with so many well-paid former American government officials acting as eyes and ears of the Japanese government or industry, Tokyo has unparalleled knowledge of what's happening inside the United States government. Often the lobbyists will know the progress of an issue before mid-level Washington officials do."[13]

The U.S. face of the Japanese lobby is illustrated in another way. A report, released in 1989, dealing with ways to handle U.S. Japanese trade problems was prepared by the Committee for Economic Development, a respected U.S. group of business and academic leaders, and a counterpart group from Japan. Heading U.S. delegates who helped prepare the report was William D. Eberle, former U.S. trade representative, who was president and half owner of a Washington consulting firm, Manchester Associates. Nissan was one of its clients. Leader of the Japanese team for the report was the chairman of Nissan. There was no reference to Eberle's relationship with Nissan in the report or at the news conference to announce it. There was deceit, intentional or accidental, in ignoring this connection.

Currying of influence by the Japanese through U.S. lobbyists with ties to the executive and legislative branches might be more palatable if there were a counterpart. There seems to be no reciprocity. The *Times* reported that a U.S. businessman asked an official of Japan's Ministry of Trade and Industry what would happen in the reverse—if his U.S. company hired a former high-level Japanese government official to represent it in Tokyo. "The official replied, 'It would not happen, but if it did we would pay him not the slightest heed. We would treat him courteously, but he would become a social leper.' "

From a former U.S. Senator, Republican John Heinz of Pennsylvania, came this comment: "It's a national tragedy. So many people who once worked to further the national interest go to work for Japan. In Japan, anyone doing that would be ostracized for life."[14]

Influence Peddlers among Faculty of the Washington Campus

Then there's the "graduate school of influence peddling," as it was dubbed by *The Wall Street Journal*, operating in our nation's capital. The executive director, Antoinette Pace Durkin, says it offers educational seminars to give corporate executives an understanding of "how the process works." For sure, it's a PR communication program that allows for questions of ethics.[15]

Its name is The Washington Campus—even though it has no campus. Meeting facilities in hotels and clubs, and even congressional offices, serve as classrooms. The faculty? Its members include members of Congress and their staffs, senior White House and other executive branch officials, lobbyists, nationally recognized political consultants, journalists, college professors, and corporate representatives. Their pay? Well, it's in dollars, of course, but it's not referred to as a salary or contractual fee. It's called an honorarium, except for members of Congress, who were forced to give up honoraria (U.S. representatives in 1991, U.S. senators in 1992) in exchange for hefty salary increases. For them, the pay becomes teaching income. Now, isn't that pretty smooth?

Among the regulars on the faculty has been Sen. Donald Riegle, Michigan Democrat, who received $1,000 for a 45-minute talk on the workings of Congress and his life as a legislator. He spoke 22 times, probably with the same general comments each time, in 1989. Over five years, his earnings in honoraria came to $90,000 from The Washington Campus.

Riegle was chairman of the Senate Banking Committee and had a policy of refusing honoraria from firms whose products or services might be of concern to his committee. Despite this, in March, 1990, he took home $1,000 from The Washington Campus in exchange for a talk to Citicorp executives. He's also taken part in programs presented to representatives from John Hancock Mutual Life Insurance Co. and Aetna Life and Casualty Co. All of these corporations have close interests in pending legislation and hearings of Reigle's committee. The rationale for his appearances before them was that the remarks were generic, not slanted to the financial community.

Another faculty member is Kevin C. Gottlieb, who served as staff director of Reigle's committee in 1989 and 90. Gottlieb was a member of Riegle's staff and accompanied his boss on a visit to operations of Lincoln Savings & Loan in March 1987. Reigle's contacts with Lincoln and Charles Keating, chairman of its parent corporation, brought him $76,000 in a campaign contribution (later returned) from Keating. The relationship also qualified him as a member of the Keating Five, senators whose alleged influence-peddling activities with the Federal Home Loan Bank on behalf of Lincoln received close scrutiny by the Senate Ethics Committee.

There is more about Gottlieb. After he resigned from Riegle's staff in mid-1987, and for 18 months before he became staff director of the Senate Banking Committee, he received $85,000 in consulting fees from the American Bankers Association. His other income in that time included $105,000, earned as chairman of Riegle's 1988 reelection campaign and $535,000 as head of the Outdoor Advertising Association, trade group for billboard companies.

The list of faculty and guest speakers has included more names of note. There are Roger B. Porter, assistant to President Bush for economic and domestic policy; Sidney L. Jones, assistant secretary of treasury for economic policy in the Bush administration (members of the executive branch can't accept speaking honoraria); Anne Wexler, assistant to President Carter for public liaison; David R. Gergen, assistant to President Reagan for communications; and Charles E. Walker, former deputy secretary of the treasury. Gergen is editor-at-large, *U.S. News & World Report*, and Wexler and Walker are lobbyists. Others from Congress are Republican Sen. Robert Dole, senate minority leader; Democratic Rep. Richard E. Gephardt, House majority leader; and Democratic senators Ernest F. Hollings and Timothy E. Wirth.

The fee charged by The Washington Campus for the 1990–91 series was $2,500 per person for a six-day session "limited to participants selected from among upper-middle or top-level executives who apply or are nominated by their organizations." The charge included daily breakfast and lunch, two receptions and dinners, and local transportation.[16] Shorter sessions are presented for individual companies for a fee of $1,300 per person.

Some companies are strong "repeat" supporters. United Technologies Corp. sent 22 groups between 1985 and 1990.

Some groups are sizable. Five management committee members and five senior officers of John Hancock attended one three-day session.

The idea for The Washington Campus came from William Seidman, former chairman of the Federal Deposit Insurance Corp., who founded the nonprofit organization in 1978. He had served President Ford as economic advisor and in that position became convinced that businessmen needed a better understanding of "how Washington worked." A consortium of colleges and universities joined with him. He and his wife obtained funding from several companies and foundations. Although Seidman is no longer active, he's an honorary member of the board; Mrs. Seidman was still a board member in 1992.

There is a summer program of The Washington Campus for which 100 graduate business students from the member universities are selected to attend a four-week intensive session. Tuition cost is $1,500. The curriculum for 1990 offered four courses: "Policy Development in the Executive Branch," "Congress and the Legislative Process," "The Formation of Economic Policy," and "Government Regulation." The faculty and guest lecturers include some of the same persons who talk to the business representatives and others in government, public policy, business, and journalism.

Imitators followed what they apparently viewed as the success of The Washington Campus. Universities in the Washington area and think tanks, such as the Brookings Institution, offered similar seminars. The fascination even extended to politicians. Sen. Tim Wirth, Colorado Democrat, offers the Wirth Washington Seminar, where for a $250 per person fee fellow Coloradans can absorb the wisdom of senators, regulators, White House advisers, and other big fish in the capital pool.

There apparently is a mystique surrounding Washington figures that leads those from outside the beltway to want to see them, touch them, talk to them—as well as ask them for favors. Catering, even pandering, to such desires seems amiss in an ethical world. The intentions of Seidman and others in offering their seminars may have been honorable. But suggestions of influence peddling have weakened the ethical standings of his and similar programs.

Closeout note regarding influence peddling: A caustic comment came from *The Wall Street Journal* on the quitting by Henry Guigni of his job as the U.S. Senate sergeant-at-arms at age 65. He reportedly was to join a Washington lobbying firm, which led the paper to say, "We don't begrudge Mr. Guigni his new riches, but we do wish his benefactors in Congress would drop their pretense that Capitol Hill is anything but an influence peddling pleasure palace. . . . If it were something better, no one in Washington would think it worthwhile to pay a 65-year-old former policeman $300,000 to 'find new business.' "[17]

Deceit/Deception: Kant Advised That All Deception Is Morally Wrong

Deception and deceit are among the uncomplimentary adjectives used to describe PR communicators and the work they do—and to comment on their kind of ethics. Deceit has no specified life span. Sometimes it is short-lived, may consist of only one incident, flash through the public mind for less than a day; in other instances the public relations subterfuge of an individual or organization may be sustained for some years.

PR professor and author Scott Cutlip points to J. Edgar Hoover, longtime director of the Federal Bureau of Investigation and a high-profile PR communicator, as a "master of concealment." He was an example of one who was able to control the news at the source, claims Cutlip, so that he could set the public agenda, or keep items off it. Hoover was a "prolific weaver of a cocoon of myths that cloaked his battles against criminals, subversives and all those with whom he disagreed."

The deceit, the concealment, was unknown during Hoover's service as FBI head, according to Cutlip, because of the tight control enforced by Hoover on all information from his office. With the assistance of his "able public relations officer," Louis B. Nichols, said Cutlip, there was an "unending publicity campaign" that transformed Hoover's G-Men into household words. Not until after Hoover's death, said Cutlip, did the press and public have access, primarily through the government's Freedom of Information Act, to Hoover's "ruthless, underhanded . . . tactics" against those of whom he disapproved. The new information shattered the myth-making, bringing to the fore such items as "Hoover's detestable persecution of Martin Luther King, whom the G-Man regarded as an 'immoral opportunist.' "[18]

MISLEADING BEHAVIOR IN THE BUSINESS WORLD

There are those in PR who do trade on deception and deceit in order to succeed for the minute, to win in the short run— regardless of how damaging to future success may be the harm done. In the business world, we hear the criticism of the CEO who leans on deception and on the company's CPA firm to allow the reporting of healthy operating figures for a quarter, even though the deceit is responsible for less favorable numbers in future quarters.

In the marketing department, you may find an instance of deception in the introduction of a new product. The product may be announced in ads, in special mailings, or at a trade show with much hype and hoopla. Visitors to the industry show may find only a prototype is on exhibit. As the promised date for the product to arrive on the shelf or in the showroom passes, plus numerous days or weeks, prospective buyers ask questions, lose faith, feel deceived and betrayed. It's worse still if, after the product finally is for sale, buyers put it to use and find it wanting—if the product doesn't perform as billed, fails to match the manufacturer's claims.

Such a series of unfortunate afflictions is rare for any single product. Most new products hit the market on schedule and live up to the claims made for them. When they don't the fault is more often poor judgment and unreasonable calculations on the part of earnest and well-meaning staff members, or in their uncritical acceptance of ill-conceived recommendations of others, than deliberate deception. Whatever the causes, the organizations and perhaps those associated with the projects suffer loss of credibility.

Business firms use polls, studies, and surveys to sell products. How reliable are these gatherings of opinion? Are you influenced to buy Levi's 501 jeans if you hear they're preferred by a majority of college students? *The Wall Street Journal* said, "Examination of hundreds of recent studies indicate that the business of research has become pervaded by bias and opinion. The result is a corruption of the information." The manipulation and deceit is the result, at least in part, of loaded questions and the vested interests of the sponsors, those who make the products that are the subject of surveys. Look at the results of studies to determine whether cloth or disposable paper diapers are more environmentally desirable. Two studies concluded that those of cloth had less adverse environmental impact; two others favored the disposable kind. As you may already have guessed, the first two were sponsored by the cloth-diaper industry, the others by the paper-diaper industry. The paper quoted Eric Miller, editor of the newsletter *Research Alert* and reviewer of 2,000 studies a year: "There's been a slow sliding in ethics. The scary part is, people make decisions based on this stuff."[19]

Some companies make environmental claims for products that "are either unsubstantiated, misleading, or plain lies," according to "Business & Ethics," a business-page column prepared by faculty members of the University of Denver Graduate

School of Business. The writer charged that companies create ethical dilemmas as they strive to enhance their environmental image. The result: customers are "bamboozled." Besides false or misleading product claims, related unethical actions included wasteful packaging for even environmentally friendly products, production processes that hurt the environment, and corporate cultures that are insensitive to the environment.[20]

Fool the Eye—When Things Aren't What They Seem

Another kind of PR deception is the manipulation of photographs, thanks to modern-day digital image technology. In decorative arts, there is the French term, *trompe l'oeil*, or fool the eye, which describes means taken through imaginative painting to heighten interest in a wall or ceiling of a room, for example. Fool the eye in the decorative sense has been admired for years, even centuries; in today's photography, the technique is more denounced than accepted.

The Poynter Institute of St. Petersburg, Florida, which presents seminars primarily in reporting, writing, and editing for newspaper reporters and editors, offered a conference titled "Photojournalism Ethics: Manipulating Reality" in 1991. The program announcement asked: "Is it real? Or is it digitized?" and went on, "Digital image technology: magic production tool, or device to create pictures that lie? . . . Digital image technology is not only changing visual presentation for print and broadcast journalists. It's also creating significant ethical debate among photographers, editors, managers, directors, and educators."

Among the better-known examples of faked photos:

The photo of Nancy Reagan and Raisa Gorbachev, wives of U.S. and Russian presidents, respectively, in which they appeared quite chummy on the November 25, 1985, cover of *Picture Week* magazine. This was a composite photo depicting something that didn't happen. In fact, there was considerable coolness between the two when summit meetings of their husbands brought them together.

The electronic moving of one of Egypt's great pyramids closer to another by *National Geographic* magazine to create a picture that better fit its cover layout.

There was irony in the incident of photo manipulation at the *St. Louis Post-Dispatch*. Robert C. Holt III, director of technology and photo operations, removed a can of Diet Coke from a photo of Ron Olshwanger, winner of the 1989 Pulitzer Price for photography. He said he was asked to get rid of the soda can because it was distracting. "I could have easily cropped it . . . but I wanted to see if I could do it (with manipulation)." The paper later adopted a policy to regulate manipulation of photos.[21]

The computer went to work for a 1989 issue of *TV Guide* magazine, and when it was through there on the cover was the face of TV talk-show hostess Oprah Winfrey with the body of actress Ann-Margret. The body, swathed in a gauzy dress, was taken from a 10-year-old publicity shot. The trickery of the composite photo was revealed after the designer of Ann-Margret's dress recognized the creation. The magazine apologized—after the damage was done, and 15 million readers deceived.

At ABC News, it was another kind of simulated photography. The network in the summer of 1989 purported to show U.S. Diplomat Felix Bloch, at the time under investigation by the Federal Bureau of Investigation, passing a briefcase containing top-secret information to a Soviet agent. The videotape looked and sounded authentic. How were viewers to know it was a phony surveillance film? After the first run of the tape on "ABC World News Tonight," introduced by Peter Jennings, the word *simulation* was superimposed as a disclaimer at the top of the screen—except that the label failed to appear on the still photo of the two men exchanging the briefcase. Jennings apologized on the air for the fakery four days later, but ABC suffered severe criticism.

There are fool-the-eye culprits in advertising, too. One was the British Columbia Ministry of Tourism, which sponsored an advertisement with the headline, "If you go down to the woods today, you're in for a big surprise," superimposed over an inviting woodlands scene. Readers would have been surprised to learn the photograph was staged: "The mist was simulated using smoke machines, the rays of sunlight were produced with floodlights, and the deer were brought in from a nearby petting zoo."[22]

More widely publicized was the deception of North American Volvo, with the "blatant rigging of its 'monster truck' " ad, which appeared in print and on television. The ad showed a pickup truck with oversized tires driving over the top of a row of cars. The pickup crushes the roofs of all of the cars except the Volvo. The roof-support pillars in the other cars were severed or weakened. The Volvo roof remained intact because it was supported with lumber and steel, unseen by the viewer.

Another Volvo ad depicted a six-ton truck lowered onto the roof of a Volvo auto with the message, "How well does your car stand up to heavy traffic?" The car holds up under the weight; it doesn't sag—with good reason. The car was propped up by jacks that were in the shadows and hidden from view. A Volvo spokesman said that without the jacks the tires would have exploded and the spring would have compressed. There was also this rationale from Volvo: The ad was intended to show the strength of Volvo's roofs and bodies, which weren't reinforced. It wasn't intended to say that the tires and suspension systems could support the load.

In response to a suit by Texas Attorney General Jim Mattox, Volvo admitted the monster truck ad was rigged. The company put the blame on its ad agency—Scali, McCabe, Sloves of the WPP Group—which was forced to resign the $40 million account. Volvo was the agency's biggest and oldest client. The

Federal Trade Commission fined Volvo and the agency $150,000 each for misleading the public.

Many ad specialists saw these and other ads that depended on trick photography as falling "into an ethical gray area."[23] When there is misrepresentation, and manipulation, the gray fades and there's really a black-and-white ethical issue.

Freebies and Payola

PR manipulation is found where there is an exchange of favors, a quid pro quo—a situation is which there is the acceptance of a product or service by one party in return for giving a commercial advantage to the other. We're talking about the "freebie."

You may spot a freebie in the relationship between a travel writer for a newspaper or magazine and a resort, a tourist board or association, an entertainment park, a cruise line, or an airline. The writer is offered such freebies as free travel, lodging, meals, and side trips with the hope on the part of the sponsoring organization that he or she will knock out a laudatory news or feature article.

Journalists who write on fashion, automobiles, business, entertainment, and sports have been tendered similar enticements by those whose products, services, or events they write about.

In the travel industry, for years "junkets" (all-expense trips) were offered to writers who might not otherwise be able to afford such excitement. Sometimes the writers descended on a vacation spot as a group, finding their pleasures there on their own. Or an individual writer might make the visit alone. Either way, the sponsor looked for the return on investment in pieces published after the writers returned home. The expectation of a favorable review may not have been openly discussed, but it would be hard to say there wasn't a kind of informal understanding.

Many publications now have editorial policies against *subsidized travel*, the more respectable term. One paper with such a policy is *The Seattle Times*, whose travel editor, John B. MacDonald, says: "We believe that publishing an article resulting from a subsidized trip is simply weak journalism and is not in the best interest of our readers. We believe a reader shouldn't have to wonder whether a story is being distorted by financial pressure or whether the newspaper is beholden to special interests. We don't want even an appearance of impropriety."[24]

Staff and free-lance writers are affected by these policies. Such major travel magazines as *Conde Nast Traveler* and *Travel & Leisure*, which contract with well-known writers at substantial rates for travel articles, have advance agreements on paid expenses. Free lancers who depend upon newspapers for sales usually are paid at lower rates that would cover only a portion of their expenses.

"No free lancer I know can survive without some assistance with transportation," according to Barry Anderson, a free lance travel writer and former president of the Society of American Travel Writers. "It's ironic that most newspapers pay free lancers embarrassingly low rates, and not expenses, yet their travel pages are among their biggest revenue generators. . . ."

One paper that recognizes the free lancer's need for subsidy is the *San Francisco Examiner*. Travel editor Don George said, "I want to continue to use these writers, and since I cannot pay them enough to cover the costs of their trips, I think we must recognize the necessity of subsidies . . . and do our best to ensure that such subsidies do not improperly influence the stories we publish."

Speaking as a public relations representative for the travel industry, Mac Seligman, writing in *Public Relations Journal*, declared, "We must reassure journalists who accept offers of travel arrangements that all we truly want is objective coverage" and "must respond intelligently to objections to subsidized travel."[25]

Public Relations Journal is published by the Public Relations Society of America, the world's largest public relations association, which gives guidelines to members on subsidized travel in its Code of Professional Standards for The Practice of Public Relations. The code states that members "shall not engage in any practice which has the purpose of corrupting the integrity of channels of communications . . ." and the code prohibits "any form of payment or compensation to a member of the media in order to obtain preferential or guaranteed news or editorial coverage." However, it is permissible "to offer complimentary or discount rates to the media (travel writers, for example) if the rate is for business use and is made available to all writers" and if it is understood that "no preferential treatment or guarantees are expected or implied, and that complete independence always is left to the media." The guidelines seem to waffle on extending such rates for personal use with the advisory that "considerable question exists" as to their propriety.[26]

Freebies for at least some journalists who cover the auto companies appear to have fewer restrictions than those for travel writers. In a catch-all statement of what existed in May 1990, *The Wall Street Journal* said, "Welcome to the world of automotive enthusiast journalism, where the barriers that separate advertisers from journalists are porous enough for paychecks to pass through—as well as airline tickets to Japan, free rooms at fancy resorts, gift certificates, clocks, briefcases and, of course, free use of some of the hottest new cars on the market."[27]

The paper's reference was to writers and editors of the major magazines for car buffs: *Car and Driver*, the largest; *Motor Trend*; *Road & Track*; and *Automobile*. Growing steadily in circulation, these publications claimed 2.9 million readers in 1990. The editor of *Car and Driver* was quoted as saying he encouraged staff members to work as " 'consultants' to auto companies, the better to get early access to new cars and inside dope."

What's in it for the auto companies? You've only to read their ads to know the answer. It's those quotes on car performances published in the auto buff books.

"Months before a new car is launched," said the paper, "manufacturers start lobbying in earnest for favorable coverage." In preparation for the introduction of the Infiniti division, Nissan in August of 1989 invited buff book writers for free stays at the Four Seasons Hotel, Beverly Hills.

Probably most sought by car manufacturers, and utilized to the fullest, were the annual awards. *Motor Trend* "selects a domestic and an import "Car of the Year"; *Car and Driver* published a "Ten Best Cars" list; *Automobile* chose an "Automobile of the Year" and "Automotive All-Stars." Ads quoting the best lines from the magazines in their judging of the cars are released as soon as possible after the choices are announced.

The paper's description of freebies as it affected employees of *Car and Driver* changed in early 1991. William Jeanes, editor, said in a letter to auto companies that "no one who works here" would accept work for pay from an automaker, its advertising agency, or another of its agents. He added, "We would prefer that you not grace us with any gift that goes beyond the souvenir memento level." Jeanes did say it was okay for the magazine's reporters to attend press trips as guests of the auto manufacturers, and to test drive new cars.

The editor of *Automobile* magazine, David E. Davis, Jr., responded to *Car and Driver* with the comment, "Mr. Jeanes has taken himself a little too seriously and probably went too far." *The Wall Street Journal* labeled Davis "a stout advocate of accepting free trips, merchandise, and speaking fees from car companies." Other auto magazines indicated their policies would not change.[28]

Sports writers and editors, or, taken collectively, sports journalists, have had a reputation as heavy freebie-takers, the result of their portrayals in movies, television, and comic strips. The Associated Press Sports Editors Association and many newspapers and magazines have been working to change this image with ground rules that put a more ethical footing under those of their craft.

Tim Wulfemeyer found positive and negative results in the acceptance of freebies by sports journalists. Among the positive, the practice allows coverage of events that would be too expensive to report otherwise. He pointed to the case of *The Louisville Times* and *The Courier-Journal*, which found that the cost for the 70 people they had covering the Kentucky Derby would be $50,000. "The papers decided they didn't want ethics that badly."[29]

One of the negatives was "the potential indebtedness that can develop." "Freebie givers are not generous for the sake of being generous," he said. "They want something in return—publicity, better treatment, a favor, etc."

Wulfemeyer reported on the results of a survey of 100 sports journalists in National Football League cities: About 90 percent of those responding thought the employer should cover all expenses of a reporter covering an event, except that 74 percent thought it OK for the reporter to have a free pass to enter. All thought it unacceptable to receive free tickets for family, friends, or colleagues. High majorities said that gifts from news sources should be refused and that it was unethical to accept free travel from a sports organization.

Expenses of a reporter on a sports assignment—travel, lodging, food, admission, any others—should be covered by the news organization, according to guidelines on freebies proposed by Wulfemeyer. Sports journalists should not accept complimentary tickets, he said, and should not request or accept discounts on merchandise, club memberships, or services. He further recommended they refuse or return any gifts.

Ethics reportedly is the major theme of annual gatherings of the Associated Press Sports Editors. At the 1989 meeting, said James Warren, many editors said they heard for the first time of the Nabsico/RJR Pick-The-Winners media contest. Apparently, their golf writers already were quite familiar with it. The contestants—who numbered about 150 fulltime writers, free lancers, and others who covered for the media—accumulated points for picking the winner on the PGA or Senior PGA golf tour. The prize was a cruise for two on Royal Caribbean Cruise Line.

"It's outrageous," said one sports editor. He and others saw the conflict of interest for a writer covering golf events to accept a cruise as a prize from a major sponsor. Another editor said, "I didn't know about it and will see that it stops" at his paper.[30]

The editors found much else on ethics and freebies to talk about. There was the report of a just-completed survey that presented situations for editors to react to. For example, a team winning a world series orders commemorative rings valued at several hundred dollars each for the players and also for those in the media who cover the team. What should the reporter do? Only four of the 145 who responded to the survey said the reporter could accept the ring.

There was mixed reaction to allowing a writer to coauthor an authorized biography or autobiography of a sports star whom the writer covers. The largest number, 51, said such participation by a writer was "probably unacceptable conduct"; 41 said it was "acceptable conduct"; 26 said it was "clearly unacceptable," but "not worthy of making an issue over"; and 23 said it was "clearly unacceptable." At odds with these numbers, 81 thought it clearly unacceptable for a reporter to host a radio or television show of a coach.

The sports editors heard about the annual meeting of the Outdoor Writers Association of America, which preceded theirs by a week. "Every function they had was underwritten by some corporation," said a sports editor who attended. "A sign in the lobby listed all the corporate hospitality suites. The group relies heavily on the generosity of the people they're supposed to cover." The outdoor writers allow corporate and government officials to be members, with higher annual dues than writer-members. "Why should I, as a reader, believe our glowing reports about a certain product?" asked an editor.[31]

The ethical public relations dilemma of freebies exists, of course, because of two parties, the giver and the receiver. The giver is a business organization—such as a manufacturer of autos, sports equipment, or other goods, a member of the travel industry, a fashion apparel house, or the sponsor of an event. The businesses apparently see nothing unethical in their offerings. But would they give cash bribes in hope of receiving the desired favorable mentions by the media? Those in the media who are the receivers are placed in what may be for many an uncomfortable position. They may feel they shouldn't accept the offered item. But, it's something they would like to have. And, to use the classic rationalization, everyone else is taking. So their ethical standards bend a little.

Leaking to Manipulate the News

Leaking of information to the news media can be of several kinds. There are ethical forms of leaking, done when it's the proper thing to do, and there are unethical varieties, when there are ulterior motives behind the acts. The determinant is the purpose of the leak.

A PR communicator who has a boss or client who insists on issuing deceptive or false information that could lead to personal injury may act anonymously to give complete and accurate information to the media and the public. A citizen may find out and leak information about an unannounced, sub-rosa meeting of public officials to discuss matters that by law should be talked about in an open session. For the PR person, this may directly precede the turning in of his or her resignation. These kinds of leaks merit ethical approval.

Fred Friendly tagged another kind of leaking, one that is patently unethical, as resulting in irresponsible reporting by the news media. Friendly, a former president of CBS News, and Edward R. Murrow, professor emeritus, Columbia Graduate School of Journalism, described a kind of leaking that is the "sloppy habit of permitting 'unnamed sources' to spread undocumented attacks on a wide variety of public officials and others who have neither been formally charged nor indicted."

He cited two examples. One was the leaking of information from a government source to ABC News that led the network to present the simulation of Felix Bloch as an accused spy passing secret information to a Soviet agent. The videotape scenes showed were actually of two ABC News staff members. At the time, Bloch was under investigation by the FBI, which had refused to comment on the case. This telecast, said Friendly, "triggered newspaper reporters and broadcasters to print and show material that has convinced millions of readers and viewers that Mr. Bloch is a superspy."

The other example was of the unofficial word leaked from the U.S. Navy that the 1989 explosion on the U.S.S. *Iowa*, in which 47 sailors died, was caused by the sabotage of a frustrated homosexual sailor. This leaked information was widely printed and broadcast, but did not appear in the Navy's official version of the cause of the disaster.[32]

A government leaker par excellence appears to have been Ollie North, the U.S. Army colonel who came to national attention in connection with the alleged sales of arms to Iran, with profits going to assist the Contras in Nicaragua. In testimony at the Irangate hearings in 1987, North justified the Reagan administration in its deception of Congress by declaring that members of Congress often leaked sensitive information. As an example, he cited congressional leaks about the interception of an Egyptian plane with hijackers of the ''Achille Lauro'' aboard.

North's charges led *Newsweek* magazine to disclose one of its sources for a cover story on the ''Achille Lauro,'' in October, 1984. ''Details of the interception,'' it noted, ''were leaked by none other than North himself.'' *Time* magazine said, ''It was hardly a secret in Washington that North had provided information on many stories. 'Ollie was the biggest leaker in this administration,' one official told *The Wall Street Journal*.''

All publications to whom he had leaked had maintained the confidentiality of the source until *Newsweek* put the finger on him. A magazine staff member said, ''When a guy lies on national television, at that point you have to reassess the rules.'' North's leaking, part of his virtually uncontrolled PR operation within the White House, showed no recognition of ethical values. *Newsweek* ran the story over the objections of its Washington bureau and ''to many reporters . . . the precedent was worrisome.'' Confidential sources are important to journalists. ''You can't eat off a source's plate and then later say you don't like the food,'' commented investigative reporter Seymour Hersh. *Time*, however, noted that granting anonymity ''allows officials to manipulate the press without being held accountable.''[33] This point and the views of Fred Friendly indicate leaking as a practice has ethical potholes and pitfalls.

Our nation's presidents have hated leakers to the point of paranoia. Yet, sometimes, they themselves did the leaking—and not always intentionally. Pierre Salinger, press secretary to President Kennedy, tells about a leak involving Kennedy in the period between his election and taking office. A story appeared on page one of *The Washington Post* saying that Dean Rusk would be secretary of state in the administration. Kennedy called in Salinger and said, "That's outrageous. Who leaked that story to them?" Salinger investigated, and returned three hours later to say to Kennedy, "It was you." It ws true; Kennedy had leaked the information to Donald Graham, then the *Post* publisher, and the paper printed it (no ethical judgment on this).[34]

POINTS

• Be conscious of the many facets of manipulation and realize that probably no institution is free of the threat.

• Object to manipulation that interferes with your attempts to achieve credibility in the practice of public relations.

• Expose those whose manipulative ways cast doubts on the credibility of you and others who observe ethical conduct.

• Reason with those who contemplate or are engaged in manipulative actions. Paint for them a picture of the credibility harm they can do to themselves and all other public relations communicators.

NOTES

1. Joyce Nelson, *Sultans of Sleaze*, (Toronto: Between the Lines, 1989), p. 51.
2. Martin Schram, "Bush Mumbles, Fumbles as Tax Vow Tumbles," *Rocky Mountain News*, July 5, 1990, p. 43.
3. Stephen J. Adler, "Consultants Dope Out the Mysteries of Jurors for Clients Being Sued," *The Wall Street Journal*, October 24, 1989, p. A1.
4. Donald E. Vinson, "Psychological Anchors: Influencing the Jury," *Litigation*, 8, no. 2 (1982), p. 20.

5. Adler, "Consultants Dope Out the Mysteries of Jurors for Clients Being Sued," p. A1.

6. Ibid.

7. Ibid.

8. Ibid.

9. Judith Dancoff, "Hidden Persuaders of the Courtroom," *Barrister*, Winter 1982, p. 8.

10. Joanne Lipman, "Scandalous Ads Convert Rejection by Networks into Free Publicity," *The Wall Street Journal*, July 30, 1990, p. B5.

11. Ibid.

12. Clyde R. Farnsworth, "Japan's Loud Voice in Washington," *New York Times*, December 10, 1989, sec. 3, p. 1.

13. Ibid.

14. Jill Abramson and Eduardo Lachia, "In Trade Talks, Japan Knows the U.S. Team—Often All Too Well," *The Wall Street Journal*, February 23, 1990, p. A1.

15. Jill Abramson, "Washington Campus Pays Legislators, Lobbyists to Teach Executives the Ins and Outs of Influence," *The Wall Street Journal*, May 7, 1990, p. A16.

16. "Business and the Public Policy Process: How Washington Works," program for 1990–1991 series, The Washington Campus.

17. "Influence as Usual," *The Wall Street Journal*, December 3, 1990, p. A14.

18. Scott M. Cutlip, speech at the PRSA district conference, Jacksonville, Florida, June 9, 1989.

19. Cynthia Crossen, "Studies Galore Support Products and Positions, but Are They Reliable?" *The Wall Street Journal*, November 14, 1991, p. A1.

20. "Hiding Behind 'Green' Curtain," *Rocky Mountain News*, October 23, 1991, p. 34.

21. Robin Hughes, "Photo Manipulation Policies," *Fine Line*, February 1990, p. 5.

22. "The Simulated Forest," *Harper's*, August, 1991, p. 21.

23. Krystal Miller and Jacqueline Mitchell, "Marketers Test Gray Area of Truth in Advertising," *The Wall Street Journal*, November 19, 1990, p. B1.

24. Mac Seligman, "Travel Writers' Expenses—Who Should Pay?" *Public Relations Journal*, May 1990, p. 27.

25. Ibid.

26. "Register Issue," *Public Relations Journal*, 1991–92, p. xvii.

27. Joseph B. White, "Car Magazine Writers Sometimes Moonlight for Firms They Review," *The Wall Street Journal*, May 15, 1990, p. 1.

28. Ned Templin, "Car Magazine Signals End to Auto Makers' Freebies," *The Wall Street Journal*, February 5, 1991, p. 81.

29. K. Tim Wulfemeyer, "Ethics in Sports Journalism: Tightening Up the Code," *Journal of Mass Media Ethics*, 1, no. 1, (1985–86) p. 60.

30. James Warren, "Sports Writers Take Notes on Ethics," special report by the Ethics Committee of the Society of Professional Journalists, 1989, p. 24.

31. Ibid.

32. Fred W. Friendly, "On Television News, Lies and Videotape," *The New York Times*, August 6, 1989, sec. 2, p. 1.

33. Laurence Zuckerman, with David Beckwith and Wayne Svoboda, "Breaking a Confidence," *Time*, August 3, 1987, p. 61.

34. "The Presidency, the Press & the People," coproduction of KPBS-TV and University of California, San Diego, taped January 5, 1990.

Chapter Eleven

Personal Accounts of Ethical Dilemmas in Public Relations; Issues that Can Create or Avoid Them

Ethical dilemmas in public relations may confront the chief executive officer, the manager, or the rank-and-file employee. Each may find pressures based on financial considerations, personal loyalties, or other reasons to engage in a cover-up, conflict-of-interest situation, deceit and manipulation, or other unethical conduct. The alternative, a choice based on the individual's personal values, is to take the high road, do what is felt to be right, honorable, and ethical. But there may be problems with this choice because of the unfavorable reaction that can be expected from those applying pressure. Either choice may be unpleasant and disagreeable.

In a survey we conducted of members of the Public Relations Society of America and International Association of Business Communicators, a few of the respondents said they had experienced ethical dilemmas in their work, and described them.[1] These are presented to indicate how different, yet how challenging, the dilemmas and their resolution can be. Following these personal contributions are views of public relations practitioners on ethical dilemmas in PR.

Randy Baker, director of public affairs with The Promus Companies Incorporated, described his "ethical discomfort" under the title, "The Ethics of Time Accounting: A Period of Personal Discomfort."[2] He wrote: "Some years ago when I was working for a major trade association, half of my time was to be billed to the trade group and half to a contract we had with a branch of the federal government. The reality of my work assignment, however, was that oftentimes about 80 percent of my time was devoted to tasks separate and apart from the contract.

"Initially this didn't bother me very much. It seemed to be a rather commonplace pattern of work in Washington. In time, however, I began to feel dishonest with myself and said something both to one of my superiors and to the bookkeeper who handled the administrative paperwork. My superior's response was that clearly I was in error in my assessment of the time I was allocating to my respective tasks because of the immensity of the government project; the bookkeeper's response was just to make sure everything on paper was 50–50.

"I chose not to rock the boat but jumped at the first opportunity to move onto a project where all of my efforts and time were clearly and unquestionably billable to a different grant. Given many years' hindsight, I think I did the right thing, but clearly I would not willingly accept a position again where the possibility of deceptive time allocation might exist."

Beth West gives us an account of the ethical dilemma she encountered early in her career.[3] She is manager of public relations of United Gas Pipe Line Company, Houston, Texas, and in 1990 chaired the accreditation committee of the International Association of Business Communicators. Her contribution:

"My first job was as a media buyer for a small advertising company in South Texas. One afternoon my boss called me to his office to tell me he wanted me to go to dinner that evening with a client, the president of a national food processing company.

"The next morning my boss asked how the evening went; when he realized I had not gone to bed with the client, he was furious. According to him, not only was I lacking a cooperative attitude, but I also had (1) failed to gain any useful information during pillow talk; and (2) not given him any leverage with the client.

"A few days later, a media rep from a local radio station came in when I was alone in the office. He told me that if I would 'be nice' to him, he would give me information which I could use as leverage with my boss.

"I gave notice the next morning and began a search for a job with a firm that wouldn't be embarrassed to put all the requirements of the job on paper. Incidentally, a year or so later, the president of the advertising firm was sent to prison on a fraud conviction (he was bilking little old ladies out of their life savings.)"

"Tell Him You Don't Know—An Ethical Dilemma for PR Practitioners" is the title Jack Blake gave his experience.[4] Blake, director of information for the Credit Union National Association in Madison, Wisconsin, presents this story: "You don't have to lie to him about it," legal counsel said. "Just tell him you don't know."

" 'It,' in this case, was a politically sensitive trade association issue, and 'him' was a persistent, sometimes abrasive reporter for a gossipy, controversy-seeking trade publication.

"The trouble with counsel's solution was that I *did* know.

"I was involved in the discussion for two reasons: First, to lend public relations counsel to management and our association officials on this controversial issue, and second, to cover the story for our association newsletter. As an editor, I could accept any management decision on the issue, even if it was print nothing. As public relations counsel, though, I felt obligated to uphold the ethics of my profession—and lying to reporters, even obnoxious ones, wasn't among them.

"Fortunately, as a trade association, we're not subject to the SEC-type disclosure rules that corporations face, nor the "Freedom of Information Act" requirements of government agencies. While we didn't have to say anything, we couldn't prevent a reporter from getting the information from other sources—and I knew this one would. So, I argued, it would be better to take charge of the story, tell the reporter what we wanted him to know, and try to minimize the controversy.

"We finally agreed that I'd call the reporter before he called me and give him our side of the story.

"Still, I was in a quandary. Was counsel's remark a comment, a suggestion, or a command? In our organizational hierarchy, counsel outranked both me and my boss. I knew there were some aspects of the story I wasn't about to tell the reporter, but how should I frame my refusal?

"My solution came to me as I was dialing the reporter's number. I read our draft release to the reporter, and then told him: 'Now, before you start asking, there are some questions I may not answer. Whatever I tell you will be the truth, but I might not tell you anything. Now go ahead and ask.'

"When he asked a question that I didn't want to answer, I would respond, 'I can't answer that' or 'I can't tell you that.' Not 'no comment,' which sounds like a cop-out, or 'I don't know,' which (in some cases) would have been a lie. When he asked for my assessment of the issues' probable outcome, I told him I wasn't in a position to speculate. I held my ground and stuck to the content of the release, and the interview finally ended.

"That was more than a decade ago, and since then I've stuck to the principle: Don't lie, just don't tell.

"It still works."

A different kind of ethical dilemma in public relations, based on the demands of a client, was offered by John Budd, Jr.[5] Budd returned to counseling from the corporate world as vice chairman of the "new" Carl Byoir & Associates, Inc., public relations counseling firm in New York City. He is now chairman and CEO of The Omega Group, characterized as the public relations field's first "think tank." Budd, a 1988 recipient of the PRSA Gold Anvil Award, describes the situation:

"Some years ago at the original Carl Byoir & Associates we were retained by a developer to help him effect a change in zoning laws in a residential community. His plan for proposed garden apartments was attractively designed to blend in with the countrified nature of the community and he was amenable to a variety of accommodations to esthetics, e.g., camouflaged parking. But after months of hearings, meetings, and negotiations, the community just could not overcome the psychological block to a zoning change, more afraid of setting a precedent than objecting to the developer's plans and spirit of cooperation.

"Increasingly frustrated, he finally determined that a citizens' revolt (his words) was in order, and he proposed taking on the administration because of its denial of free enterprise, etc. We counseled that this was not only irrelevant to his problem, but was foolhardy and irresponsible. He was adamant. He said we were his counsel; he was paying us and we were obliged to do his bidding.

"It became an impasse. He would not listen to reason. Demanded action.

"We resigned the account! Told him not only was the idea farfetched and professionally unsound but it represented an adversary action that had no public benefit and we would not be a party to it.''

A dilemma with a satisfactory conclusion is the kind we hear from Fred Alexander, manager of corporate communications for Nantahala Power and Light Company, Franklin, North Carolina:[6]

''As the volunteer chairman of a nonprofit organization's promotion committee, I was asked to submit false invoices to a government agency for reimbursement. The interesting aspect was that the way the organization wanted to spend the money was, in my judgment, more beneficial in achieving the grant-giver's purposes. But, the grant uses were specific and could not be changed. Even one within the government agency said when the subject of change was brought up, 'Don't tell me what you're going to do. Let me tell you again what the invoices must look like for reimbursement.'

''I wrote a memo recording the requests to submit false invoices to a vendor with copies to the organization head and the person pressuring me. I did not actually send one to the vendor. My hope was that a conversation between the two recipients would end the situation. I don't know if the head read it or not. But, the pressure continued.

''Finally, I met with the pressuring person and said, 'You know, I just don't feel comfortable inside turning in one kind of invoice and spending the money another way. It could be very harmful to the organization and all concerned if this came out during an audit.'

''The response I got really surprised me, 'Well, if you feel that way, I guess we shouldn't do it.' No argument. Nothing. It seemed like a trial balloon to that person, at least by the response. To me, it was so serious that I intended to resign my post rather than have any part of it.''

"Test Your Ethics Quotient" is the name of a column in *Communication World* monthly magazine published by the International Association of Business Communicators. This feature has two parts: It poses an ethics question and asks readers to write in with their ideas for handling the situation; and it prints what is considered to be the best response to a previous question. The question in the June 1989 issue was, "Name that Purloined Tune" and here is the detail. "One of your co-workers invites you to preview a videotape discussing retirement issues. The tape is well done. Its feeling is amplified by a familiar melody that carries the mood so well you find yourself humming the tune after the presentation is over. Just for your information, you ask how the company got permission to use the song, and how much it cost. Your co-workers says, 'Don't worry—the video will just be used internally, so no permission is required.' In fact he asked an attorney and was assured that so long as the song isn't used to make money, it will be okay.'"[7]

A later issue presented the response of Lorraine Boyd, director of communications, The Westside Community Schools, Omaha, Nebraska, who said, "I was recently faced with a similar situation when I produced a video for student recruitment. While not strictly for 'in-house' use, it was for a nonprofit organization, and use is free. While I realize that much of what you described goes on all the time, it makes me uncomfortable.

"I asked those putting our video together if we had permission to use the highly recognizable music in our video. They said they had a verbal agreement for use in nonprofit productions. Still not satisfied, I called the music company and explained the situation. I offered to pay, though my budget was not large.

"They gave me permission for use, gratis, as long as we didn't sell it, and asked that I put our agreement in writing for their files, which I gladly did. Now I don't have to worry every time I show the video or give it away. And I know I've done not only the ethical thing, but the courteous thing as well. Do unto others. . . ."[8]

ISSUES THAT SPAWN ETHICAL DILEMMAS

Budd, who is also a founding fellow of PRSA's College of Fellows, has done some thinking about contemporary issues that present ethical dilemmas for PR executives in counseling firms and listed the following in his 1991 Gold Paper of the International Public Relations Association:

Bait and switch—Is it ethical to make a client proposal with senior staff, then assign to the account young, relatively uncredentialed staffers?

Churning—Is it ethical to create/make work to add up the chargeable hours? The unwanted press kit to be widely disseminated, the unneeded audit or survey?

Playing client pool—Clients set the objectives but should they also dictate the implementation tactics? If so and you go along even when your best professional judgment says it's not the way to do it, is it ethical? Do you counsel or conform? Fear of "rocking the boat" internally is not much different.

Client caveat emptor—Is it ethical to accept an assignment that is transparently undoable?

Read my lips—Is it ethical to issue misleading statements that, while not technically false or inaccurate, will certainly be perceived as straightforward facts?

It's his dollar—Is it ethical to countenance sloppy, slipshod, or even professionally wrong actions by staff?

Dirty tricks that work—You know the budget of a competitor's bid. Is it ethical to come in just under it—or if you're hiring counsel, is it ethical to quote a competitor's bid in an effort to play one against the other?

Trojan horse—You have the opportunity to give free-lance work to a competitor's staff person, in return for inside data. Ethical?

Wine, roses, and accounts—Without ever overtly soliciting, you "arrange" occasions to flatter a competitor's client CEO (a speech here, an award there, a chance meeting then). Your long-range objectives are obvious. Is it ethical to do this?

Plant and sow—You leak negative information about a competitor. Even if true, is it ethical?

Just say "no"—Is it ethical to violate your own best professional judgment and not tell a client—or the CEO—no in fear of upsetting the relationship?

Who's the editor, anyway?—The client hires you as an expert, then tells you how to word the release. It's bad journalism and it will find the round file. Do you try to persuade him to let you do it, or do you "go along" in interests of client harmony?

Preempting preferred—A competitor is planning a major announcement—or a press party. Is it ethical to upstage that organization by holding a major press event the day before?

All head; no legs—You write a headline on the story that dazzles the client with its self-serving adjectives and you tell him it's going to a high-leverage publication, but you know it will never use that headline. Is it ethical to lead the client (or your boss) astray like this?[9]

These ethical dilemmas in public relations are real-life examples of issues that are complex and not readily responsive to doctrinaire codes of conduct, Budd tells us. They are responsive only to the personal judgment and values one holds. Ethical decision making, he believes, "is an amalgam of your values, morality, and standards." Giving honest consideration to these factors, one will likely make decisions that are ethical. Clouding all of this, cautions Budd, is a recent development—the conversion of public relations counseling firms from private to publicly held companies and the greater profit pressures. If each quarter's operating results have to be better than the past, there is a new impact on ethical decisions that is worrisome to Budd— and should be to all who find themselves in such situations.[10]

ATTENTION TO ISSUES THAT CAN AVOID ETHICAL DILEMMAS

Another public relations counselor, Davis Young, also a PRSA Fellow, emphasizes that PR communicators are in the business of enhancing trust. They have an ethical responsibility of a special kind, he states, because so many people depend upon those in public relations as they make key decisions in their lives: for example, in voting, taking jobs, buying products, making investments, choosing schools. As those in PR meet their ethical responsiblity, they may avoid confrontations with ethical dilemmas. "If ours is the business of enhancing trust," he says, "then our effectiveness is in direct relation to whether or not people trust us." Young, chair of the 1991 annual conference of PRSA on the theme of ethics, calls for practitioners to devote attention to several issues, an exercise that will aid them in meeting their ethical responsibility and handling dilemmas, and in enhancing their personal credibility and trustworthiness. Young's list includes:

- Avoid overpromising.
- Set parameters for program or project expectations in advance.
- Agree on standards of measurement and embrace (not resist) accountability.
- Put as much emphasis on full, accurate, and understandable disclosure as you do on timely disclosure. (Avoid selective disclosure on a timely basis.) Recognize that half truths are half lies.
- Achieve a balance between the steak and its sizzle. Put more emphasis on substance and less on bells, trains, and whistles.
- Go out of your way to avoid the appearance of impropriety.
- Recognize there are no quick fixes, easy answers, or magic solutions to tough communication problems.
- Pay as much attention to the spirit of the law as to the letter of the law.
- Confront ethical issues by placing them in the context of the best long-term interests of employers or clients.
- Keep learning—professional development never stops. Failing to take advantages of opportunities for continued learning is cheating oneself. Surely this "is an ethical issue of great magnitude."[11]

Practitioners will find help in working their way through personal ethical dilemmas with the aid of an ethical dilemmas workbook, whose coauthors are counselors James E. Lukaszewski and Ronald W. Watt. They pose nine situations in which one is confronted by ethical issues and raise questions to be answered in resolving the dilemmas. One scenario: One of your largest clients, someone you've had a relationship with for a number of years, has a unique problem—one, however, with which you have a fair amount of experience in your career. The client offers you the opportunity to consult "on the side" to help it through a difficult period of adjustment and reorganization. When you decline because of (your) company policy, the client makes a job offer on the spot—the implication being that if you don't accept one or the other, the client's relationship with your firm may be in jeopardy.[12]

Here are the questions for *you* to ponder in deciding the ethical course: What are the ethical principles and standards of conduct at issue? How would you manage this ethical problem? What are your responsibilities? What should you do? Who should be advised or consulted? How could this have been avoided? What could it mean for you or your company?[13]

POINTS

• Facing an ethical dilemma will make you uncomfortable. You'll wish you didn't have to decide between the choices, neither of which may be agreeable or satisfying. No, it's not as easy as deciding whether to lease or buy a new car, or which brand of fax machine to purchase.

• Anticipate contradictory tugs at your conscience as you weigh the factors surrounding an ethical decision. Let these emotions stimulate your thinking, help you to arrive at the option you'll feel right about.

• If your conscience alerts you that you're about to take part in an unethical action, don't assume that you're trapped and have to go along with those who propose it. Look for ways that you can challenge the action without suffering retaliation or punishment.

• Talk with your associates—fellow managers, your boss or client, and those who report to you—about real, potential, and hypothetical ethical dilemmas. Discuss alternative steps that can be taken to end them in an appropriate manner.

• When you're looking for an ethical solution to a dilemma, keep in mind the factors that build credibility and trust and measure them against the proposed resolution.

NOTES

1. Random sample mail surveys conducted by author in November–December 1989 and May 1990.
2. Correspondence with Randy Baker, January 8, 1990.
3. Correspondence with Beth West, January 9, 1990.
4. Correspondence with Jack Blake, 1990 (undated).
5. Correspondence with John Budd, Jr., January 11, 1990.
6. Correspondence with Fred Alexander, June 25, 1990.
7. "Test Your Ethics Quotient," *Communication World*, June 1989, p. 14.
8. "Test Your Ethics Quotient," *Communication World*, July/August, 1989, p. 51.
9. John F. Budd, Jr., "Ethical Dilemmas in Public Relations," *Gold Paper* no. 8, International Public Relations Association (June 1991).
10. John F. Budd, Jr., adapted from *Gold Paper* no. 8.
11. Davis Young, adapted from article, "We Are in the Business of Enhancing Trust," *Public Relations Journal*, January 1986, p. 7; and presentation, "Confronting the Ethical Issues that Confront You," professional development seminar, PRSA national conference, November 9–10, 1987, Los Angeles, Calif.
12. "The Ethical Dilemmas Workbook #1," Professional Standards & Business Practices Committee, Counselors Academy, Public Relations Society of America, November 4, 1991.
13. Adapted by James E. Lukaszewski and Ronald W. Watt from material of the Ethics Resource Center.

Chapter Twelve

Examples of Ethics Codes and Their Makers

Ethics in public relations finds full flower when institutions and their PR communicators express their intentions for ethical conduct through codes of ethics or standards. The code—which can be, and usually is, an important public relations document for the institution—offers opportunity to develop the desired ethical stance, and to provide for its maintenance and endurance. A code sends a message to the parties of interest that the institution asks and expects a high level of ethical operations from all of those who are directly a part of or in contact with it. The code is a bid for credibility with the organization's publics. Administration of a code's provisions, however, can cause ethical dilemmas and threaten the credibility of an organization. Managers may become involved with codes at any or all of several stages in their development: participation in discussions about needs that will be fulfilled and purposes served for the organization by adopting a code; developing and writing provisions of a code; communicating about the contents and ramifications of a code to the intended audiences; and the enforcing of the code.

WHERE YOU FIND CODES OF ETHICS

Segments of society that have adopted codes of ethics fall into three broad categories:

Business and nonprofit corporations, which sound the ethics call to employees, from the lowest to the topmost, and to other groups within their communities.

Membership organizations (which also may be incorporated), which advise those with mutual interests who have voluntarily joined, professionals and those who aspire to professionalism, and those otherwise linked by common vocations.

The public sector, where local, state, and national bodies proscribe for those in elected and appointed positions.

Most U.S. business corporations have a comparatively recent acquaintance with formal codes of ethics. One of the earlier and better known set of ethical principles is the Credo of Johnson & Johnson, put forth by the firm's head in the 1940s. The credo provided the basis for the challenging business decisions faced by the company and was an aid in enabling the firm to preserve its credibility during the Tylenol crisis (Chapter 3).

The post–Watergate years, beginning in 1973, saw a sharp increase in the developing and posting of codes by business corporations. The defense-contractor scandals of the mid- and late 1980s continued the impetus to increase ethical awareness and practice for those doing business with the army, navy, and air force. In 1979, a study of 650 of the largest U.S. corporations disclosed that 73 percent had put into writing standards of conduct or codes of ethics. Interestingly, 50 percent of these had been adopted during the previous five years. For defense contractors, the percentage with codes in 1979 was the same as for the larger group of corporations. The picture in the defense industry changed rather rapidly, however, and, by the end of 1985, 92 percent of the firms that sold to the Pentagon had adopted codes.[1]

The corporate consciences of nondefense firms—aroused in part by the insider trading scandals on Wall Street—were stirring through the 1980s also. By 1988, 85 percent of large U.S. companies across all major industries had adopted ethics codes, according to a survey of 2,000 companies conducted by the Ethics Resource Center.[2]

The ravenous attention to ethics by business spawned "what well may be the hottest new business of the year," said *Newsweek* in 1988. ''What kind of hot commodity are these entrepreneurs selling?'' asked the magazine. ''It's not wonder drugs or precious metals but something many would consider just as rare: ethics. A new breed of 'ethics consultants' is thriving.''[3]

The magazine's view had a scent of hyperbole, perhaps, as these consultants didn't all spring to life in just that year. Surely, though, there was an increasing number of clients for those established earlier. Among this group of ethics consultants are Gary Edwards, who heads the Ethics Resource Center, which put down its roots in 1977; Barbara Toffler of Resources for Responsible Management, Boston, formed in 1986; and Michael Josephson of the Josephson Institute of Ethics, Marina del Rey, California, which became active in mid-1987. They were joined by specialists in certified public accounting firms and others who offered ethics consulting. Growing too was the attention focused on ethics at the schools of business in colleges and universities. Harvard Business School in the summer of 1988 announced a required course of three weeks in business ethics as part of its curriculum. The school said it planned to have more discussion of ethics in other courses.

CREATING BUSINESS CODES

Business codes, frequently but not always prepared with the help of the consultants, are drawn up as guidelines for the ethical conduct of employees, usually at all levels. The documents bear such titles as Code of Ethics, Code of Conduct, Code of Ethics and Business Standards. While they target employees as the main audience, the codes speak of the firms' and employees' relationships with other publics or audiences of direct and important concern—customers, suppliers, shareholders, and communities in which they operate facilities. Some firms send copies of their codes to members of these groups as a way to trumpet their corporate values.

Among the most detailed and specific in reference to ethical conduct are those of defense contractors. In many instances, these companies were driven to formulate and put into practice more ethical operations after they received citations from the government and court convictions for illegal acts in fulfilling contracts. For some who sell largely to the government, codes are the keystones of comprehensive ethics programs. One of the oldest and most extensive is that of General Dynamics, described in Chapter 4.

Sometimes, unwelcome developments within a nondefense business prompt executives to move toward an ethics program. Nynex, one of the six regional phone companies, acted in 1990 after suffering ''a troubling string of incidents including graft, trips by its purchasers to sleazy Florida parties paid for by suppliers, and questionable financial transactions between its regulated and unregulated subsidiaries.'' *The New York Times* said besides the negative publicity and the cost to the company in millions of dollars of penalties, the incidents came when New York Telephone, the largest subsidiary, was asking a rate increase, the first in five years.[4]

There are positive reasons for businesses adopting ethics programs. Three major reports on corporate ethics published in the late 1980s offered the ''strongly stated motive'' that ''good ethics is good business.'' The Conference Board said that executives who were interviewed ''say that the enterprise in which they are engaged, and the products or services that they market, ought to serve an inherently ethical purpose.'' In a report of the Business Roundtable was the statement that ''a good company reputation for fair and honest business is a prime corporate asset . . . corporate ethics is a strategic key to survival and profitability in this era of fierce competitiveness in a global economy.'' Further, said the Business Roundtable, respondents to its study saw no conflict between ethical practices and acceptable profits, ''indeed the first is a necessary precondition for the second.'' Touche-Ross (now Deloitte & Touche) reported on its survey that "63 percent . . . believe businesses actually strengthen their competitive position by maintaining high ethical standards."[5]

A corporate missionary for the good-ethics-is-good-business belief is James E. Perrella, executive vice president of Ingersoll-Rand Company. "Many people, including many business leaders, would argue that such an application of ethics to business would adversely affect bottom-line performance," he said in a speech at the University of Illinois at Chicago. "I say nay . . . good ethics, simply, is good business. Good ethics will attract investors. Good ethics will attract good employees."[6]

A typical corporate ethics program begins with the writing of a code or set of standards and its approval by the board of directors. A statement at the beginning of the code will express the company's ethical commitment or responsibility to its key "publics." The code then will present ethical forms of conduct for employees as related to such specific topics as conflict of interest; acceptance of entertainment, gifts, or payments by employees from suppliers or offered to suppliers by employees; insider information; and antitrust. The code also spells out degrees of discipline for an employee found to have violated it. These can range from a warning, to termination, to reimbursement for losses or damages, to referral to authorities for possible civil or criminal action.

The company selects a director or administrator to supervise operation of the ethics program. The code is published and distributed to employees, who sign cards acknowledging receipt of the code. There may be a booklet of guidelines and interpretations of the code, presenting brief cases of conduct that violate the code along with those that would be in compliance, which is distributed to employees.

For information and indoctrination purposes, employers hold a series of employee meetings—starting with upper-level management and continuing through rank-and-file workers. Those who conduct the meetings introduce and discuss the code and take up questions about implementation of the code. Employees are encouraged to report suspected violations of the code, either to their supervisor or on a hot line to the office of the corporate ethics director or ombudsman that some companies provide. Company employee publications give frequent attention to the ethics program with reminders of its importance and the necessity for employees to be constantly aware of its provisions.

A review of a sampling of communications for internal distribution published by corporations for their ethics programs reveals the earnestness and sincerity that go into their preparation. The tone is serious, but as friendly as can be allowed. The writing is intended to be understood by persons of widely differing backgrounds. Sentences from two of them: ''The Standards depend on the sense of honesty, fairness, and integrity brought to the job by all employees,''[7] and ''Prompt reporting of violations (of the Code) is considered to be in the best interest of all.''[8] The business ethics policy of another firm is equally direct: ''We don't want liars for managers, whether they are lying in a mistaken effort to protect us or to make themselves look good. One of the kinds of harm that results when a manager conceals information from higher managements and the auditors is that subordinates within his organization think they are being given a signal that company policies and rules . . . can be ignored. A well-founded reputation for scrupulous dealing is itself a priceless company asset.''[9]

ETHICS PROGRAMS AMONG NONPROFIT SERVICE GROUPS

The American Red Cross provides detailed ethical guideposts for volunteers and paid staff members. ''The work of the American Red Cross is fueled by something very precious: the trust of the American people,'' says a booklet titled ''Ethics: Our Commitment at the American Red Cross.'' ''To maintain that trust, and be the best stewards of their donated gifts, we must work by only the highest of ethical standards."

The Red Cross ethics program is administered by an ethics officer at the national headquarters in Washington, D.C. Components of the program include group discussions of difficult case-study situations, consultation on specific issues, a lending library of literature on ethics, and a listing of ethics experts around the country who can be recruited to help local Red Cross units. "The program," states the booklet, "is to teach that each of us is responsible for making careful, ethical choices in our daily work."

A Red Cross code of conduct with guidelines applies to volunteers and paid staff to help them avoid conflicts of interest. It provides that none of the personnel will allow use of the organization's name, emblem, or property for personal gain; accept financial gain or benefit as a result of Red Cross affiliation; use affiliation with the Red Cross "to promote any partisan politics, religious matter or public issue not officially held" by the organization; disclose confidential Red Cross information; or knowingly influence the Red Cross for personal gain or for the benefit of another corporation with which the person is affiliated.[10]

United Way of America has a United Way credo that states eight beliefs about the operation of United Way and "volunteers and professionals of United Way subscribe to these fundamental precepts as a guide to our daily action." United Way professionals also pledge "to adhere to and abide by" a code of conduct. The code asks professionals to maintain high standards of personal and professional conduct; respect individual differences; fight against discrimination, fraud, and mismanagement of resources; be thorough and objective in the use of facts; strive to grow in knowledge and skills; avoid conflicts of interest; exercise a positive attitude and compassion and foster "open communication, creativity, and dedication to the United Way Mission"; and serve the public "with respect, concern, courtesy, and responsiveness."[11] (As recounted in Chapter 5, ethical transgressions that violate the code have occurred.)

ETHICS GUIDES FOR MEMBERSHIP GROUPS

There is a longer history of codes among the membership organizations. Claim to the oldest such code can safely be made by the American Medical Association (AMA), which adopted its original code in 1847. There were major revisions in several years, and a revised format for what became Principles of Medical Ethics in 1957.[12] The AMA's code of ethics is composed of three integrated components: "Principles of Medical Ethics," "Current Opinions of the Council on Ethical and Judicial Affairs," and "Reports of the Council on Ethical and Judicial Affairs."

Directing words to its publics about Principles of Medical Ethics, "the cornerstone" of its code of ethics, the AMA says, "The Principles instruct physicians to practice medicine with competence, compassion, and respect for human dignity. They impose an obligation to expose colleagues who are deficient in character or competence and to seek changes in laws which are contrary to the best interests of patients. They also demand the safeguarding of patient confidences and the sharing of advances in scientific knowledge with colleagues. Finally, the Principles recognize a responsibility of physicians to participate in activities contributing to an improved community."[13]

The earliest written code of ethical principles for medical practice, according to the AMA, was conceived by the Babylonians around 2000 B.C. in the Code of Hammurabi. The Oath of Hippocrates, a brief statement of principles "cherished by physicians," is believed to have been conceived in the fifth century B.C., during the period of Grecian greatness.

Moving into the early 20th century, we find accountants and lawyers concerned with ethical guides for members of their associations. The American Association of Public Accountants, a forerunner of today's American Institute of Certified Public Accountants (AICPA), adopted its first ethical rules in 1905. AICPA members now have a Code of Professional Conduct that became effective in January, 1988.

The American Bar Association (ABA) adopted 32 Canons of Professional Ethics in 1908. These were based principally on the code of ethics that the Alabama State Bar Association approved in 1887. The ABA revised the canons and they became part of the Model Code of Professional Responsibility, adopted in 1969 and amended nine times. A number of amendments were required because of decisions of the U.S. Supreme Court and lower courts relating to such subjects as the provision of group legal services and provision of additional legal services not only to indigents but also to persons of moderate means; and because of Supreme Court decisions relating to lawyer advertising.

The preamble of the ABA code speaks to the public as well as to members of the association: "Lawyers, as guardians of the law, play a vital role in the preservation of society. The fulfillment of this role requires an understanding by lawyers of their relationship with and function in our legal system. A consequent obligation of lawyers is to maintain the highest standards of ethical conduct." The code consists of three interrelated parts— Canons, Ethical Considerations, and Disciplinary Rules. "While these cannot apply to nonlawyers," says the preamble, "they do define the type of ethical conduct that the public has a right to expect not only of lawyers but also of their non-professional employees and associates. . . ."[14]

Not far behind was the National Association of Realtors (NAR), which adopted a code of ethics in 1913 that has been amended more than a dozen times since. Accompanying the sections of the code are "standards of practice," which "serve to clarify the ethical obligations imposed by the various articles." In both the articles and the standards of practice there is frequent use of the term *REALTOR*, "a registered collective membership mark which may be used only by real estate professionals who are members of the National Association of Realtors and subscribe to its strict code of ethics." The NAR has a membership of 800,000, who find a principal marketing benefit is access to Multiple Listing Services, a valuable information source for a majority of home sales.

The preamble of the NAR Code of Ethics and Standards of Practice declares that the REALTOR "should recognize that the interests of the nation and its citizens require the highest and best use of the land and the widest distribution of land ownership," that such interests "impose obligations beyond those of ordinary commerce." REALTORS are told that in the interpretation of this obligation they "can take no safer guide than that which has been handed down through the centuries, embodied in the Golden Rule."[15]

There also are ethics codes of membership organizations for those in the public relations trenches, whose titles and business cards designate them as working in public relations, corporate/public affairs, communications, or related responsibilities. The major membership groups for these individuals are the Public Relations Society of America, with 15,000 members, and International Association of Business Communicators, with 11,000 members.

The PRSA Code of Professional Standards for the Practice of Public Relations contains 17 articles "to promote and maintain high standards of public service and ethical conduct among its members." The current code was adopted in 1988 and replaced a code of ethics in force since 1950 and revised several times thereafter. Among the specifics of the code: A member shall act in accord with the public interest; "exemplify high standards of honesty and integrity"; "deal fairly with the public, with past or present clients or employers and with fellow practitioners"; "adhere to the highest standards of accuracy and truth"; and shall not "knowingly disseminate false or misleading information," "engage in any practice which has the purpose of corrupting the integrity of channels of communications or the processes of government," or "guarantee the achievement of specified results beyond the member's direct control."

There is an Official Interpretation of the Code for all members plus official interpretations of the code as it applies to those who engage in political public relations and financial public relations. The latter interpretation was prepared by a society committee working with the Securities and Exchange Commission.[16] Separately, PRSA members who are counselors and members of the Counselors Academy adopted interpretations to the code as it applies to them.[17]

Some PRSA members, using the code to reflect their philosophy of operation, report they routinely give a copy of the code to a prospective client; others say they hand it to new clients in their first meetings. PR counselor Joe Epley favors "taking a proactive stance to promote and enhance the code as our way of life." At his firm, it's required that all employees, whether practitioner or receptionist, agree to abide by the code's provisions. In contracts with clients, he reports, there are two pertinent paragraphs: One states "We will not do anything" in violation of the code; another states that the client will not "ask us to do anything" that would be in violation of the code.[18]

IABC has a much shorter code of ethics. In force since 1985, the IABC code sets forth seven points "developed to provide IABC members and other communication professionals with guidelines of professional behavior and standards of ethical practice." Major provisions: "Communications professionals will uphold the credibility and dignity of their profession by encouraging the practice of honest, candid, and timely communication . . . not use any information that has been generated or appropriately acquired by a business for another business without permission . . . abide by the spirit and letter of all laws and regulations governing their professional activities . . . not condone any illegal or unethical act . . . respect the confidentiality and right-to-privacy of all individuals, employers, clients, and customers . . . not use any confidential information gained as a result of professional activity for personal benefit or for that of others . . . and should uphold IABC's standards for ethical conduct in all professional activity."[19]

Among other membership organizations with codes that relate to ethics in public relations are the International Public Relations Association, North American Public Relations Council, American Society of Journalists and Authors, Inc., Society of Professional Journalists, American Society of Newspaper Editors, Associated Press Managing Editors, National Association of Broadcasters, Radio-Television News Directors Association, American Advertising Federation and Association of Better Business Bureaus International, and American Association of Political Consultants.

ETHICS CODES FOUND AT ALL LEVELS OF GOVERNMENT

In government, at the federal level there are ethics laws that apply to those who are part of a presidential administration, during their service and after they leave for private employment. The U.S. Senate and House have ethics rules for the guidance of the members. Critics of the effectiveness of the laws affecting those in the administration and rules for those in Congress have called for tougher provisions.

An executive order signed by President Bush in 1989 established "fair and exacting standards of ethical conduct" for all executive branch employees. Sections of the order cover principles of ethical conduct, authority of the Office of Government Ethics in administering the order, and responsibilities of agency heads in observing the regulations. The first item under the principles notes that "public service is a public trust, requiring employees to place loyalty to the Constitution, the laws, and ethical principles above private gain."[20]

The Office of Government Ethics distributes regulations on standards of conduct to the agencies in the branch and works with them in preparing annual ethics training plans. The office gathered nearly 200 ethics officials of the agencies for a three-day conference in 1991, the first such in almost a decade. The office publishes, as necessary, revised editions of the publication, "How to Keep Out of Trouble, Ethical Conduct for Federal Employees."

While the titles of the legislation vary, 36 states have passed measures as codes of ethics or standards. These laws apply to defined groups of public employees, which are variously described. The state codes cover such matters as conflict of interest, campaign financing, lobbying, and personal financial disclosure.

County and city units of government also have enacted laws or codes of ethics that cover elected officers. In June 1990, voters in the city of Los Angeles adopted an ethics measure called "the most comprehensive package of ethics and finance reform in the country." Provisions called for greater financial disclosures by city officials, a ban on their outside employment and partial public financing of election campaigns, and gave substantial pay raises to top-ranking officials. Action toward development of the ethics package came after controversy over outside financial dealings of former mayor Tom Bradley.[21]

INTEGRATING ETHICS INTO THE OPERATIONS—MAINTAINING SENSITIVITY

Those in each of the three groups—business and nonprofits, membership organizations and the public sector—face challenges as they integrate an ethics program into their operations and keep those affected sensitized to the tug of ethics in day-to-day operations.

"The CEO has a unique responsibility," said William F. May, retired chairman of American Can Company. "He's a role model. What he does, how he lives, and the principles under which he operates become pretty much those the rest of the corporation emulates. . . . A CEO must also make his expectations explicit. He needn't sit in judgment, but he can guide the performance and operation of his people."

To this, William Smithburg, chairman of Quaker Oats, stated, "Setting a good example is not enough, however. The CEO must also ensure clear, consistent communication of the corporation's values to all employees."[22]

The communications to employees of which Smithburg speaks are of several kinds. Among the common ways corporations address ethics are in employee newsletters and magazines, on information boards and closed circuit video screens. Other frequently found communication methods are supervisor-employee talks and section or department meetings. Management representatives may attend company-sponsored seminars, sometimes away from their work sites, and discuss ethical issues from the perspectives of themselves and those who report to them. The thoroughness with which employers provide ethics information and training for employees varies among the firms. Edwards, of the Ethics Resource Center, found in a survey of financial services companies that while 90 percent of those polled had codes of conduct or other policy statements only one third had training programs dealing with ethical issues confronting the banking industry.[23]

For membership organizations, it's the carrot, not the stick, to arouse and keep alive members' sensitivity to the desirability of abiding by their codes. The ethical note is sounded in articles appearing in publications for members. The subject may be the basis for a speech at one of the regular local chapter meetings of members, the theme of workshops and seminars, of audio and video tapes, and the topic for speakers or panels at the annual national gatherings of members.

In government, where the basis for ethical conduct is in the law and regulations, one might expect to find less need to maintain awareness of the statutes by those who are affected by them. Not necessarily so. In California, for instance, the chairman of the Fair Political Practices Commission appointed in 1991 placed a high priority on education, saying, ''The commission performs no more important task than education. We must emphasize the importance of interpreting the act in a reasonable and responsible manner. We must give clear and concise explanations to those who seek our guidance . . . before anyone can respect the law they must first understand it.''[24] The Texas legislature, which passed a new ethics law in 1991, also created the Texas Ethics Commission and granted it interpretative as well as administrative and enforcement authority.

Workshops and seminars presented by private consultants help maintain sensitivity to codes for many in each of these groups. Those attending programs of the Josephson Institute of Ethics (JI) have included senior corporate executives, business school faculties, state legislators, lawyers, judges, school administrators, newspaper reporters and editors, upper-level employees of the Internal Revenue Service, Rotarians, and Girl Scouts officials. Of the 80 programs JI provided in 1990, one third were given to government groups, 15 percent to education, and 15 percent to business groups.[25]

"OUTSIDERS" DISCUSS CODES

Codes of ethics have many supporters among organizations that have adopted them. Some may raise questions and suggest ways to improve the administration or effectiveness of an ethics program. Most would rather work with the ethics guides, however, rather than for their dismantlement.

Skeptics and doubters are more likely found outside the organization. There's the question, for example, of whistle-blowers. An employee who reports what he or she believes to be a violation of the code is promised confidentiality and freedom from reprisals, for example, protection of job status. Not all whistle-blowers can report this treatment. Skepticism was laced in comments about business codes by *Business Week*, which took the view that "adopting a code of conduct provides no assurances that it will be followed. Often sound-alike statements suggestive of the Boy Scout oath, such codes blandly instruct employees to be loyal, law-abiding, honest, and trustworthy. As such, they may only remind employees of existing laws and end up in the back of an employee handbook for all to forget. Even advocates concede that many codes are employed as mere window dressing."[26]

The magazine pointed out that enforcement of a code can mean that a company stands behind employees "who forfeit a sale because they refuse to slip a customer a bribe or skimp on costs by cutting corners on pollution controls." Then, it added, "fewer companies can point to a firm stand here. Most adopt a fairly narrow view of corporate responsibility." This related view of Donald R. Cressey, sociologist at the University of California, was presented: "These codes stress crime against the company or unethical behavior against the interests of the company. They give much less attention to crime on behalf of the corporation."

After examining arguments levied against codes of ethics for "communication-oriented" organizations, Richard L. Johannesen found several he thought were typical. Among these arguments: Codes are often filled with meaningless language, "semantically foggy cliches," and thus their practical value is limited; "there is the danger that a code will be viewed as static, as settling matters once and for all"; many codes lack enforcement procedures; and "many codes are dismissed as mere public relations ploys aimed just at enhancing the group's image of responsibility with the public."

From his own view, Johannesen found "useful functions of precisely worded ethical codes." Highlights of the pro stance:

• Codes can educate new persons in a profession or business by acquainting them with guidelines for ethical responsibility based on the experience of predecessors, and by sensitizing them to ethical problems specific to their field.

• Codes can narrow the problematic areas with which a person has to struggle.

• The very process of developing the formal code can be a healthy one that forces participants to reflect on their goals, on means allowable to achieve those goals, and on their obligations to peers, to clients, or customers, to employees and to the public at large.

• An appropriate and voluntary code may minimize the need for cumbersome and intrusive government regulation."[27]

POINTS

• If your employer or client is without an ethics program, urge the adoption of one.

• As selling points, emphasize that the program offers employees or members of an institution direction in deciding to do what is right; that without one the message may be, Don't worry about what's right; just don't get caught.

• Remind the decision maker that an institution without a code of ethical conduct is advertising itself as one that's not concerned with ethics.

• Also, since credibility and ethics are so closely linked, stress that the organization with a program carefully planned and monitored can enhance its credibility.

• If you're part of an organization with an ethics program in place, counsel on the need for maintaining close oversight that assures it's accomplishing its goals, that it's for effect, not show.

NOTES

1. Appendix N, "Final Report and Recommendations on Voluntary Corporate Policies, Practice and Procedures Relating to Ethical Business Conduct," Ethics Resource Center, Inc., undated, p. 264.
2. "Ethics Policies and Programs in American Business," Ethics Resource Center, 1990.
3. Todd Barrett, "Business Ethics for Sale," *Newsweek*, May 9, 1988, p. 58.
4. Barnaby J. Feder, "Helping Corporate America Hew to the Straight and Narrow," *The New York Times*, November 3, 1991, p. F5.
5. Karen Hamilton and David Krueger, "Recent Corporate Reports on Business Ethics: An Ethical Assessment," *Business Insights*, Spring–Summer 1989, p. 32.
6. "Perspectives," *Ethics Journal*, May/June 1991, p. 7.

7. "General Dynamics Standards of Business Ethics and Conduct," General Dynamics, p. 1.

8. "Code of Ethics and Standards of Conduct," Martin Marietta Corporation, p. 3.

9. "Business Ethics," Policy Manual, Exxon Company, U.S.A., Board of Directors' Meeting, September 24, 1975.

10. "Ethics: Our Commitment at the American Red Cross," American Red Cross, 1988.

11. Code of Conduct for United Way Professionals, and United Way Credo, undated.

12. "Current Opinions of the Council on Ethical and Judicial Affairs," American Medical Association, 1989, p. vii.

13. "Medical Ethics—A Leadership Role," publication of the American Medical Association, undated.

14. "Model Code of Professional Responsibility and Code of Judicial Conduct," American Bar Association, 1986, pp. ix–xi and pp. 1–2.

15. "Code of Ethics and Standards of Practice," National Association of Realtors, 1988.

16. "Register Issue," *Public Relations Journal*, 1991–92, pp. xvii.

17. "Counselors Academy's Interpretations to the PRSA Code of Professional Standards," Counselor's Academy, PRSA, October 1990.

18. Correspondence with Joe Epley, April 24, 1991.

19. "Ethics," International Association of Business Communicators, May 1985.

20. "Presidential Documents," *Federal Register*, 54, no. 71 (April 14, 1989).

21. "Ethics Package Is Adopted by Voters in Los Angeles," *The Wall Street Journal*, June 7, 1990.

22. Hamilton and Krueger, "Recent Corporate Reports on Business Ethics: An Ethical Assessment," p. 32.

23. Gary Edwards, "The Need to Revitalize Bank Ethics," *The Bankers Magazine*, July/August 1991, p. 4.

24. "The Guardian," Council on Governmental Ethics Laws, August 1991, p. 7.

25. "A Vintage Year of Success and Growth for JI," *Ethics in Action*, November–December 1990, p. 3.

26. Daniel B. Moskowitz and John A. Byrne, "Where Business Goes to Stock Up on Ethics," *Business Week*, October 14, 1985, p. 66.

27. Richard L. Johannesen, "What Should We Teach about Formal Codes of Communication Ethics," *Journal of Mass Media Ethics*, 3, no. 1 (1988), pp. 59–62.

Chapter Thirteen

Advantages and Faults of Ethics Codes

Commitment is the key word behind any organization's ethics program, and managers will find that the degree of commitment will affect its success or failure. They will discover that the greater the degree of commitment, the more advantages in credibility and other factors accrue to the organization; conversely, the lesser the amount of commitment, the fewer will be the advantages and the more faults will be found.

WEIGHING ADVANTAGES VERSUS FAULTS

"A lot of companies see these [ethics] policies as being preventive medicine that's worth the money," Michael Hoffman, director of the Center for Business Ethics at Bentley College, Waltham, Massachusetts, told *The New York Times*. "But they also see them as something that can attract favorable reaction from investors, consumers, and regulators, and help recruit the best and the brightest." Carl Skooglund, a quality engineer who became the first corporate ethics director for Texas Instruments said, "We have had a written code for over 30 years but we wanted a formal focal point for reinforcing what we felt was a strong culture."

On the negative side can be problems resulting from employee use of hotlines on which they can report suspected violators of codes. These have been dubbed "snitchlines" or "ratlines."

Not everybody likes whistleblowers, though they are essential in weeding out code violators.

Occasionally, a caller can create a problem by providing information in such detail and so pinpointed that the allegation can't be checked into without disclosing the caller's identity. The nature and degree of the violation are taken into consideration when the ethics administrator decides how to proceed.[1]

How do you obtain the advantages of commitment? Proponents of a company's commitment "to fair play, openness, and decision-making," faculty members of the University of Denver Graduate School of Business, have proposed a six-point strategy for establishing an ethics code. They lead off with "be specific, translate ethical values and beliefs into specific standards of behavior for specific situations." They suggest involvement of employees in writing the code and urge that it be reinforced without exception. They call for a code that is consistent, applying "to all employees regardless of rank. Double standards cripple the code's effectiveness." Further, they say, the code should be accessible to all employees and periodically reviewed—this to help management determine if "the code is influencing employee behavior."[2]

A principal fault with a code is uncovering the violator. How does an organization know when someone violates its code of ethics? Some violations may surface accidentally, say through a misfiled report or an unintended comment that exposed a culprit. Others may come to light through outcry from the party who was on the receiving end of unethical conduct. Violators also become known because of complaints registered by fellow employees or by members within organizations. Since not every employee wants to snitch on another, and a member may hesitate to point the finger at a peer, violations of ethical conduct undoubtedly go unreported.

Still, this unofficial system for baring those who transcend the bounds of ethic codes has worked. In business, nonprofit, membership, and government organizations, those who chose to forego ethical conduct have been revealed. Yet identifying the violator is only the first step. In some instances, the difficulty in enforcing ethical rules is as great as that in tracking down the transgressors.

Employers—business corporations, nonprofits, and a portion of the public sector—can exercise the greatest amount of control over individuals, the employees, who violate ethical rules. They can issue ethical edicts that apply to employees and expect them to be followed, and can discipline the nonfollowers. Elected and other public officials are subject to the controls and discipline in the ethics laws and regulations that apply to them. Perhaps the greatest enforcement problems are with the membership groups, who do not have the direct disciplinary control, as do employers. Some professional membership organizations, such as the American Medical Association and the American Bar Association, do have the support of provisions in the licensing laws that govern members' ethical missteps that are illegal. Members can lose their license to practice. Also, these organizations, along with the National Association of Realtors, Public Relations Society of America, and others, have well-defined procedures for investigating and acting on cases of alleged noncompliance with the codes. For members of the International Association of Business Communicators, compliance with the code of ethics is voluntary and there is no provision for enforcement.

TALES OF TWO MEMBERSHIP ORGANIZATIONS IN CODE ENFORCEMENT

A look at steps taken to enforce code violations in two membership organizations in the communications field depicts the problems that can arise. The Society of Professional Journalists (SPJ), 17,000 members strong, worried, stewed, and fretted over 14 years about adding an enforcement procedure to its code of ethics—and finally dumped the proposal. And then it deleted a section that called for censure of those who were found to have violated the code. The background and reasons well illustrate the code enforcement problem for a voluntary membership organization.

SPJ began as a college journalism fraternity known as Sigma Delta Chi in the early 1900s. Today, the society continues to have student chapters on many campuses and also has professional members employed in news organizations—on daily and weekly newspapers, in radio and television news departments. SPJ adopted a code of ethics in 1926 that went through three revisions in the 1970s and 1980s. The code's opening sentence states the belief that "the duty of journalists is to serve the truth." Standards of practice are set forth under these major headings: responsibility; freedom of the press; ethics; accuracy and objectivity; fair play; and pledge.

The ethics section opens with the statement that "journalists must be free of obligation to any interest other than the public's right to know the truth." To implement this, there is a ban on freebies, which "can compromise the integrity of journalists and their employers. Nothing of value should be accepted." Members are cautioned about accepting secondary employment, political involvement, holding public office, and service in community organizations if the activity would compromise integrity. There's an acknowledgment that confidential sources of information will be protected and the pronouncement that "plagiarism is dishonest and unacceptable."

In the section on accuracy and objectivity is the declaration that "truth is our ultimate goal." Objectivity in reporting is cited as a goal and "there is no excuse for inaccuracies or lack of thoroughness." Included in the portion on fair play are admonitions to guard against invading a person's privacy, to give the accused a chance to reply if the news media communicates unofficial charges affecting reputation or moral character, and to make prompt and complete correction of errors.

Finally, there is the pledge section, which was the site of the problems that set off much debate and probably a few headaches. In a revision of the code of ethics at the annual meeting of members in 1973, when many of the above provisions were enacted, the society approved this sentence: "Journalists should actively censure and try to prevent violations of these standards, and they should encourage their observance by all newspeople." This became known as the censure clause. This was to be the enforcement language, the "teeth," so the code would not be just another set of high-sounding principles that could be ignored.

Whatever censure was expected didn't materialize. Journalists, just as those in other membership organizations, hesitated to call attention to the sins of their peers. There was a program of ethics education, which consisted mostly of having copies of the SPJ code posted in newsrooms around the country. So, in 1983, the society thought it time to take another look, to do something with meaning about code enforcement.

A task force was charged with drafting an SPJ ethics grievance procedure, one that would spell out a method to handle ethics complaints against members. The procedure that was developed defined an ethics violation and proposed a three-tier process—review of complaints and their resolution (expected in 90 percent of the cases) at local, chapter levels; further review or appeal as necessary at regional board levels; and, for complaints still unresolved, review by a national ethics council, to be formed. The national council might recommend to delegates at the annual convention the expulsion of a member.

This proposal was on the agenda of the national directors of SPJ in 1984. The board tabled it and voted to survey chapters to ask if they favored having the procedure. Chapter response was weak. Of the replies received, 54.8 percent opposed the grievance procedure.

There were several concerns of members that emerged from the conduct of the survey and the attendant attention. Some pointed out that code enforcement would affect only SPJ members, and that there were many journalists outside the organization who would be unaffected. There was some doubt about the ability of local chapters to handle inquiries into ethics violations. There was also the fear expressed that grievance procedures might invite lawsuits. After hearing a report on the survey, and receiving an opinion from the society's lawyer that the enforcement procedure might lead to expensive litigation, the board unanimously voted down the grievance procedure proposal in May 1985.[3]

The code of ethics was still intact, however—the pesky censure clause was still there, for another two years. Members at the annual meeting in 1987 voted to remove the censure language. The revised pledge said that by programs of education and other means the society shall "encourage individual journalists to adhere to these tenets, and shall encourage journalistic publications and broadcasters to recognize their responsibility to frame codes of ethics in concert with their employees to serve as guidelines in furthering these goals."[4]

Members of SPJ still have their code of ethics to live by, to guide them in the direction of responsible journalism, accuracy, objectivity, and fair play. The code has had a salutary effect, serving as a model for codes adopted by numerous newspapers throughout the United States. Many individual journalists will observe it, even though they don't want to point the finger of accusation at violators.

As a contrast, we look at another membership organization in the communication field, Public Relations Society of America (PRSA), the world's largest association of PR communicators. The bylaws of this society have a well-defined procedure for enforcement of its Code of Professional Standards for the Practice of Public Relations, described briefly in Chapter 12. Adherence to the code is a condition of membership in the society. With payment of annual dues, a member agrees to abide by the society's bylaws and its code, and the rules for its enforcement.

PRSA provides for judicial panels made up of accredited members of the society, who are appointed by the president, with approval of the board of directors at its annual meeting. Each panel has the power to conduct disciplinary proceedings and to hear complaints relative to violation of the code or of the society's bylaws "on complaint made by a member or by the Board of Ethics and Professional Standards." After a hearing, the panel may make recommendations to the board of directors regarding disciplinary action against a member for violation of the code or bylaws.

The role of the Board of Ethics and Professional Standards (BEPS) is to make investigations concerning violation of the code or bylaws, to bring complaints before the appropriate judicial panel, and to prosecute. This board also may take a complaint of any violation directly to the board of directors.

Confidentiality and closed sessions are required for proceedings of the judicial panels and the two boards. In cases in which a member receives a warning, admonishment, or reprimand, the board of directors may decide to give information about the disciplinary action to society members. When there is censure, suspension, or expulsion of a member, the board must tell members of the action.

How well have the enforcement methods worked? Were complaints of alleged violations of the code by members considered? Were disciplinary actions taken?

PRSA reported that 200 cases became formal BEPS or panel cases from 1950 through 1989. There were 34 cases referred to the judicial panels. Of these, members in two cases were expelled, two were suspended, three were censured, and four were reprimanded or admonished. The remaining 23 cases were dismissed for several reasons. After hearings, one was dismissed for inconclusive evidence, two because the individuals against whom the complaints were lodged were no longer members, six for insufficient evidence, and four upon a ruling of no violation. Six cases were closed after members resigned while cases were in progress, three were withdrawn, and one was settled without a hearing.

Complaints and investigations involved all articles of the 17-point code. The article cited most frequently was the one requiring a member to deal fairly with clients or employers, past or present, with fellow practitioners and the general public. Next most frequently cited was that stating a member shall conduct his or her professional life in accord with the public interest. Following in close order were cases dealing with charges of a member knowingly disseminating false or misleading information, and failure to adhere to accuracy and truth.

A PRSA study of its ethics file published for the years 1950 through 85 concluded the code, and its enforcement procedure, "is a good one," and at the same time noted it is a living document that can and will be improved.[5] Critics of the PRSA code have their opinions.

Just about the loudest of the critics is Jack O'Dwyer, whose firm publishes *Jack O'Dwyer's Newsletter*, subtitled "The Inside News of Public Relations," and *O'Dwyer's PR Services Report*. The latter publication demanded "Article 14 of the PRSA code must go!" in the headline over an editorial that stated reasons for the position. What O'Dwyer referred to as the offending article in the code says, "A member shall not intentionally damage the professional reputation or practice of another practitioner."

O'Dwyer pointed out the problem of this article in connection with one of the more publicized cases taken up by PRSA's board of ethics and professional standards. The case arose from a full-day meeting of four PRSA members, including a former president of the society, with William Casey, former CIA director; the subsequent public criticism of the five by another society member, Summer Harrison; and the PRSA investigation of her for speaking out. The meeting of the PRSA members and Casey, who was a member of President Reagan's cabinet as well as head of the U.S. overseas intelligence group, occurred in 1983. This gathering wasn't revealed until September 1988 in a report issued by the Committee on Foreign Affairs of the House of Representatives. A story on the meeting was then published in the September 28, 1988, issue of *Jack O'Dwyer's Newsletter*.

After reading of the meeting, Harrison released to the news media a criticism of the members' participation, claiming that the meeting of the four with Casey was a violation of the code and thus unethical. Article six of the code prohibits a member from engaging in any practice that might corrupt "the processes of government." She cited this and other articles to support her position. One PRSA member at the meeting said the purpose was "to 'educate' the American public about what was going on in Central America." It's against the law for the CIA to operate domestically, but the PRSA members said they met with Casey as a member of the president's cabinet. The question raised: "Which hat was Casey wearing?" The ethics board decided that the members did not violate the code by their meeting.

The BEPS followed up with Harrison in a letter that asked her for information supportive of her statements. Harrison replied with an 11-page letter, which she again made public, and this got her into hot water with the ethics board. She said she would not have released copies of it if she had been told she was under investigation for possible violation of the code. (A person under investigation should treat related material as confidential.) There was a further exchange of letters, in one of which the board informed Harrison she was under investigation, and the cloak of confidentiality descended and was respected. The case became moot when Harrison resigned from PRSA in April 1990.

Back to article 14 of the PRSA code and the demand for its riddance. The O'Dwyer editorial said some society members think Harrison violated that portion of the code when she criticized those who went to the Casey meeting. The editorial points out, though, that PRSA's legal counsel told the publication that members "do not give up the right to criticize other members of the PRSA ethics process" when they become members.

Besides article 14, the publication calls for PRSA to "consider dropping its entire secretive ethical process" and "modernize and promote criticism of members' ethics."[6]

Marvin Olasky, another critic of the PRSA code of ethics, maintains that the code has not helped even "the public relations of public relations." The code, he adds, appears as "one more indication of hypocrisy in an occupation scorned for promoting imagery rather than substance."

Olasky avers that adherence through the code to "generally accepted standards of good taste," has allowed "many questionable practices to continue." Olasky quotes Paul Ylvisaker from his talk to the 1976 national convention of the society: "I read your Code of Professional Standards. I read it very carefully. And I compliment you. . . . But I read one thing that scared the hell out of me. It says here, 'A member has the affirmative duty of adhering to generally accepted standards of accuracy, truth, and good taste.' In other words, if you can document that the general standards are not so sharp, you're off the hook."[7]

That phrase, *generally accepted standards*, has been labeled a "hotly debated provision" of the PRSA code by coauthors Scott Cutlip, Allen Center and Glen Broom. They say it's "the bone of contention among thoughtful practitioners. Its elasticity permits more than one unethical practice to go unpunished."[8]

Countering the critics, Donald B. McCammond, a former BEPS chairman, said the code "is a highly positive element in maintaining and demonstrating the professional quality of public relations,"[9] and "this system of guarding a higher ethical code for public relations works, and works well."[10]

POINTS

• A manager in a business corporation involved in installing an ethics program should be sure it suits and fits the needs of the organization, that it's not just a copy of a plan selected because it worked well at another firm.

• In looking for ways to get the best possible use from a hotline, hold a series of meetings with small groups of employees, explain the reasons for having this, and the confidentiality safeguards. Ask for suggestions on how to obtain cooperation and acceptance from the total work force.

• If you belong to a membership organization that has an ethics code, give it your support. Ask that ethics be discussed in the newsletter, by speakers, in workshops, and other ways.

• When you know of unethical conduct by someone you work with or share membership with, don't look the other way. Be sure of your facts, then take up the wrongful act with whoever is appropriate to deal with it.

NOTES

1. Barnaby J. Feder, "Helping Corporate America Hew to the Straight and Narrow," *The New York Times*, November 3, 1991, p. F5.
2. "Ethics Codes Work with Commitment," *Rocky Mountain News*, January 22, 1992, p. 33.

3. Casey Bukro, "The SPJ Code's Double-Edged Sword: Accountability, Credibility," *Journal of Mass Media Ethics*, Fall/Winter 1985–86, pp. 10–13.
4. "Code of Ethics," Society of Professional Journalists, revised, 1987.
5. "History of Enforcement 1952–85," research project of the PRSA Board of Ethics and Professional Standards, 1987.
6. "Article 14 of the PRSA code must go!" *O'Dwyer's PR Services Report*, August 1989, p. 4; also issue of September 1990, pp. 26–33.
7. Marvin N. Olasky, "Ministers or Panderers: Issues Raised by the Public Relations Society Code of Standards," *Journal of Mass Media Ethics*, Fall/Winter 1985–86, pp. 43–44.
8. Scott M. Cutlip, Allen H. Center, and Glen M. Broom, "Effective Public Relations," 6th ed. (Englewood Cliffs, N.J.: Prentice Hall, 1985), p. 458.
9. Donald B. McCammond, "A Matter of Ethics," *Public Relations Journal*, November 1983, p. 46.
10. Donald B. McCammond, "The Growth of Ethical Awareness," *Public Relations Journal*, January/February 1985, p. 8.

Chapter Fourteen

Moving toward the Credibility Factor: Barriers, but Also Progress

You've polished your credibility shield; you have ethics in public relations working to assure credibility for you and your organization. You may even have inspired fellow practitioners to take the ethical way when they feel the pinch of a dilemma. Still there remain barriers that pull down the credibility of all of you.

THE INCOMPETENT—AREN'T THEY UNETHICAL?

Unethical conduct in public relations has many faces. So far, attention has been paid to those most commonly observed— and criticized: deceit, conflict of interest, lying, manipulation, breaking the law. There's another kind of unethical conduct, perhaps as prevalent and maybe more insidious: incompetence.

Competency is a relative term in judging a person in public relations. The word connotes more than knowledge acquired at school or through experience. The personal, the emotional, qualities of the person affect his or her competency. These factors are difficult to judge. There isn't a test or exam that will tell us who matches or beats the passing level of competency, only who has the ability or knowledge or psychological fitness to perform competently. The test of competency is in the workplace, where the pass-or-fail grade is determined by how tasks are completed. There are no figures on the number of PR communicators who might be rated incompetent, or at least less than fully competent. Some might think the younger, less experienced people would be those most greatly afflicted by incompetency. Others could tell you that on the average this group would have above-average formal education and should be ranked among those thought to be more competent. But no one knows.

One might ask: Isn't the incompetent in PR a management problem for an employer or client to deal with, to discipline or dismiss the offender, just as with any other employee or retained counselor who has other failings? True, to an extent. But the employer or client may not always know when the PR person gives poor advice about the resolution of a public relations problem or fails to initiate plans that are adequate to maintain or bring about desired change in relationships with one or more of the publics of interest. An organization may incur loss of time or costs in dollars or shattered relationships with key publics before the discovery that it has been depending upon the advice and other services of an incompetent person.

Counselor Pat Jackson speaks to all this when he says, "The biggest ethical problem today is failure to learn the new skills necessary to really serve the personalized, behavior-motivating client needs—and so, selling them on what the practitioner can do, usually publicity." He then asks, "What would we say if our doctors treated us for measles, because they know how, when we really had cancer? I see no difference."

He points out that there's a corollary in medicine to the question of whether staying abreast of state-of-the-art practice is an ethical issue. "The specialty medical societies that have refused to adopt voluntary reexamination or reaccreditation," he says, "have almost all done so because of the fear that most of their members could not pass—because they don't keep up the way they should. A bit frightening, what?"[1]

Another public relations counselor, Joe Epley, says its unethical for him or one of his peers to offer service they are not capable of fulfilling. "If you are not sure you can meet a commitment, don't deceive your client or yourself by attempting it," he says. "When we promise that we can do things and then don't, we are lying to our clients. That's dishonesty."[2]

Commenting on another aspect of competency is Joan B. Taylor, a public relations development director in the health-care field. She says she found "to my dismay that those in positions of authority in public relations were not only not qualified . . . but when confronted with a situation handled the media poorly through lack of experience and training." Though it appeared that a hospital spokesperson favored one reporter over another, or tried to cover up an incident, "he was 'unethical' out of ignorance." She advocates that such an ill-equipped person improve his or her ethical performance through training in classes and seminars.[3]

How do you know if the PR person is competent? Checking with individuals or organizations whom the person has served is probably the most reliable way. What kind of credibility does the person have? Do others speak well or ill of him or her? Does the performance match the promise? Persons with credibility have satisfied customers or bosses or clients.

IS PUBLIC RELATIONS A PROFESSION?

Many public relations practitioners aspire to professional status for themselves and designation of public relations as a profession—titles that connote competency. Most, however, realize the fantasy that is part of this longing. Many practitioners use the terms *professional* and *profession* in describing the work they do and the field they toil in (and you find application of the terms in this book). There probably are few, however, who seriously believe they have now attained such status.

Edward L. Bernays, a public relations pioneer who opened a publicity office in New York City in 1919, coined the term *public relations counsel*. He believes public relations is a vocation, not a profession, which he defines as "an art applied to a science in a manner that puts public interest ahead of personal gain."[4] "Regrettably," he says, "it is not, although it could be and should be."

Bernays cites several markings of a professional: an individual who is practicing a vocation after graduation from study of that field in a university; has taken and passed an examination by the state; taken the equivalent of a Hippocratic oath "attesting to following our ethical procedures, and may be disbarred from the profession if the oath is broken." Having said this, Bernays laments. "Any paperhanger can call himself or herself a public relations practitioner. Fifty-one different titles are used in the field to designate a public relations practitioner. None of them indicates that the user of the specified title knows anything about the field."[5]

Coauthors Scott Cutlip, Allen Center, and Glen Broom dissect the criteria that qualify an occupational group as a profession and also find the practice of public relations lacking. They do see enough of a glimmer of the qualities necessary for such classifying that they find: "Our thesis is that public relations is an emerging profession." They base this conclusion in part on their observations that practitioners increasingly demonstrate a mature concept in their work and conduct themselves in an increasingly professional manner. They add that professionalism is an important goal for those entering the field.

The coauthors offer their criteria to "measure the advance of the contemporary practice" toward the goal of professionalism. These include:

- Specialized educational preparation to acquire knowledge and skills, based on a body of theory developed through research.
- Recognition by the community of a unique and essential service.
- Emphasis on public service and social responsibility over personal gain and private special interests.
- Autonomy in practice and acceptance of personal responsibility by practitioners.
- Codes of ethics and performance enforced by a self-governing association of colleagues.[6]

IS LICENSING THE ANSWER?

Bernays' qualities necessary to mark a public relations person as a professional differ in one major point from the criteria of Cutlip, Center, and Broom. He proposes that the aspiring public relations professional be required to take and pass a state examination. Licensing. Bernays was an early proponent of licensure, advocating it in a magazine article in 1953. He sees licensing as a thread that could stitch public relations to observance of ethics and status as a profession. A defined code of ethics would be part of the fabric accepted by the public relations persons after registration and gaining a license to practice.

Once the public relations professional is licensed, believes Bernays, he or she knows the framework and bounds within which to stay in order to continue to hold the license. The person who is accused of breaching the regulations regarding ethics or other matters and is found guilty must discontinue practice. Bernays points out that such a system removes behavior and adherence to moral standards as a matter of individual choice. He fears that without licensing there will be many in public relations whose "desire to make a living is greater than their awareness or application of any ethical code."

He offers this analogy. The regulation of the legal profession "has made me feel I can go to any lawyer and feel protected by his ethics. And, the same in medicine. If I'm in Arkansas and I want to see a doctor and I see the sign of an M.D., I feel I can go into that office without too much inquiry.

"If I'm in Arkansas and looking for public relations assistance and I see an ad for a public relations firm in the yellow pages of the telephone book, I have to make a long examination and investigate individuals from direct and indirect sources."[7]

While coauthors Cutlip, Center, and Broom omit licensing from their criteria for professionalism, they do treat licensure in another section of their book. "Codes of behavior will lack wholly effective means of enforcement until there is legal certification of practitioners," they say. Having taken this stand, they continue by pointing out that controlled access is the sign of a recognized profession and "that there must be controlled access, through licensing, to the title of 'certified public relations counselor.'" They think this is the only way to separate "frauds and flacks" from legitimate practitioners. There's an additional claim they make—that there should be licensing to protect society as well as to promote the cause of professionalism.

The Cutlip–Center–Broom discussion on licensing also takes note of basic legal questions that are involved in licensing public relations people. After examining these, they give the gloomy summary that the law is not ready for licensing of public relations people and that "licensure will not soon provide a means of elevating the ethics and competence of practitioners."[8]

Licensing was one of the agenda items at a Public Relations Society of America Symposium on Demonstrating Professionalism held September 5–7, 1986, in Itasca, Illinois, where members in favor of and against licensing presented papers. Bernays spoke on behalf of the committee for licensing and registration that he helped form and chaired. "As far as I'm concerned," he said, "licensing or registration is no longer a debatable question.

People who think otherwise express opinions based on ignorance or prejudice.''

Paul Forbes, counselor of Falls Church, Virginia, in his paper
listed arguments for mandatory licensing and registration with
legal sanctions, and opposing views for continued reliance on
''a voluntary approach to public relations ethics and professionalism.'' Among the pro arguments: licensing would define the
practice of public relations, would establish uniform curricula;
would set uniform ethical and professional standards; would
provide for the decertification of violators of ethical standards;
would protect the consumer of public relations services (clients
and employers) from imposters and charlatans; and would protect qualified practitioners from unfair competition from the unethical and unqualified.

Arguments against licensing and registration, and for contin-
uation of the voluntary approach, included: makes it difficult to
define public relations; places too much emphasis on education;
accreditation is sufficient to establish standards; courts are available to deal with malpractice; and legislatures are not interested
in limiting the field.

His pros and cons also touched on the relationship between
licensing and the First Amendment. Those against licensing believe that any licensing in the communications field is an infringement of First Amendment rights, while the pros says that
licensing ''would not control anyone's right to deal with the
media or government, or to speak out in any way, there would
be no infringement of First Amendment rights.'' Atty. Jerald A.
Jacobs, in giving an overview on licensing versus self-regulation,
said he believed a government-issued license was ''unrealistic
given the First Amendment and the broad nature of the activities
public relations professionals are engaged in.'' He thought that
state governments would be averse to prohibiting those without
a license from engaging in the issuance of press releases or in

consulting with organizations on how the public and the press would view their policies and programs.''

Of the approximately 85 practitioners who attended the symposium, the majority did not ''feel licensing is the way to proceed (at least in the near future).'' There was, however, a consensus that the subject should be studied to learn the benefits and problems.[9] One veteran counselor who opposes licensing, Larry Newman, a former board member of PRSA, has said that if licensing takes place, he'll change the title of his work to ''institutional consultant.''[10]

A state senator in Massachusetts introduced in the 1992 legislative session, on behalf of Bernays, a bill to license public relations practitioners. Under its provisions, ''applicants would have to pass 'good character' requirements (no criminal record) and a test of their knowledge of communications theory . . . in order to use the terms public relations, communications, or corporate communications in their title, the experts would need a bachelor's degree, with a PR concentration, and two years of experience, among other things.''[11] The proposal failed to reach the senate floor for action.

PRSA PUTS IT ALL TOGETHER

How long must the world of PR communicators wait for the advent of licensing? No one knows, just as no one knows whether this final rung on the ladder of professionalism will ever be attained. There are steps that men and women in public relations can take, and are taking, however, to prepare themselves to meet other prerequisites of professionalism, such as put forth by Bernays and Cutlip, Center, and Broom. In front of other PR organizations in readying members for professional status is the Public Relations Society of America.

By the early 1990s, PRSA had put together a comprehensive package for professional development of members:

- Accredited status for members, the highest category of membership, with an "Accreditation Primer" to assist members to prepare for the accreditation exam and a continuing education program to assure they can maintain this level of membership.
- Professional development aids, including seminars, video library, and home study courses, which offer continuing education credits.
- Monthly journal with articles on current topics of interest.
- Fourteen interest sections for members with specialty areas of practice.
- Information and research services.
- Annual national conference with speakers and workshops, and audio tapes available.
- Annual awards to members, whose entries are judged by peers, that recognize outstanding public relations projects.
- The Code of Professional Standards.
- The Public Relations Body of Knowledge.

The *Public Relations Body of Knowledge*, initially completed in 1988 and expanded through yearly updates, is of special breakthrough, milestone significance. Coauthors Catherine Pratt and Terry Lynn Rentner declared "PRSA's Herculean efforts in gathering and organizing the diverse threads of research and information pertinent to the study and practice of public relations have resulted in a seminal document of critical importance to public relations."[12]

Members of the PRSA committee who began the project saw that professionalism in public relations was limited because of the lack of agreed-upon subject matter defined as most applicable or distinctive to the field. They, and the task force of volunteers that provided a comprehensive outline for codifying the knowledge, engaged in "the first nationwide effort to detail the public relations body of knowledge."[13] The *Public Relations Body of Knowledge* is a resource that is expected to be widely used by practitioners and by educators and students.

Writings and research on ethical and social responsibility issues are part of the first section, "Foundations of Public Relations." Titles of the other sections, not always couched in words that sound terribly user-friendly, are "Organizational and Management Context," "Communication and Relationship Context," "Public Relations Practice," "Elements and Functions of Professional Practice," and "Organizational Contexts for Professional Practice." Abstracts of the articles and books listed in the *Public Relations Body of Knowledge*, on computer disks and stored in a data bank at PRSA's headquarters in New York City, are available to members.

POINTS

- If you suspect a person practicing public relations for you is incompetent, exercise close supervision, ask questions about what's being done and why and how. Act before the organization's, or your, credibility is threatened.

- Look for reasons to account for incompetency in another. You may be able to counsel with the person about learning opportunities that will improve his or her performance.

- Prepare yourself to be among the most competent by continuing to learn, keeping abreast of developments in public relations programs, and keeping posted on what's happening in technology and new ideas that affect public relations. You can perform ethically and in other ways as a professional, even though your activities aren't regulated through a license.

- It is shortsighted to think of establishing credibility only for you or your organization. Look around, act to convert another you observe straying from the ethical path.

- Speak out on putting ethics to work in public relations. Be a missionary for credibility. Place the topic on the agendas of meetings in your own organization and of other groups with which you are affiliated.

NOTES

1. Correspondence with Pat Jackson, March 8, 1990.
2. Correspondence with Joe Epley, April 24, 1991.
3. Correspondence with Joan B. Taylor, December 4, 1989.
4. Phone conversation of author with Bernays, March 5, 1992.
5. Edward L. Bernays, book review, *Public Relations Review*, 17, no. 2 (Summer 1990), p. 83.
6. Scott M. Cutlip, Allen H. Center, and Glen M. Broom, *Effective Public Relations*, 6th ed., (Englewood Cliffs, N.J.: Prentice Hall, 1985), pp. 449–63.
7. Conversation with author in Bernay's office, April 9, 1991.
8. Cutlip, Center, and Broom, *Effective Public Relations*, p. 461.
9. "Demonstrating Public Relations Professionalism," Foundation for Public Relations Research and Education, Inc., Public Relations Society of America, February 1987.
10. Conversation with Larry Newman, February 22, 1990.
11. Suzanne Alexander, "Some Think Many of These Folks Have Too Much License Already," *The Wall Street Journal*, March 19, 1992, p. B1.
12. Catherine A. Pratt and Terry Lynn Tentner, "What's Really Being Taught About Ethical Behavior," *Public Relations Review*, Spring 1989, p. 57.
13. James K. Van Leuven, "Public Relations Body of Knowledge: A Task Force Report," *Public Relations Review*, Winter 1988, pp. 11–17.

Index

Also available from Business One Irwin . . .

MASTERING THE ART OF Q&A
A Survival Guide for Tough, Trick, and Hostile Questions
Myles Martel, Ph.D.
How to prepare step-by-step for nearly every type of communication—speeches, presentations, media appearances, and more—so you can have the right answer every time!
ISBN: 1-55623-141-5

GETTING THE WORD OUT
How Managers Can Create Value with Communications
Frank Corrado
Shows how to relate Communications to the bottom line—and increase profits. You'll discover how to communicate effectively with employees, customers, the media, and your community.
ISBN: 1-55623-785-5

CREATING DEMAND
Powerful Tips and Tactics for Marketing Your Product or Service
Richard Ott
Double the effectiveness of your advertising at no additional cost! Ott gives you new ways to stimulate demand for your products or services so you can allocate precious resources to maximize appreciable return.
ISBN: 1-55623-560-7

AFTERMARKETING
How to Keep Customers for Life through Relationship Marketing
Terry G. Vavra
Shift your focus from pursuing new customers to building lasting relationships with current customers. You'll discover a clear mandate to help you gain category leadership in the radically changing marketplace of the 90s.
ISBN: 1-55623-605-0

SECOND TO NONE
How Our Smartest Companies Put People First
Charles Garfield
New from Charles Garfield, whose ongoing study of hich achievers was the basis for his 1986 *Time* magazine bestseller, *Peak Performers: The New Heroes of American Business*. Garfield reveals how our smartest companies are thriving in the midst of intense competition. He examines how innovative teamwork and partnership strategies will help any organization achieve peak performance in the 1990s and beyond.
ISBN: 1-55623-360-4

Available at fine bookstores and libraries everywhere.